Feminine Capital
Unlocking the Power of Women Entrepreneurs

Barbara Orser and Catherine Elliott

Stanford Business Books
An Imprint of Stanford University Press • Stanford, California

Stanford University Press
Stanford, California

Special discounts for bulk quantities of Stanford Business Books are available to corporations, professional associations, and other organizations. For details and discount information, contact the special sales department of Stanford University Press. Tel: (650) 736-1782, Fax: (650) 736-1784

Printed in the United States of America on acid-free, archival-quality paper

Library of Congress Cataloging-in-Publication Data

Orser, Barbara, author.
  Feminine capital : unlocking the power of women entrepreneurs / Barbara Orser and Catherine Elliott.
    pages cm
  Includes bibliographical references and index.
  ISBN 978-0-8047-8378-1 (cloth : alk. paper) — ISBN 978-0-8047-8379-8 (pbk. : alk. paper)
  1. Businesswomen. 2. Women-owned business enterprises. 3. Self-employed women. 4. Entrepreneurship. I. Elliott, Catherine, 1960- author. II. Title.
  HD6072.5.O77 2015
  338'.04082—dc23
                    2014042781

ISBN 978-0-8047-9431-2 (electronic)

Typeset by Bruce Lundquist in 10/15 Minion

This book is dedicated to the late Gwynneth Joyce Wallace,
a friend, community leader, and nurturer of dreams.
For everything there is a season.

To our children, Emily and Hannah Young, Michael and
Amanda Grant-Orser, and David Riding, this book
demonstrates the power of friendship and perseverance
in fulfilling one's dreams.

We extend heartfelt thanks to our husbands, Allan Riding and
Andrew Young, for their support in the creation of this book.
Merci.

Contents

Figures, Tables, and Learning Aids

Learning Aids

Acknowledgments

It is our hope that this book serves to stimulate discussion about the substantive contributions of women entrepreneurs and to illustrate the relevance of gender and entrepreneurship research to business practice, education, training, and public policy. We are indebted in this task to the thousands of entrepreneurs whose experiences are captured in the studies and scenarios profiled throughout the book. Having heard their stories and experiences?—as women, as entrepreneurs, as entrepreneurial feminists—we were motivated to share their insights. There were also many other "behind the scene" contributors. Each study had a support team, and to our coauthors, research assistants, and librarians we extend our gratitude.

We also wish to express our special thanks to Sandra Altner (CEO, Women's Enterprise Centre of Manitoba) and Allan Riding (Deloitte Chair in the Management of Enterprise Growth at the University of Ottawa Telfer School of Management). Three more members of the university project team are deserving of special mention: Cecilia Tellis (librarian, Telfer School of Management) and graphic designers Michael Anstis and Safae McLellan (docUcentre). Editorial assistance was provided by David Horne. A special thank you to Margo Beth Fleming and James Holt of Stanford University Press, and to Patricia Greene and Julie Weeks, who provided timely and constructive feedback on the book proposal and manuscript. With their generous input, we were able to forge ahead with clearer concepts and direction.

Much of our work has been influenced by scholars in the Diana Group. A note of thanks is also extended to members of the Canadian Taskforce for Women's Business Growth and numerous "women-in-enterprise champions" around the world who are working to better support women's entrepreneurship through public policy.

We wish to acknowledge those agencies that have financially supported our research, including Atlantic Canada Opportunities Agency, Department of Foreign Affairs, Trade and Development, Embassy of the United States, Industry Canada, Mount St. Vincent University Women's Enterprise Centre, Social Science and Humanities Research Council of Canada, Status of Women Canada, University of

Ottawa Telfer School of Management, U.S. State Department, Western Diversification, Women's Business Initiative, and Western Diversification Women's Enterprise Initiative. Thanks are extended to colleagues Dean Francois Julien (University of Ottawa), Dean Micheál J. Kelly (now, Wilfred Laurier University), and Assistant Dean Alain Doucet. Over the past ten years, their support has enabled the completion of several large-scale projects that have helped to formulate our thinking around the concept of *Feminine Capital*.

Barbara Orser and Catherine Elliott

Feminine Capital

Globally, two hundred million women are engaged in business ownership.[1] Across North America, women retain ownership in half of all small businesses.[2] In the United States alone, over eight million female-owned firms generate $3 trillion a year in economic impact.[3] Women are creating jobs, products, and services, and are investing earnings in their families, firms, and communities. In doing so, they are changing the landscape of venture creation around the world, one venture at a time.

Despite these encouraging statistics, from our perspective, being female is too often deemed to be an entrepreneurial handicap. When compared to male-owned ventures, female-owned enterprises are judged to be smaller, less successful, and less likely to grow. With women around the globe making progress on their own terms, however, it is time to redefine entrepreneurship and what it means to be successful.

Traditionally, entrepreneurship is defined as enterprise creation, including actions taken to create for-profit, nonprofit, social, ecological, and sometimes publicly funded ventures. "Fear of success," "risk adversity," and "failure to delegate" tend to dominate discussions about the reasons for gender differences in enterprise performance and notions about women's entrepreneurial identity. These apparent psychological flaws have little value in explaining women's economic progress. It is time to recognize feminine capital as an asset.

Feminine capital captures that which is feminine within one's experience and identity. It is an aggregation of ways of knowing, roles and expectations, values, and behavior that is both individual and collective. These assets have social and economic value. Feminine capital can be developed, just as risk-taking behaviors within venture creation can be learned. This book celebrates the feminine. We do so by describing women's experiences in the world of venture creation.

Feminine attributes traditionally are associated with females, behavior that is reinforced through socialization. For this reason, we listened to the experiences of women to better understand the nature of feminine capital. In conversations with, and studies of, thousands of women business owners we learned that entrepreneurs embrace a continuum of perspectives about how gender has an impact on the ways that they do business. For some, they perceive that being female has no influence on their business practice. For others, it's all about being female. Women are making the conscious decision to not let others' perceptions about aspirations and behavior limit their commercial success. Underlying the way in which some women do business is a sense of determination and passionate belief in the importance of their enterprises. In certain cases, perceptions about inequality and women's subordination have triggered entrepreneurial inclinations. A common ambition of many women entrepreneurs is the desire to empower others. Entrepreneurship is seen as a mechanism for creating opportunity, economic self-sufficiency, and equity-based outcomes. These *feminist entrepreneurs* are change agents who employ entrepreneurship to improve women's quality of life and well-being. By doing so, they enrich our understanding about contemporary feminism. They are showing us how venture creation can lead to social and economic transformation.

We conducted other studies that compared the experiences of male and female entrepreneurs. While research tells us that gender is associated with differences in enterprise performance, we found more similarities than differences between groups. Building on these studies and an emerging literature about gender and entrepreneurship, this book explores three questions:

- What is feminine capital?
- How is feminine capital transforming entrepreneurship?
- How does entrepreneurship inform feminism?

This book takes a fresh look at the intersection between entrepreneurship and feminism, and how female entrepreneurs are infusing new values in business practice. Stories and scenarios are used to explain concepts and theories that are presented throughout the book. "Reflections" are questions intended to link these ideas with your own perspectives and experiences. Drawing on four decades of research that examines entrepreneurship, the book consolidates the most important lessons learned. These insights will help you as a business owner, student, scholar, or future entrepreneur to challenge dated assumptions and to recognize your own unique talents and skills.

How This Book Came to Be

Our first encounter with feminist entrepreneurs came from an unexpected source—the women of Wolfville, Nova Scotia, a small town in Atlantic Canada. It was among these business owners that we recognized the power of feminine capital. Conducting interviews was not initially part of a holiday, but surrounded by the panoramic beauty of the Annapolis Valley, we were introduced to the founder of a community-based theater troupe.[4] Then we were introduced to six more local entrepreneurs. All had founded business or social enterprises. All spoke about the need for social change. They all told us about their efforts to earn a living while improving the lives of others. These women were calling on their knowledge as caregivers, community champions, artisans, and former employees to develop new products, new markets, new services, and better processes. Some were creating "by women, for women" enterprises. They saw themselves as feminists, women of Wolfville, and women of the world. Their commitment to equity through enterprise was inspiring.

Arriving back in Ottawa, we decided that we would seek out more women who share such entrepreneurial perspectives. Surprisingly, it was not difficult. Reaching out to our North American contacts in small-business training agencies, we asked if the directors would forward our request to speak with female entrepreneurs with a double bottom line, one that includes helping other women. The email produced more responses than the study could absorb. Never had so many business owners contacted us to tell their stories. Diamond extractors in Northern Canada, midwestern manufacturers, and west coast retailers described the ripple effects of their enterprises. Motivated by their insights, in this book we draw on the lessons we learned from the many business owners who sought to talk to us, as well as from other findings of our ongoing research program. Collectively, our studies document the experiences of over twenty thousand entrepreneurs.

One lesson is that for many women, venture creation is not gender neutral.[5] Yet recognizing feminine capital in the venture creation process is not obvious. Its impacts are subtle. Its magnitude is obscure. At the surface lie visible markers of gender. But gender effects are realized in many ways: in entrepreneurial decisions and assumptions, within identity and perception, and through actions and interaction. Gender is linked to the firm by way of governance and corporate culture, and is reproduced through institutional relationships within financial intermediaries, government, and academe. In other words, gender is embedded within the venture creation and exchange process.

Organization of This Book

To position our research findings, the first section of the book (Chapters 1 to 4) introduces the concept of feminine capital. Chapter 1 starts by debunking misperceptions about gender and entrepreneurship. The masculine archetype is exposed.[6] We then explain how expert thinking contributes to the invisibility of feminine capital. The tenets of neoclassical economics, women in management, and entrepreneurial feminism are presented. Chapter 1 is the most theoretical of the chapters. This information is included at the outset of the book, as we believe that it is useful to understand the conceptual foundations upon which the rest of the book is built. For those readers who seek practical insights only, you may wish to jump directly to Chapter 2. In this chapter, we explore how being female influences entrepreneurial identity, a building block for enterprise creation. We also explore the links among definitions of success, attitudes to business ownership, and entrepreneurial intention. We then introduce the *Entrepreneurial Identity Framework*—a tool that will help business owners map out how their perceptions of success and intentions reflect their identities as entrepreneurs. Chapter 3 delves into opportunity identification. We describe how women entrepreneurs are capitalizing on their wisdom, know-how, and the Internet to commercialize ideas. Motivated by the desire for change—in themselves, families, and others—women are launching enterprises that align personal values with market opportunities. Pathways to venture creation are explained. Then in Chapter 4, we shift the focus from theory to practice, describing tactics for building enterprises that align with founders' values and expectations. Innovative business models that fuel sustainability and enterprise growth are illustrated through three in-depth case studies. Many of the approaches that women are using are radically different from traditional, profit-focused pathways. This information can help you to broaden your vision of venture creation and guide decisions such as where you should invest your time, creativity, and capital.

The second section of the book (Chapters 5 and 6) explores the gendered nature of resourcing enterprises. This section is important, given that many entrepreneurs face limited time and money; an absence of peers and colleagues from whom they can learn; and significant personal, professional, and financial risks.[7] Chapter 5 deals with relationships, ways of creating value-added networks, advisory teams, mentors, associations, and other forms of social capital. Best practices in mentoring and protégé relationships are shared. Chapter 6 is all about money, including types and uses of financing. Innovative financing strategies and the challenges of achieving financial literacy are also discussed.

Up to this point in the book, we focus on individual actions, the power within that enables entrepreneurs to create wealth and social change. However, entrepreneurial success is not solely the consequence of one's intentions. In Chapter 7 we broaden the conversation to include institutional influences on enterprise performance, such as politics, policies, and training programs. *Power in policy* implies that public policy can be better leveraged to support women's entrepreneurship. In this chapter we make a call to action, describing why it is important for women business owners to engage in policymaking and ways in which you can influence public policy. This information is important, given that public policy has an impact on multiple aspects of enterprise performance and that few policy frameworks explicitly address issues associated with women's entrepreneurship. Finally, in the closing chapter (Chapter 8), we summarize the key themes of the book by revisiting feminine capital and entrepreneurial feminism—the foundational concepts advanced in the book—to explain how women's entrepreneurship is changing the ways we think about wealth.

Each chapter contains tips, diagnostic tools, and checklists, as well as practical scenarios that illustrate alternative approaches to doing business. We also summarize ideas and highlight related studies in a series of learning aids, figures, and tables. Explaining feminine capital necessitates new perspectives and language about venture creation. To provide clarification of key terms, a glossary is presented at the end of the book. We encourage you to read the glossary and chapter notes, as this book introduces a number of new concepts.

Before proceeding, take a moment to reflect on your views about being female and entrepreneurship. Think broadly. If you are an entrepreneur, how, if at all, does gender affect the ways you do business? To what extent is the process of venture creation gendered? If you are a student, reflect on how gender is reflected in curricula, including entrepreneurship course content, case studies, and speakers. We encourage you to write down your reflections, as we will revisit this question in Chapter 8. Consider which of the categories in Table I.1 best capture your perspective.

More Reasons for Writing This Book

Several more observations played roles in our motivation to write this book. We have heard academic colleagues and policymakers at the highest levels proclaim, "There are no gender issues in entrepreneurship." It is as if venture creation remains unadulterated by social, cultural, and historical influences. Whether the statement

Table I.1: Gender and venture creation

	No Gender Influence	Gender Awareness	Gendered Process
Gender Influences	There are no gender differences. Male and female founders make similar decisions.	Gender differences exist but do not influence decisions or actions.	Gender influences dimensions of venture creation: founder motives, product or service design and delivery, and governance.
Potential Impact on Venture Creation	Gender plays no role in the venture creation process.	Being female may or may not enhance or impede the venture creation process.	Being female enhances or impedes the venture creation process and hence, enterprise performance.
Continuum of Opinions			

is echoed behind closed doors, in the classroom, or at a public podium, a substantive body of research does not support this contention. Too often, business owners assume that their own life circumstances and experiences reflect the realities of other entrepreneurs. We have pondered what motivates or gives intellectual license to such a proclamation, particularly within the academic community that is in the business of creating and disseminating evidence-based knowledge. On the topic of women's entrepreneurship, single-study findings, anecdotes, and personal opinion trump validated studies. This is not without consequence. Such a perspective cuts off discussions of why, for example, there remain persistent gender differences in enterprise performance or why females are significantly less likely to consider venture creation as a career choice.

Females constitute over half of North American business students. Many colleges and universities have introduced entrepreneurship courses across faculties. Such courses reflect the reality that many graduates will experience self-employment or business ownership at some point during their careers. Universities also face increasing pressure to commercialize faculty members' and students' intellectual property. Yet insights about gender influences in venture creation are essentially absent within entrepreneurship curricula and technology transfer operations. As a result, many faculty and students retain the perception that there are no gender issues. Statistics prove otherwise.

We anticipate that this book will be of interest to small-business owners who seek to grow their enterprises. Information will also assist academics, industry associations, and sector councils that wish to better understand the professional needs of students and members. The book presents an upbeat and practical view on how entrepreneurship can inform feminist thinking. This last motive reflects an observation that many regard feminism as passé. Others claim, "I'm not a feminist, but—" Our studies taught us that many women business owners are reclaiming feminism. Feminist entrepreneurs are embracing an action orientation, one that infuses values of equity within the act of venture creation.

Entrepreneurial decisions must be considered within the broader context of women's legal and property rights, family responsibilities, culture, and politics. Once you have completed the book, we encourage you to reflect on how the lessons learned resonate with your own circumstances and the extent to which being female influences your entrepreneurial practices. We invite you to share your experiences and perceptions with other entrepreneurs in order to create a collective understanding about the ways in which feminine capital is enacted in venture creation. By doing so, you can contribute to insights that will inform business practices, training, research, and policies to create even more prosperous ventures and social change.

Reframing Entrepreneurship

To begin our exploration of how feminine capital influences the venture creation process, we open by introducing five women who are among those whose stories we will follow during the course of this book. Three have founded operating enterprises, of which two are *intrapreneurs*, entrepreneurs who are responsible for creating innovative services and products within institutional settings. Two more of the entrepreneurial heroines are fictitious, composites that embody the experiences of the women whom we interviewed through the course of our research. Each of the five stories reflects a unique perspective about the venture creation process. After becoming acquainted with these entrepreneurial heroines, we step back in time to expose early stereotypes about female entrepreneurship. We do this because a historical perspective helps to illuminate antiquated assumptions about what it means to be entrepreneurial. Stereotypes continue to influence entrepreneurial intentions, sometimes pushing business owners to act in prototypically masculine ways.[1] In addition, stereotypes help to explain why some female entrepreneurs, even those who are experienced and well educated, are less likely to believe that they possess the skills and knowledge needed to become an entrepreneur.[2] Finally, we present summary tables to frame how we think about entrepreneurship. These tools will help you to reflect on the roles that feminine capital and feminism play in the venture creation process.

The Nature of Feminine Capital

Susan Ross

Susan is a stay-at-home mother who is thinking of starting a professional services business. At the same time, she is weighing the pros and cons of returning to corporate employment. Prior to leaving the workforce, she was employed as the product manager in a global consumer packaged goods company. Susan's decision is one that many women face. Should I continue working in the home? Should I start a business? Should I return to paid employment? The decision is not easy. Susan may be aware that most women who leave the labor force for family responsibilities rarely catch up to the earning capacity of colleagues who stay. This leads her to favor venture creation. But business ownership rarely offers health or other benefits coverage. There are more trade-offs to consider. Many new enterprises do not survive the first few years. Given the discontinuance rates of startups, lower self-employment wages, and often lack of pensions and other benefits, Susan must think about the opportunity costs of venture creation. These include forfeited wages, professional reputation, and time and capital invested, not to mention the stress associated with potential business failure. Susan is also aware of the advantages: the satisfaction of creating a new venture, autonomy, the opportunity to employ others, and the possibility of earning more than salaried colleagues.

Asha Sing

Asha is the president of a mid-sized, international wholesale operation for shoes. The firm has a proven track record of performance. She is seeking growth opportunities. During a recent customer visit, Asha noticed that the buyer referred all questions to her male vice-president. Having realized this (after several attempts to engage him in conversation), she stepped back to let the two men speak. In reflecting on this incident, Asha realizes that this customer simply does not wish to do business with a female president. On a personal level, she has no time to worry about what she refers to as "knuckle-draggers," those who treat female business owners as subordinates. At the professional level, she must determine how best to respond to such a client.

Maria Guidi

Maria owns a small construction firm with a growing list of local clients. She likes the idea of keeping her business small. A representative from WEConnect International—a nonprofit advocacy organization that promotes supplier diversity initiatives—has suggested that she apply for certification as a majority female-owned firm. Certification may facilitate business with global corporations. She has mixed feelings, however, about this opportunity. She is concerned that the firm may not have the capacity to meet international standards and fulfill the obligations of a large contract. At the same time, Maria knows that being small has its downfalls. Enterprise growth might enable her to diversify risk across more customers. Growth might increase her compensation. Staying small makes it difficult to attract investors, retain talent, and secure lead clients. Lead clients can be used to signal that her products meet industry scrutiny. Finally, few investors, other than family and friends, are interested in supporting a lifestyle firm—one that is not seeking growth. Yet young, rapidly growing firms also tend to be turned down for bank (or debt) financing compared to relatively stable enterprises.

Elaine Jolly

After thirty years of practicing medicine, Dr. Elaine Jolly sees the need for a full service women's health center. The health care model she envisions will be different from that offered anywhere in North America. Building a multidisciplinary women's health center in the face of hospital budget cuts and rationalization is a monumental task. For Elaine, opportunity takes a different form. In building the center, she must sell the merits of a female-only health care service to the hospital board that is composed primarily of male colleagues. She would like to draw on female patients for support, as she anticipates that they can best understand and communicate the value of women's health care. But a demanding clinical practice leaves her little time to acquire and practice political, fundraising, and board management skills. She must determine how to best sell her vision to colleagues and board members who will ultimately determine the relevance and viability of the center.

Cynthia Goh

Cynthia Goh is a professor of chemistry and medical science at the University of Toronto. She is an academic entrepreneur. Her scientific innovations have led to new medical diagnostics. She is also the cofounder of two nanotechnology firms. Startup challenges for Cynthia have been many. An early challenge was working within the university bureaucracy to commercialize academic knowledge. This was initially frustrating for Cynthia, who finds that developing technology is inherently creative and rewarding. When asked how, if at all, being female might influence the commercialization process, she suggests it is best to not notice. "In many cases, I think if you ignore them, challenges do go away." Taking this pragmatic perspective, Cynthia believes that there are no rules and not just one way to create business success. Focusing on gender is not productive.

· · ·

Each of these stories provides insight into the gendered nature of entrepreneurship. For example, Susan's decision between starting a business or returning to paid employment is riddled with trade-offs that many mothers face. Maria's story illustrates that staying small can have an impact on enterprise-wide strategy. Elaine Jolly is strategically leveraging feminine capital within her vision for an integrated women's health center. Her desire to support women's needs is reflected in the center's service delivery practices, governance, and operational processes. For Asha, being female informs her response strategy, and Cynthia Goh's ignoring gender is a conscious decision.

Recognizing Female Entrepreneurship

To understand how being female can influence entrepreneurial endeavor, it is useful to recall that entrepreneurship is not a new phenomenon. How we think about entrepreneurship today is rooted in early economic and management theory. While feminine duties traditionally have focused on family responsibilities, throughout the ages women have assumed commercial entrepreneurial activities—trade, harvesting, crafting, midwifery, and, in more recent centuries, small-business ownership. Artifacts testify to the entrepreneurial activities of indigenous women in early settlements. Upon arrival in New England and New France, female colonists established schools, hospitals, and religious orders. In mid-1600, Lady Sara Kirke managed an international fleet of ships, carrying out commerce through military campaigns and political turmoil, despite being subject and servant of the king. Yet the stories of entrepreneurial women are largely forgotten. How many entrepreneurial heroines can you name?

Every nation has a roster of industrial superstars, barons, and captains of industry. Most North American students learn about innovators and high-tech billionaires Bill Gates (Microsoft), Marc Zuckerberg (Facebook), and the late Steve Jobs (Apple). The gregarious British tycoon Sir Richard Branson of Virgin Group is another familiar face to many. Canadians have watched leaders such as Blackberry co-founders Jim Balsillie and Mike Lazaridis. But the list of accomplished entrepreneurial heroes rarely includes innovators such as Nobel Laureate Marie Curie, whose work led to the therapeutic application of radiation for cancer treatment. How about the brave women who helped to test the contraceptive pill in the development work of Carl Djerassi (inventor of the pill)? Arguably, radiation therapy and the pill are among the most important medical innovations in history. How about media entrepreneurs Oprah Winfrey, Amber Chand (Baby Einstein), writer J. K. Rowling (Harry Potter), cosmetic pioneers Estee Lauder and Mary Kay Ash, or Anita Roddick and Heather Reismen, who refined customer-focused retailing with the founding of The Body Shop and Chapters/Indigo Books? The list of entrepreneurial heroines is long, but all too often they are not as visible as male role models. The absence of women in our collective memory is, in part, the product of how the media and scholars have systematically ignored female entrepreneurship.

Women's economic invisibility is also not new. Its roots can be traced back to early political philosophers, such as Adam Smith, and economists, such as Joseph Schumpeter.

Rational Economic Man

Adam Smith is credited as the first to describe free market economics.[3] At the epicenter of the free market stands the rational economic (masculine) man. The purported reason for enterprise creation is to fulfill man's desire for wealth, convenience, and luxury through the smallest amount of self-denial.[4] Free market economics (the invisible hand) have driven financial policy and market structures throughout the world. But the mechanics of female entrepreneurship had no place within free market economics. From seventeenth-century rural cottage spinners to nineteenth-century factory weavers, women who ventured away from domestic duties were generally viewed as convenient, low-wage labor in the growing industrial apparatus. Feminine capital resided in the home.

In the early twentieth century, organizational behaviorists turned their attention to how the rational economic man foraged for ways to enhance efficiency and profit through standardizations of inputs and outputs.[5] Building on foundations of Smith's neoclassical economic theory, Joseph Schumpeter is credited for advancing the notion of the *entrepreneurial spirit*,[6] a spirit that enables "creative destruction."[7] This spirit was described as aggressive and dominant, typically masculine characteristics.

Over the past century, entrepreneurship has been viewed as an individual endeavor or process. New wealth is created by the destruction of existing wealth. Only a few possessed the constitution to helm this process. Entrepreneurial men, rational and heroic, epitomize success as "a will to conquer." As men laid claim to that which was enterprising, rarely were prototypical feminine qualities such as loyalty, kindness, and compassion used to characterize rational man and, subsequently, the entrepreneur.

In the mid-1900s, scholars continued to build on these theoretical principles to explain entrepreneurial success as the product of "need for achievement," "propensity to take risks," and "locus of control."[8] Early management studies about entrepreneurial leadership typically employed male-only or male-dominated samples. The iterative nature of scientific conversation further entrenched masculine nomenclature in the concept of entrepreneurial orientation.[9] Commercial decisions were distinct from and in conflict with, feminine behavior. Motivation was predicated solely on financial outcomes. Firm structure was typified as hierarchical with a clear division of labor, roles, and responsibilities.

Like Darwin's theory of natural selection, survival of the fittest implied that entrepreneurial women were expected to remain in the likeness of rational economic men. The feminine was ignored, if not silenced.[10] Only now are scholars unearthing the insights of early female writers such as Mary Parker Follett (1868–1933), who wrote on the holistic nature of collaboration and competition, reciprocal relationships, "power with" rather than "power over," and alternative dispute resolution mechanisms.[11] These are some of the leadership practices that we describe as elements of feminine capital.

Women in Management

Removed from the gaze of academe, by the mid-1900s North American women sensed the phenomenon of what Betty Friedan coined "the problem that has no name."[12] Her 1963 groundbreaking book, *The Feminine Mystique*, shone a spotlight on the lives of middle-class American housewives, women living with material comfort and unhappiness. Their desire to work outside the home ushered in the second wave of feminism. While the first wave secured the right of women to vote, the second demanded economic opportunity. Women wanted more.

The 1970s and 1980s witnessed the mass entry of women into paid employment, spurred by economic necessity and the desire to work outside the home. Simultaneously, primarily female academics began to capture women's professional experiences through research. Few studies, however, challenged established theory. Much of the research in the social sciences simply entailed adding a study variable labeled "sex" to established study protocols, without regard to the impact of structural, historical, and cultural influences on enterprise performance.[13] The fundamental desire for wealth, convenience, and luxury was assumed to apply to all.[14] Studies employing surveys and other diagnostics constructed from male-

Table 1.1: Early masculine and feminine nomenclatures

Bem Sex Role Inventory		Schein Sex Role Descriptive Index	
Masculine	**Feminine**	**Characteristics of Managers That Are More Similar to Men Than to Women**	**Characteristics of Managers That Are More Similar to Women Than to Men**
Self-reliant	Gentle	Logical	Modest
Analytical	Warm	Consistent	Neat
Defends own beliefs	Sensitive to the needs of others	Emotionally stable	Aware of the feelings of others
Assertive	Tender	Frivolous	Not vulgar
Strong personality	Does not use harsh language	Leadership ability	Humanitarian values
Leadership abilities	Shy	Direct	Intuitive
Willing to take risks	Eager to soothe hurt feelings	Well informed	Creative
Independent	Soft-spoken	Objective	Cheerful
Forceful	Flatterable	Aggressive	Sophisticated
Makes decisions easily	Loves children	Analytical ability	Helpful
Self-sufficient	Compassionate	Self-reliant	Understanding
Dominant	Understanding		
Willing to take a stand	Yielding		
Ambitious	Sympathetic		
Competitive	Loyal		

only samples produced mounting evidence of gender differences in enterprise performance.[15]

Early attempts to capture the feminine within the management literature are presented in Table 1.1. The table presents traits drawn from diagnostics that have been used to examine the characteristics of successful managers and entrepreneurs. The left-side columns are selected attributes taken from the *Bem Sex Role Inventory*, characteristics thought to reveal that which is masculine and that which is feminine.[16] The right columns list attributes synonymous with "being managerial and male" and "being managerial and female." These word associations are drawn from the *Schein Sex Role Descriptive Index*.[17] These dated diagnostics continue to be used by social scientists.[18] This is unfortunate in that the lists are premised on the notion that masculine and feminine are independent or oppositional dimensions. They position the masculine within decision-making roles and the feminine within passive or supportive roles. The private or domestic sphere is defined as feminine. We argue that the feminine and masculine fall within a continuum of influences and that feminine capital can be realized in commercial settings and entrepreneurial roles.

Underperformance Rationales

Another legacy from this period is the view that female entrepreneurs are less successful. Comparing females to males creates a norm that diminishes the economic and social value of women entrepreneurs. Here are some of the claims that fall under this umbrella:

- Female-owned firms underperform.[19] For example, accountants and financial analysts draw on resource-based and investment theory to explain gender differences in enterprise performance; comparatively small initial investments produce commensurate smaller economic returns.
- Economists observe that female-owned enterprises incur relatively high transactional costs, costs such as negotiating and information gathering that are incurred by all firms competing in the marketplace. Relatively high transaction costs are associated with weak economies of scale due to firm size.
- Marketers report that, relative to male competitors, women business owners underprice goods and, in particular, services. Small profit margins then limit opportunities to reinvest in the firm and owner and staff compensation.
- Financial analysts speak about lack of credit histories, which stymie access to credit that is often required to fund firm growth. This then impedes the ability of owners to compete in capital-intensive industries, such as manufacturing.[20]

Figure 1.1: Female deficiencies: Theoretical rationales

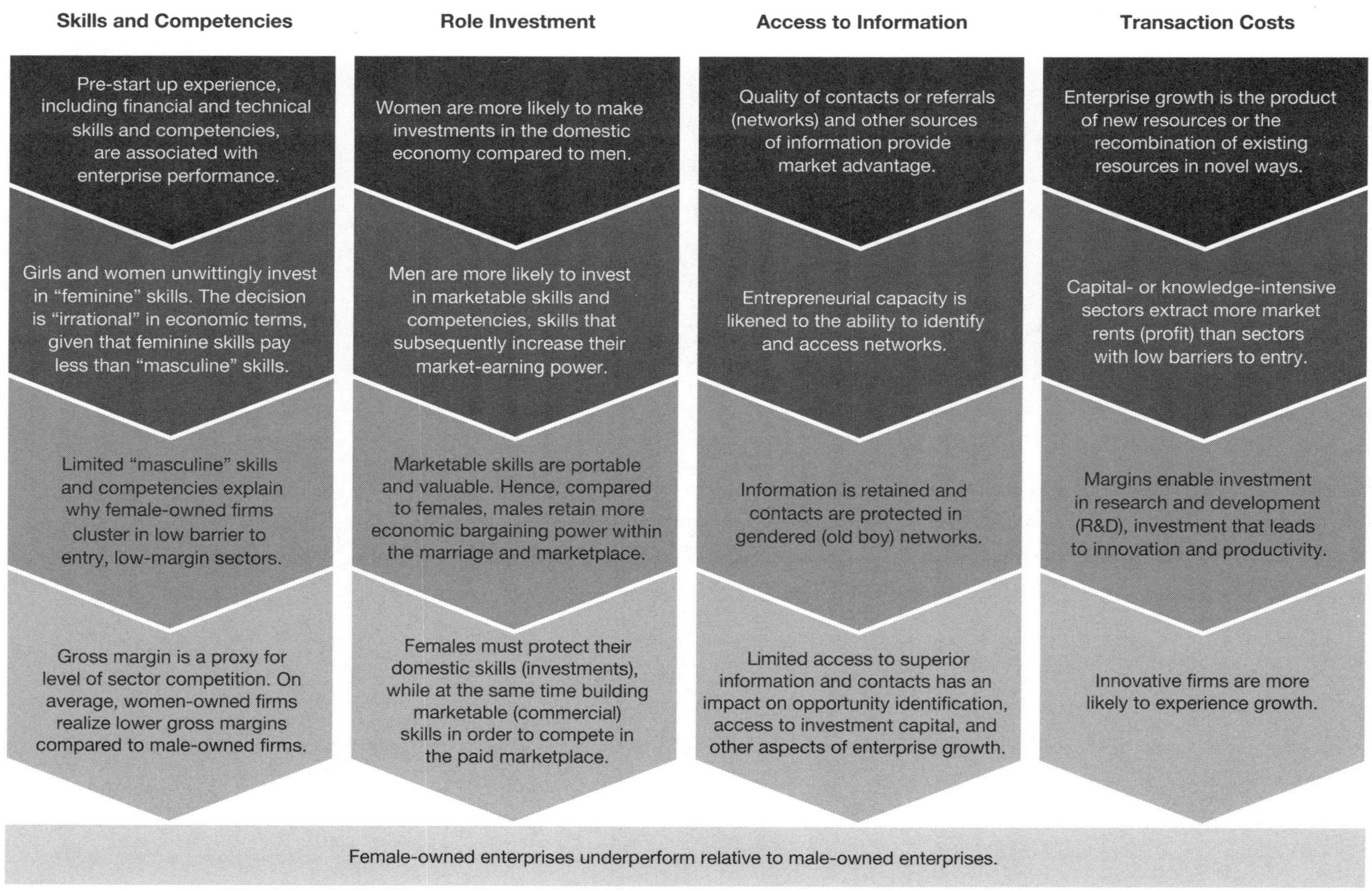

Skills and Competencies

Pre-start up experience, including financial and technical skills and competencies, are associated with enterprise performance.

Girls and women unwittingly invest in "feminine" skills. The decision is "irrational" in economic terms, given that feminine skills pay less than "masculine" skills.

Limited "masculine" skills and competencies explain why female-owned firms cluster in low barrier to entry, low-margin sectors.

Gross margin is a proxy for level of sector competition. On average, women-owned firms realize lower gross margins compared to male-owned firms.

Role Investment

Women are more likely to make investments in the domestic economy compared to men.

Men are more likely to invest in marketable skills and competencies, skills that subsequently increase their market-earning power.

Marketable skills are portable and valuable. Hence, compared to females, males retain more economic bargaining power within the marriage and marketplace.

Females must protect their domestic skills (investments), while at the same time building marketable (commercial) skills in order to compete in the paid marketplace.

Access to Information

Quality of contacts or referrals (networks) and other sources of information provide market advantage.

Entrepreneurial capacity is likened to the ability to identify and access networks.

Information is retained and contacts are protected in gendered (old boy) networks.

Limited access to superior information and contacts has an impact on opportunity identification, access to investment capital, and other aspects of enterprise growth.

Transaction Costs

Enterprise growth is the product of new resources or the recombination of existing resources in novel ways.

Capital- or knowledge-intensive sectors extract more market rents (profit) than sectors with low barriers to entry.

Margins enable investment in research and development (R&D), investment that leads to innovation and productivity.

Innovative firms are more likely to experience growth.

Female-owned enterprises underperform relative to male-owned enterprises.

More explanations for the underperformance of female-owned enterprises are posed by different management disciplines. Organizational behaviorists report on limited management or leadership experience prior to startup or limited applied knowledge about engineering and technology, while industrial psychologists point to constrained intentions, modest performance expectations, and low entrepreneurial self-efficacy. The list of structural and cultural deficiencies is long—and growing. Deficiency rationales create language that diminishes women's entrepreneurship. Contributions are dismissed. One can think about such rationales within a balance sheet, in which being female is moved from being an asset to being a liability to enterprise performance. The implicit message is that female entrepreneurs simply don't measure up to expectations.

In Figure 1.1, we present another view of the deficiency rationale. While the foundational argument for each logic stream differs, added together, all position female entrepreneurs as underperformers when compared to male entrepreneurs. The first column draws from human resource theory to expose women's lack of marketable skills and competencies. The second, a role investment rationale, explains why female-owned firms are poor investments. The third deficiency scenario, access to information, clarifies how certain parties in commercial transactions (such as female-owned firms) have relatively limited access to value-added information (such as market intelligence). Think of "old boy networks." This advantages one of the parties (male-owned enterprises) over another. The fourth deficiency stream describes variations in transaction costs associated with creating competitive (female-male) advantage or disadvantage. While these four different arguments appear to have explanatory power, they are all built on the underlying assumption that women-owned enterprises underperform, compared to the "standard" venture (that is, masculine status quo). The result? Women entrepreneurs are further discredited.

REFLECTIONS

In reviewing Figure 1.1, reflect on how some of the deficiency rationales may affect you as a business owner, an aspiring entrepreneur, an intrapreneur, or a student. If you currently own a business, for example, do any of the streams of influence speak to your own experiences? If so, what have you done in response? What strategies have been the most successful and why? If you are considering venture creation, think about ways in which you can mitigate these deficiencies. Planning ahead will pay off as you set up your enterprise. For instance, if you have limited management experience, consider whom to contact to access initial support for key aspects of the startup such as client development. If you are concerned about having adequate time to invest in the emergent firm, consider how best to discuss with family, friends, or business partner the importance and anticipated demands of the new venture (for example, how will each positively and continuously contribute to your success?). With respect to access to information, what formal networks should you tap into prior to starting up? Can you build a business model to withstand rapid growth and relatively high transaction costs? If you are not sure how to respond to these questions, read on. The following chapters offer many ideas, tips, and tools to help you answer these questions.

Be aware that biased assumptions of female-owned enterprises, such as those illustrated in Figure 1.1, continue to hold weight in the media, corridors of government, and academe. You may assume that this type of thinking is old school. Not so. One example, published in a prestigious journal in 2011, employed the rationale of preference-driven constraints to explain women's financial underperformance.[21] Yet the concept of preference implies that women *choose* to manage small and unprofitable enterprises. This is not always the case. Women can encounter subtle yet insidious pressures to stay small, such as from partners who are unwilling to take on more domestic responsibilities or cofounders who lack vision. And we are yet to meet a woman who prefers to make less money than more. The notion of preference is one more concept that lends credibility to beliefs about female deficiencies and the underperformance of women entrepreneurs. Given such thinking—even within top-ranked management journals—it is easier to understand why many women around the world feel that they are not taken seriously as business owners.

The focus on underperformance and a failure to recognize feminine capital as an asset discourages more fruitful research, studies that would benefit all entrepreneurs. Being female is seen as problematic. Underperformance hypotheses[22] legitimize political and government indifference to recognizing the contributions of women to the social and economic fabric of the global economy. For these reasons, we turn to feminist criticism for an alternative view of entrepreneurship.

Feminist Criticism

During the 1990s, management researchers began to call for a reexamination of the venture creation process. Critics noted that female-dominated sectors typically were excluded from scientific inquiry, an omission that served to overvalue male business activities and undervalue enterprises associated with female entrepreneurs.[23] Feminist criticism provides fertile ground for rethinking about entrepreneurship. Eileen Fischer and Rebecca Reuber were among the first to argue that feminist theory, rather than biology (male-female cohorts), offers a more robust explanation for enterprise performance.[24] Concerns were also voiced about "linguistic differencing" of male and female entrepreneurs,[25] sex role stereotyping of the successful entrepreneur, and an absence of focus on power imbalances within entrepreneurial relationships.[26] Unlike women in management research, feminist criticism explicitly challenged "gender arrangements" such as masculine notions of what it is to be an entrepreneur.[27] The linguistic lexicon of entrepreneurship did not include feminine attributes.

Feminist criticism was a good theoretical fit, as feminism and entrepreneurship have much in common. Feminism seeks to address subordination and enhance economic well-being. Women entrepreneurs achieve this same end through the creation of personal wealth. Both feminism and entrepreneurship entail opportunity recognition. Opportunity recognition is exemplified in alliances founded by women, alliances that embody the common desire for both economic and social change. Opportunity recognition is evidenced in the growing number of women-only venture capital pools, television networks, and charitable foundations. Opportunity recognition is captured in emerging policy and legislation to mandate representation of women on public and private boards.

In explaining entrepreneurship, most contemporary studies reflect one of two feminist viewpoints: liberal feminist reasoning or social feminist thinking. The tenets of the two feminist paradigms follow. We then describe how entrepreneurship can inform feminism, when entrepreneurs are seen to effect social and economic change for women. When reading this next section, again reflect upon your own views about the influence of gender in venture creation. You can use this information to question or strengthen your thinking about how being female has an impact on enterprise performance.

Liberal and Social Feminism

Liberal feminism assumes that all human beings are "equal and they are essentially rational, self-interest-seeking agents."[28] This perspective is rooted in liberal political philosophy, reflected in the work of social activists such as Mary Wollstonecraft and John Stuart Mill.[29] From this vantage point, in order to start and grow enterprises, women entrepreneurs must overcome or circumvent systemic barriers. To the extent that women business owners can do so, enterprise performance would be equivalent to that of male counterparts. According to this view, differential enterprise performance would reflect that women are disadvantaged relative to men due to overt discrimination, fewer opportunities, and systemic cultural and institutional barriers.[30] As such, women would fail to achieve full potential in the marketplace. In practical terms, liberal feminism suggests that *if* women entrepreneurs acquire commercial acumen and social capital equivalent to those of male entrepreneurs, there will be no systemic gender differences in enterprise performance. Performance differences can be accounted for by sector influences such as margins and growth rates. Advocates who follow a liberal feminist perspective fight for policy and program changes that will remove individual-level constraints (for example, funding day care and small-business training).

A second paradigm, social feminism, suggests the need to dig deeper into women's experiences to understand women from their *own* perspectives.[31] The philosophical origin of social feminism is based on reproduction theory, in which feminine traits are seen as beneficial resources that can be used constructively. Men and women are seen to be essentially different. However, social feminism contends that gender is socially constructed; being female cannot be separated from the influences of history, culture, and the broader society. Gender differences are also evidenced in values and motives and differences in power and autonomy that remain within the home (female or private sphere) and workplace (male or public sphere). The central premises of social feminism applied to women's entrepreneurship include the following:

- The feminine is constituted in the very nature and operational practices of enterprises.
- Being female is evidenced within entrepreneurial motives, opportunity recognition, sector choice, organizational structure, and growth strategy.
- Gender influences are therefore embedded within the many factors that contribute to enterprise performance.

It is therefore reasonable to expect differences in the underlying nature, construction, and outcomes of male- and female-owned enterprises. From the social feminist perspective, advocacy focuses on changing patriarchal structures and legislation that advantage males (such as tax and investment schemes in sectors that systematically exclude many female-owned enterprises). Policy directives should also fund female-only small-business training.

Liberal and social feminist criticisms do not, however, complete the story of women's entrepreneurship. There is a third perspective from which entrepreneurship can be viewed, one which we coin "entrepreneurial feminism."

Entrepreneurial Feminism

Entrepreneurial feminism introduces entrepreneurship into feminist thought. We listened to women describe a new wave of feminism, one in which entrepreneurial women are embracing economic self-sufficiency and social change. Women are employing venture creation as an aspirational means to improve the well-being of others, particularly girls and women. For some, feminism has come full circle. Where once patriarchal laws and attitudes historically prohibited women's rights to vote, retain property, or pursue careers, women now are embracing entrepreneurial feminism as a means to contribute to family life while participating in the formal economy, changing the way business is done and building communities of like-minded business owners.

A diversity of feminist values is being realized in entrepreneurial settings, a view predicated on ethical considerations. Liberal feminist and social criticism report on women's entrepreneurship within the *existing* owner ↔ firm ↔ market paradigm. Entrepreneurial feminism embraces an alternative view. It proposes an action orientation: female entrepreneurs are infusing feminist values *within the act* of venture creation. Contrary to neoclassical economics (recall rational economic man and the invisible hand), in which choice is seen as distinct from moral behavior, entrepreneurial feminism turns such thinking on its head.

Entrepreneurial feminism posits that the exchange process is gendered, on the basis of relational capital and mutual trust. Entrepreneurial feminism is a conscious and deliberate response to address women's subordination through enterprise creation. In our research, the feminine is partially evidenced in the sharing of power in relationships and through owner authenticity to self and entrepreneurial creativity. Feminist values reflect the need for economic and social independence. Competition is dependent on cooperation through agreement on rules, whereby women are not only subjected to but also influence market structures, as it suits individual purpose.

In our research with feminist entrepreneurs, inclusivity was evidenced in the way in which these women expressed their desire to work with men and women. They often do so within the existing market structure, using traditional business practices. At the same time, many described how they express feminist values through their enterprises. Another common theme was a desire to empower women, to effect change through business ownership. As one participant said when we asked her to define feminism,

> I think a feminist is someone who promotes women's opportunity. And I usually promote everybody's opportunity. But, again, I have a particular bias or interest towards encouraging women and providing opportunities for them to see beyond their horizons.

Table 1.2 presents an evolutionary view of the tenets of neoclassical economics, social feminism, and entrepreneurial feminism. We do not include liberal feminism for several reasons. There is little empirical evidence to support liberal theory in practice. Even among those economies recognized as supporting a high level of gender equality, (for example, female enrollment in post-secondary education, entry- and mid-level job opportunities for women, maternity benefits, provision for day care), women remain less likely to engage in business ownership compared to men. The entrepreneurship gender gap is evidenced in indices that monitor

Table 1.2: Theoretical foundations of entrepreneurial feminism

	Neo-Classical Economics	Social Feminism	Entrepreneurial Feminism
Principles	The enterprise is autonomous. Firms relate to society only through the marketplace.	Women are socialized to assume supportive rather than leadership roles. Women entrepreneurs face other unique barriers such as being newcomers to the commercial marketplace.	Egalitarian, partnership-based decision making is reflected in commercial transactions, webs of relationships, connectedness, cooperation, empathy, and trust. Owners act to coordinate and share knowledge and skills, rather than competing for resources.
Entrepreneurial Values	Owner values are reflected in their profit-seeking orientation (that is, minimizing risk and maximizing return on investment). Entrepreneurs are characterized as heroic, self-reliant, assertive, forceful, dominant, and willing to take risks.	Entrepreneurial values are reflected in gendered definitions of entrepreneurial self and identity; power differentials in the home and marketplace; and level of authenticity, self-efficacy, and creativity.	Values are reflected in mutuality of relationships, economic independence, social action, and synthesis of opposites. Many women business owners act in accordance with internal wisdom and promotion of conflict resolution (such as intra-group support).
Dynamics of Market Exchange	Decisions are objective and distanced from personal biases and emotion.	Commercial decisions are not distinct from, and therefore can conflict with, ethical behavior and values. Owners' values partially explain differences in enterprise performance.	Market exchange is predicated on social relationships and utilitarian outcomes. Women seek to re-create rules of the marketplace to make up for historical subjugation. For example, markets can be viewed as dependent upon cooperation rather than competition.
		Time	

women's economic and social progress. Several are describe in Chapter 7. As such, entrepreneurial feminism is positioned as an evolutionary synthesis of neoclassical economic theory and the adoption of social feminist thought. It serves as a reference as we continue to build our arguments about feminine capital.

REFLECTIONS

We encourage you to take time to review Table 1.2. To what extent are your views embedded in neoclassical economics? Do your views reflect social feminist principles? To what degree might your business practices adhere to the principles and values described as entrepreneurial feminism? How do these theoretical foundations inform your opinions about creating opportunities for women? We have observed an evolution in thinking about the role of venture creation in addressing women's subordination. Do you know any feminist entrepreneurs?

Having introduced entrepreneurial feminism, let us return to the stories that we described earlier in the chapter. We consider Elaine Jolly to be a feminist entrepreneur. Her vision for an integrated women's health center is predicated on women's needs for specialized services, procedures, and products. She has expressed this vision by building a business case for efficient, female-specialized health care. This scenario is also a classic case of good marketing: designing services to meet client needs (that is, decisions are patient centered). From the outset, she approached venture creation by marshaling the talents and resources of women. However, not all of our entrepreneurial heroines fit the profile of feminist entrepreneurs. Not all have an explicit double bottom line: to create an enterprise and to effect change for other women. Yet all illustrate the diverse nature of feminine capital.

One of Maria Guidi's motives in applying for certification as a majority women-owned company with WEConnect International is to expand her network of like-minded, growth-oriented entrepreneurs. Feminine capital is reflected in a desire to join a women's business community that may help her and others address their sense of isolation while also meeting prospective clients. Susan's decision to start a business or return to work is an example of how being female is embedded in occupational choices and the desire to balance professional and domestic responsibilities. Asha Sing appointed a male vice-president to deal with the few clients who prefer to deal with men. Experience has taught her that getting the job done is the best response to antiquated biases about doing business with women. Cynthia Goh's decision to ignore gender suggests that there are no simple, applicable theories to explain how being female influences business practices. While her products and ventures are not targeted specifically to women, feminine capital is evidenced in how she is paving the way for other female academic entrepreneurs, by being a role model and breaking academic stereotypes. Asha and Cynthia also illustrate a subtle aspect of feminine capital, "the work around": when one confronts gender barriers in the process of venture creation, the entrepreneurial response is to determine a viable alternative route to "get the job done."

The Bigger Picture

Personal stories such as those of our five entrepreneurial heroines are constructed within a larger reality. Country-level studies offer evidence that entrepreneurial orientation is not solely an individual decision. In the bigger picture, access to resources, including knowledge about navigating sociocultural norms and cumbersome regulations, is reflected in women's entrepreneurial propensity. In 2012, the

World Bank concluded, "cultural attitudes and normative discrimination still prevent women and girls from participating equally with men as paid workers, as business operators and owners and as asset holders."[32] The magnitude of influences is captured in the *Global Entrepreneurship Monitor* (GEM).[33] GEM is a global initiative that reports on early stage entrepreneurial activities across economies. It focuses on individuals in the process of starting a business and those running young firms. The variation in the engagement (or ratio) of female to male entrepreneurs varies considerably by country. Interestingly, the gap decreases with country-specific level of economic development. That is, as countries become more developed economically, the proportion of female entrepreneurs increases. Yet, across all economies, women perceive themselves as having lower entrepreneurial capabilities.

Among the United States and Western European countries, female participation ranges from one-fourth of all entrepreneurs in Norway to the United States and Canada, where nearly half of businesses retain some female ownership. China and to a lesser extent Taiwan show high levels of female engagement. Korea and Japan are among the lowest ratios. Eastern Europe also exhibits relatively low levels of female entrepreneurial activity. Russia is an exception, where women represent 44 percent of entrepreneurs.

As we head into the next chapter, ask yourself,

- To what extent do gender, cultural, and structural factors influence my entrepreneurial intentions?
- What *other* factors might influence entrepreneurial decision making?

To inform your thinking, in the next chapter we explore three cognitive drivers of opportunity recognition: entrepreneurial intention, perceptions of success, and identity.

Intention, Success, and Identity

2

This chapter gets to the heart of feminine capital. As we learned from the women of Wolfville, Nova Scotia, feminine capital is both personal and collective. These women see themselves as local entrepreneurs and women of the world. We focus on feminine capital in the context of the individual and how self-perception affects decision making. We also describe entrepreneurial roles and explore identity and success through the words shared by female entrepreneurs. We close the chapter by considering factors that lead to entrepreneurial action. The *Entrepreneurial Identity Framework* presents a visual model of how identity, success, and intention interact, as individuals weigh the many trade-offs associated with venture creation.[1] This framework also provides a springboard for further understanding how feminine capital influences decision making and venture performance.

Identity is an individual's sense of self. Entrepreneurial identity stands at the intersection of self-image (Who am I?) and the occupational choice to be an entrepreneur (What do I want to be?).[2] We link identity with two more foundational elements of the venture creation process: perceptions of success and intention. These three elements are precursors to entrepreneurial action.[3]

Before exploring entrepreneurial identity, perceptions of success, and intention, we encourage you to complete a short exercise. On a piece of paper, write down five words that describe you. What are your notable traits or attributes? Next, write down five words that describe an entrepreneur. Having done so, compare the two sets of words.

How do the words in both lists differ? How are they similar? To what extent do the words you use to describe yourself match those typically used to describe an entrepreneur? Such reflections are useful because identity, or self-image, guides how we respond as entrepreneurs, and whether we believe that we "have what it takes" to be successful.[4] If your descriptors from the two lists were very different, you may not perceive yourself to have the attributes necessary to be an entrepreneur. But is this true? To help you better understand how many business owners go about constructing their identities, the next section delves deeper into what we have learned from our research with women entrepreneurs.

Entrepreneurial Identity

In describing their entrepreneurial identity, business owners use adjectives, clichés, and metaphors.[5] Words retain symbolic meaning, reinforce perception, and crystalize what it is to be an entrepreneur. In Chapter 1, we described how entrepreneurship is infused with language that personifies the entrepreneur as masculine.[6] It is not surprising then that females are less likely to see themselves as entrepreneurial.[7] This occurs when self-image does not match the stereotypical successful entrepreneur. Studies also tell us that low entrepreneurial identity among females, compared to males, cuts across age groups and nationalities.[8] Being female and entrepreneurial can be seen as a conflict between economic and social values.[9] Misalignment between self and identity weakens intention and, ultimately, entrepreneurial action. Social and cultural contradictions can lead to an *entrepreneurial identity gap*. We define *gap* as a schism between that which is personified as female or feminine and that which is described as entrepreneurial, as defined by masculine-oriented past practice.[10]

To examine the construction of entrepreneurial identity, we conducted a series of studies in which we asked female entrepreneurs the following question: *How, if at all, does being female influence your business practices?*[11] Study subjects included women entrepreneurs in the advanced technology sectors, startup business owners, and participants of women-focused training programs. Multiple themes emerged. The women described themselves in ways that are refreshingly powerful. The most prevalent theme was *participative leadership*—the involvement of others in business success. Female entrepreneurs talked about being connected, sharing, leading by example, and empowering and motivating others to step over boundaries and to get involved. While women did not use the word *democratic* per se, they talked about leadership in democratic terms, citing the desire to provide employees and associates with opportunities to voice opinions and participate in decision making. They gain a sense of accomplishment through others.

Some described how women "foster relationships," "understand other women," and use "intuition" and "sensitivity" to run their businesses and empower others. Women were also seen to use more holistic definitions of success in comparison with male counterparts. The majority of self-descriptive statements were optimistic in tone. These entrepreneurs saw themselves as professional, action-oriented, creative thinkers and problem solvers, visionary and determined. Bias toward action reflected an interest in change or a perceived need to initiate it.[12] These words challenge the view that women are ghettoized or sidelined to the margins of entrepreneurship. In conversations with the women we interviewed, their words resonated with action, passion, and vision. More themes emerged. Which of the following attributes describe you?

- *Action-oriented* was associated with being hard working, positive, optimistic, and driven to pursue one's ideas. *Action orientation* also referred to the ability and desire to pursue entrepreneurial ideas with passion and energy. *Entrepreneurial identity* was described using words such as *hard working, high energy, confident, assertive,* and *optimistic.*
- *Creative problem solvers* described themselves as challenging others in a constructive, positive way: being creative, being curious, having many ideas, being interested in solving problems through innovative solutions, and having the ability to dream and to use their imagination. Women were equally likely to perceive themselves to be *visionary,* demonstrating strategic thinking and clear sightedness, such as acting on calculated risks.
- Female entrepreneurs equated being *professional* with being respectful, sincere, knowledgeable, organized, intelligent, and acting with integrity.
- *Relationship-focused* women saw themselves as collaborative, fostering relationships using care and empathy to nurture employees, partners, and customers. In the words of one woman, "I like to share a lot of information so that we can find a win-win solution. I'm very fair. I recognize that everyone is in business to make money, but I also recognize that there are other drivers. . . . I come at it from a noncompetition, nonthreatening perspective."

These women were determined to make a difference through entrepreneurship. For some, this meant social change: bettering the lives of girls and women through their business endeavors. We called these business owners feminist entrepreneurs. For others, it meant bringing an innovative product to market, one that would help their clients in some important way. Irrespective of the business goals, these women described themselves as persistent and tenacious. Collective leadership was characterized as recognizing the role of others, building a strong team, being a group facilitator, sharing leadership, and developing others. Our study respondents perceived themselves as being able to motivate others and offer honest feedback. These attributes speak to feminine capital.

It was notable that many of the traits typically identified in the media, including stereotypical feminine characteristics listed in the *Bem Sex Role Inventory* or the *Schein Descriptive Index,* were not voiced in our studies.[13] In our research, female entrepreneurs also gave little attribution to traditional *maternal* characteristics (such as eagerness to sooth hurt feelings, warmth or tenderness, love of children).

It seems that assumptions about a presupposed mothering ethic may have little application in the entrepreneurial context. Maternity (associated with childrearing) does not reflect peer-to-peer business relationships, as described by these entrepreneurial women.

However, there were other comments that we heard within our studies that are worrisome. Some statements were negative in tone and content. Being female was perceived to be a liability. Illustrative quotes about female entrepreneurial identity suggest that some view themselves as "outsiders" and that women don't "ask," "think big," "have confidence," "negotiate well," or "retain power." It is telling that women voiced these depictions! Some were resigned to the fact that gender challenges are normal and part of being female in a male-dominated world. Their perceptions reflected difficult relationships with male suppliers or partners, "old boys" networks, a "lack of female role models," and self-limiting perceptions about growth (for example, "there are limits to my ability to obtain financing through conventional methods"). Some missed having a sounding board. Several observed other women who need "confidence boosts" to start a business. One described how she managed to conquer her "inner critic" through coaching and professional support, and she then parlayed her experiences into a consulting practice. As a result, she is now coaching others. Her words echo a fear of failure:

> I find some women let fear take a controlling ride from the first day. They start worrying about all the things they're not good at, they start worrying about all the things they don't know, they start worrying about all the things that could go wrong.

We are not alone in reporting such observations.[14] The entrepreneurial identity gap pervades and is instilled across all sectors, from female-dominated clusters such as health care to male-dominated clusters in advanced technology. For example,

- Female entrepreneurs in a nursing study describe how they consciously distance themselves from their role of "entrepreneur" in order to retain legitimacy and acceptance amongst female colleagues and employees.[15]
- In the advanced technology sectors, multiple studies report that being female is associated with perceptions about a lack of credentials or technical competence.[16]
- A large-scale study of male and female students in the United States, India, and Turkey reports that those students who rate themselves as more masculine than feminine (that is, rated themselves higher in stereotypical male gender characteristics) express higher intentions of starting a business.[17] Similarly, surveys of business owners report how both males and females value masculine characteristics as the dominant entrepreneurial criteria.[18]

- One British survey of female entrepreneurs reports that 40 percent believe they have experienced difficulties at startup because of gender.[19] Challenges include assumptions that women are not as technically competent and conflicts between "being a mum and an entrepreneur."

Fifty years after the publication of *The Feminine Mystique*, professional women are accepted as long as they do not challenge masculine norms.[20] And despite the global proliferation of female business owners, linguistic profiling continues to personify the entrepreneur as masculine.[21] That women do not always fit this mold results in a needlessly negative self-image, low expectations of self, and a lack of incentive to start or grow their enterprises.

Transformational Nature of Entrepreneurship

Change is afoot. More and more women are challenging stereotypes and expectations by becoming engaged in entrepreneurship. And the act of being entrepreneurial is transformative, as women business owners assemble, validate, and discard identities over time.[22] Slowly, societal expectations change. This movement is being reflected in our research results as well as those of other entrepreneurship scholars; many women report having experienced very positive changes about emerging entrepreneurial roles. For example, in an American study of entrepreneurial identity, participants described themselves as one of the following:[23]

- *Founders*: women with a passion for activities associated with assembling the resources necessary to create an enterprise. Founders are defined as "establishing a venture for commercializing and exploiting opportunities." Remember Asha Sing in Chapter 1? She is a serial entrepreneur. Prior to starting her current firm, she had founded several businesses and a trade association. Her identity reflects someone who is passionate about venture creation. Asha is motivated to establish and nurture ventures.
- *Inventors*: those who seek out new ideas and are engaged in product development. These entrepreneurs are highly committed to commercializing new concepts, techniques, processes, or technologies by constantly seeking out ideas, tinkering with product development, or scanning the environment for market-disruptive opportunities. Cynthia Goh is one example. Her nanotechnology research is cutting edge, and she is passionate about bringing innovations to market. Through her endeavors, she personifies at least three identities: academic, inventor, and entrepreneur.
- *Developers*: women who identify with activities related to market development and financial growth. These entrepreneurs experience passion when they engage in activities that enhance the firm's value proposition, some-

times through new customer acquisition. An example is Maria Guidi. She is in the process of weighing decisions about how best to grow her firm by entering new markets, diversifying her product portfolio (for example, through energy efficient, "green" homes), or both.

So while some perceive being female as a disadvantage, others see feminine capital as advantageous. And there are many different ways to be entrepreneurial. We know that through entrepreneurship, identity is reconstructed, especially in the early stages of enterprise development.[24] Research has shown that there are positive connections between self, opportunity recognition, role development, and resulting business outcomes.[25] Therefore, when women visualize themselves as "successful entrepreneurs," they are more likely to recognize the potential of their ideas as a product or service in the marketplace. More important, they are then more likely to commercialize them.

It may be that some women entrepreneurs need to consciously manage their entrepreneurial identity in order to achieve specific outcomes. To a greater or lesser degree, they need to think about how they "co-create" their identity within the social and business context in which they exchange goods.

A key take-away from all of these studies is that there is no universal answer to how being female influences entrepreneurial identity, no singular perception about how being female influences practice. Female entrepreneurs continue to produce new knowledge about what it means to be entrepreneurial.[26] Women are redefining venture creation using new language.

Feminine capital captures the multitude of experiences, values, identities, and competencies that are mobilized through the venture creation process. It remains important to positively self-define how being female affects your business practices. Doing so can have an impact on enterprise performance.

Closing the Identity Gap

The now-ubiquitous presence of female entrepreneurs lays bare the antiquated notion that being female is to be considered an "other" in the commercial marketplace. Yet in most countries, the impact of women's entrepreneurship is still barely on the radar. Feminine capital offers awareness, knowledge, and the recognition that entrepreneurship needs new nomenclature—leadership attributes and characteristics that more accurately reflect women's experiences and voices about being entrepreneurial.

The ways in which women entrepreneurs describe themselves also differ from those presented in traditional financial theory. An example is the concept of risk-taking. While some women mentioned risk, their description of the behavior was unexpected: they did not mention level of difficulty, fear of failure, or unknown outcomes. This contrasts with the popularized notion of risk-taking, as initially described by David McClelland. McClelland, a Harvard psychological theorist, sought to understand individuals' "motives to achieve" under conditions of competition. In his 1961 publication *The Achieving Society*,[27] he advanced a model of human motivation in which high *need for achievement* was associated with high levels of individual responsibility for outcomes, desire for significant accomplishment, mastering of skills, control, and high standards. These attributes were then associated with the taking of risks. Those who exhibited such qualities were deemed to be more likely to pursue entrepreneurial opportunities. Over time, his ideas evolved into preconceptions about entrepreneurial identity. They have become the accepted norm and are rarely questioned. Today, then, being entrepreneurial is commonly associated with risk and bravery, autonomy, and self-sufficiency—attributes that mirror the archetypal neoclassical male.[28]

By contrast, some of the female entrepreneurs with whom we spoke viewed risk-taking as a process of trial and error and being resourceful. Our studies mirror others that describe women entrepreneurs as focusing on risk in the context of making things happen. They mobilize resources by working with others in collaborative ways.[29] As noted earlier, many prefer a relational style of entrepreneurial leadership. They encourage participation.[30] Not surprisingly, we discovered that their vocabulary reflects this orientation. It is infused with terms such as *empowering*, *enhancing*, and *creating*:

- *Empowering* is characterized by the development of others such as subordinates or clients, enabling them through delegated authority and decision-making power.
- *Enhancing* refers to one's own professional growth and effectiveness and continuous improvement of self and enterprise.
- *Creating* teams is focused on developing teamwork, realizing synergies, and facilitating productive interpersonal relationships.

In addressing the entrepreneurial identity gap, another step is to recognize that masculine stereotypes, often reproduced through the media and academe, further discount women's contributions and capacity to translate wealth into social power.[31] There are simply too few entrepreneurial heroines—household names and faces that inspire young entrepreneurs to seek venture creation as a career option. This is evidenced in the classroom. Curricula can undermine confidence and erode the entrepreneurial intentions of students. There remains a lack of female role models in training materials, including textbooks and cases. This is problematic.

Modeling entrepreneurship as combative and competitive is not consistent with how most women describe entrepreneurial leadership. Young women can be discouraged by not visualizing themselves in this role. Success is defined within a narrow context—firm size and profit. Yet these are not performance measures that all women bring to venture creation. We see the impact when female academics, for example, are significantly less likely to commercialize their intellectual property than their male counterparts.

What we are learning is that in the process of venture creation, experience informs identity.[32] For example, let's return to two of our entrepreneurial heroines. Susan Ross has thought carefully about how the skills and competencies that she gained through the role of product manager have helped to mold her entrepreneurial identity. Elaine Jolly's advocacy for women's health care has been recognized with Canada's highest honor, the Order of Canada. Negotiating identity, for Elaine, implies balancing multiple roles of advocate, decorated citizen, clinician, teacher, founder, leader, and mother. Such negotiations are often difficult, as societal (gender) norms can be strong and insidious. One step toward discarding negative stereotypes is to create your own entrepreneurial brand identity.

Building an entrepreneurial identity requires reflection, negotiation, and watching carefully the words we use to describe others and ourselves. An example of how language can affect the construction of our identities is the term *bossy*, an adjective that is frequently given to girls and women who take a strong leadership role. The word has negative connotations, and it is seldom used to describe men. At the time of writing this book, a campaign to "Ban Bossy" had just been launched.[33] Endorsed by celebrities such as Beyoncé and political leaders such as Condoleezza Rice, the initiative proclaims that the word *bossy* is problematic. We agree. In the words of the first-grade teacher of one of our daughters, "She likes to take a leadership role in games." Referring to girls and women as leaders rather than bossy leverages the power of language.

Learning Aid 2.1 is intended to help you to create a vocabulary to define your own entrepreneurial identity. This tool is based on the affirming statements shared by female entrepreneurs.[34] The attributes were drawn from studies that examine the words that women use to describe themselves as business leaders. All are part of an inventory of positive characteristics that constitute feminine capital.

Review these entrepreneurial attributes to determine which align with your self-perception. Having done so, compare the descriptors with those that you listed at the front of the chapter. How do the lists differ? And how might these words be reflected in action? We invite you to use this vocabulary in speaking with employees, clients, and suppliers. By doing so, you affirm to others what you deem to be entrepreneurial competencies. If you are a student, discuss these attributes

Learning Aid 2.1: Recognizing your feminine capital

Instructions: The following statements reflect the attributes that women use to describe themselves as business leaders. Check those phrases and adjectives that best describe your leadership. Use these phrases to then construct a personal brand image to portray to family, employees, clients, and investors.

Self-Described Characteristics of Women Entrepreneurs

Participative: I am a woman who achieves results through others. I inspire, empower, and develop others. I am a teacher, facilitator, and mentor.

- ☐ **Builder:** I build teams of people. I bring them together, focusing on the same vision, mission, and values.
- ☐ **Coach:** I encourage and reward team members who work with me to help realize a vision.
- ☐ **Facilitator:** I help groups to reach consensus and then execute on that.
- ☐ **Motivate:** I encourage people to step over their boundaries. I get them to do things that they might not have otherwise thought of.
- ☐ **Provide feedback:** I am blunt when others are not doing as much as they can, but I'm not unkind.
- ☐ **Not alone:** I can't do it by myself. It's only when we get a group of people to band together that change happens.
- ☐ **Sharing:** I'm very sharing, and I am happy to give others the credit.

Relational: I am a woman who fosters relationships with employees, partners, and customers. I am considerate, empathic, and understanding.

- ☐ **Collaborative:** I try to be inclusive. It's collaboration at all levels.
- ☐ **Empathy:** I'm very passionate, I'm bold, but I also have a lot of empathy.
- ☐ **Relational:** The way I approach things is by being a connector and convener.
- ☐ **Service-oriented:** I do my best to be of service to others, and to be concerned about people.
- ☐ **Well connected:** Everybody knows me in the industry. It helps to bring in new opportunities.

Flexible: I am a woman who demonstrates flexibility in my interactions with others. I tolerate differences and treat everyone with respect.

- ☐ **Considerate:** I consider others' well-being, and I work at being considerate.
- ☐ **Flexible:** I'm flexible to the point of being fluid.
- ☐ **Tolerant:** I remain true to my beliefs and stand by my commitments.

Professional: I am a woman who is skilled, experienced, intelligent, and respected by others in her field.

- ☐ **Delivers:** I will not commit to or promise anything that I cannot deliver.
- ☐ **Experienced:** I have a lot of experience, across a lot of different roles.
- ☐ **Integrity:** I remain true to my beliefs and stand behind my commitments.
- ☐ **Organized:** I'm pretty organized.

Ethic of care: I am someone who is motivated by helping others and contributing to social good.

- ☐ **Social:** It's not about me. . . . I'm a social entrepreneur.
- ☐ **Make a contribution:** Leadership is about how you view your rights and what you can contribute and what you should give back.

Change agent: I am positive, optimistic, and driven to pursue ideas.

- ☐ **Energetic:** I'm high energy. I exhaust my friends.
- ☐ **Hardworking:** I'm extremely hard working.
- ☐ **Focused on execution:** Everything must be executed flawlessly.
- ☐ **Optimistic:** I think if you have a problem, you learn from it. It's full of information.

Creative thinker and problem solver: I have ideas and like to solve problems.

- ☐ **Curious:** I am curious about the world, and how to do better, and how to improve opportunities.
- ☐ **Fixer:** I'm always looking to see if there should be something to change or improve.
- ☐ **Inspired:** I am inspired by others. Others push me forward.

(*continued*)

Learning Aid 2.1: Recognizing your feminine capital (continued)

Determined: I am someone who takes an idea and sees it through to commercialization.
☐ **Driven:** I don't budge. I don't take no for an answer, I just keep going.   ☐ **Persistent:** One of my strengths is that I persevere.   ☐ **Tenacity:** I'm passionate, tenacious.   ☐ **Stubborn:** I'm very stubborn.
Visionary: I am a woman who has a strategy, who can articulate a vision to others, and who can inspire others to pursue this vision.
☐ **Clear-sighted:** I see certain things very clearly.   ☐ **Communicator:** I am able to communicate my vision to my team so that they are excited by that vision.

with colleagues and faculty. How do entrepreneurship, management, or women's studies curricula recognize the leadership attributes reflected through the words of women entrepreneurs? Recognizing these attributes in yourself, appreciating their value, and speaking about them serves to validate their importance as components of feminine capital. And the better that you understand these assets and the value of your own feminine capital, the better it can be leveraged for business success!

Entrepreneurial Success

Recall again the women that we introduced you to in Chapter 1. Maria's decision about a business startup is influenced by her desire to remain engaged in the local community through client relationships. For Susan, success is measured by work-life balance. For Asha, success means market acceptance of her products and services. Elaine Jolly values quality health care and females' empowerment over their bodies. Cynthia Goh's statements reflect intellectual dimensions of success.

While traditional economic theory postulates that rational commercial decisions are profit-oriented,[35] most women do not define success in financial terms.[36] To learn about how women define success, we spoke with hundreds of entrepreneurs and managers in small firms and large corporate settings about what they value. We heard that success entails trade-offs.[37] Success for many encompassed aspects of family (work-life balance), wealth creation, professional mobility, the environment, and emotional well-being.[38] Throughout these interviews, we also learned that success can be defined as the process of

- *Commercializing* products and services
- *Cooperating* ("Together we can build something")
- *Sharing* resources to help all succeed ("Everyone needs to be validated")
- *Building* on one's personal strengths
- *Supporting* others.

When we further analyzed our interviews with women entrepreneurs, we learned that perceptions of success tend to be influenced by education, experience, occupation, and age, as well as firm size. The more education and years of experience (sometimes referred to as human capital), the greater the value these entrepreneurs placed on commercial outcomes measured by financial indicators such as income and revenue. This makes sense. Women who invest in education seek economic and social rewards associated with professional success. Those who valued autonomy were more likely to value business ownership over corporate employment. Perhaps business ownership better allows credentialed women opportunities to capitalize on their capabilities without the barriers to advancement traditionally inherent in large corporations.

The Paradox of the Optimistic Female Entrepreneur

Our studies revealed another intriguing pattern. We found the tendency for females to rank all success criteria associated with their firms as both *more important* and *more likely* compared to male entrepreneurs. For instance, while the female study participants reported significantly *less revenue* and *fewer employment opportunities*, they consistently ranked these outcomes as more likely and more important than the males did.[39] The paradox extended to how women assessed the rewards of their labor, evidenced in international studies in which women rank themselves as relatively financially successful, even with comparatively fewer assets when compared to men.[40] This phenomenon is referred to as *paradox of the optimistic entrepreneur*. Why might this be the case?

While part of the answer may be that men and women interpret success differently, could another explanation be that women expect less value for their goods and services? Evidence of gender differences in paid employment supports this unusual explanation. Women entrepreneurs' relatively modest expectations may also reflect market signals. For instance, some argue that employers benefit from credentialed and educated women assuming subordinate roles in low-paid jobs.[41] Such expectations may extend to female business owners: corporations benefit from discounted prices predicated on modest expectations of female-owned suppliers. Perhaps as relatively new entrants to the formal economic marketplace, some women are satisfied with merely being present (open for business) rather than expecting financial rewards equal to those of male competitors.

These study findings and speculations prompt a more personal question. How do you view success?

How Do You View Success?

Here is a learning aid to help you to define success. Learning Aid 2.2 is a mapping tool that charts success criteria that female business owners cited in several of our studies.

The success criteria were statistically analyzed to reveal five underlying constructs.[42] The building blocks of entrepreneurial success could be grouped as the following:

- *Market acceptance* refers to commercial dimensions of success such as product or service quality, market acceptance, and product or service innovation.
- *Professional autonomy* reflects the ability to make decisions, maintain commercial relationships, pursue intellectual activities, and engage in community.
- *Work-life balance* pertains to time availability and managing professional and personal relationships.
- *Self-fulfillment* captures intrinsic and personal success criteria such as spiritual well-being, pursuit of intellectual activities, sense of achievement, and self-determination.
- *Financial performance* includes prototypical indicators of enterprise performance such as revenue, employee productivity, profitability, and generating personal earnings.

Learning Aid 2.2 enables you to think about how *you* define success. Complete the diagnostic by determining the *importance* of the building blocks of entrepreneurial success on the left side of the tool. Then, on the right-hand side, indicate the *likelihood* of achieving each of these success criteria in the context of business ownership. Having completed each of the sections, add up your respective scores. The tallies numerically represent what you value most and your perceptions about the likelihood of obtaining these outcomes through business ownership.

REFLECTIONS

If you are considering a business startup, look for gaps between what you believe to be important and the likelihood of attaining success. Gaps are identified as differences between the scores of what you perceive to be very important and the likelihood of achieving success. Let's see how our entrepreneurial heroines might use this diagnostic. If Asha Sing were to complete the tool, she would likely score "financial outcomes" and "autonomy" as very important and very likely. Her responses would mirror the prototypical motives of many entrepreneurs. She may also observe that self-fulfillment is scored as very important, but not likely to be achieved. This might prompt her to become more engaged in the community and think about how to have a positive impact on the lives of her employees. These are actions that might lead to self-fulfillment. Susan Ross is still in transition. She is weighing the merits of employment versus business ownership. Her scores on the importance of work-life

Learning Aid 2.2: Building blocks of entrepreneurial success

Instructions: To complete the exercise, circle the number that represents how you feel, where 1 = not important or not likely, 3 = somewhat important or somewhat likely, and 5 = very important or very likely. Add your scores for each section to determine the relative importance and likelihood of each. Then tally the scores to determine the importance and likelihood of the success attributes. What patterns do you observe?

Importance of Achieving Success Attributes						Likelihood of Achieving Success Attributes					
Market Acceptance						**Market Acceptance**					
Product or service quality	1	2	3	4	5	Product or service quality	1	2	3	4	5
Product adoption	1	2	3	4	5	Product adoption	1	2	3	4	5
Customer relations	1	2	3	4	5	Customer relations	1	2	3	4	5
Product or service innovation	1	2	3	4	5	Product or service innovation	1	2	3	4	5
Score						**Score**					
Professional Autonomy						**Professional Autonomy**					
Ability to make decisions	1	2	3	4	5	Ability to make decisions	1	2	3	4	5
Engagement in community	1	2	3	4	5	Engagement in community	1	2	3	4	5
Independence	1	2	3	4	5	Independence	1	2	3	4	5
Professional freedom	1	2	3	4	5	Professional freedom	1	2	3	4	5
Score						**Score**					
Work-Life Balance						**Work-Life Balance**					
Maintaining relationships	1	2	3	4	5	Maintaining relationships	1	2	3	4	5
Control over my life	1	2	3	4	5	Control over my life	1	2	3	4	5
Time for self	1	2	3	4	5	Time for self	1	2	3	4	5
Acquisition of goods	1	2	3	4	5	Acquisition of goods	1	2	3	4	5
Score						**Score**					
Self-Fulfillment						**Self-Fulfillment**					
Intellectual activities	1	2	3	4	5	Intellectual activities	1	2	3	4	5
Spiritual well-being	1	2	3	4	5	Spiritual well-being	1	2	3	4	5
Sense of achievement	1	2	3	4	5	Sense of achievement	1	2	3	4	5
Impact on the environment	1	2	3	4	5	Impact on the environment	1	2	3	4	5
Score						**Score**					
Financial Performance						**Financial Performance**					
Profitability	1	2	3	4	5	Profitability	1	2	3	4	5
Firm performance	1	2	3	4	5	Firm performance	1	2	3	4	5
Generating income	1	2	3	4	5	Generating income	1	2	3	4	5
Create employment	1	2	3	4	5	Create employment	1	2	3	4	5
Score						**Score**					

balance exceed all other outcomes. At the same time, she wonders if business ownership will provide adequate time for maintaining relationships with family. Hence, she might consider "work sharing" with a corporate colleague. Hence, her score on the likelihood of "work-life balance" success was relatively low compared to the likelihood of other success outcomes. Academic entrepreneurs, such as Cynthia Goh, often value "market acceptance" of their intellectual property. However, the likelihood of successfully launching an innovative product through business ownership may be less likely than if the product launch were to be facilitated through a university technology transfer office. Institutional or university support can enhance product legitimacy. Tech transfer specialists can also open doors to potential clients and investors. Hence, business ownership may make less sense than retained employment. These are strategies that Cynthia might consider.

If you own a small business, observe your response patterns, particularly within those success outcomes that you scored most important and least likely. How can you address these gaps? We hope that you find this diagnostic helpful because how you perceive success underscores entrepreneurial intentions. The next section zeroes in on the way that perceptions of success influence intention.

Entrepreneurial Intention

The Global Entrepreneurship Monitor (GEM), described in Chapter 1, presents measurable evidence that being female influences entrepreneurial intention. In ninety-seven countries, females were less likely to *intend* to pursue business ownership. This is an overwhelming number. One reason offered is higher *fear of failure* than among males. Yet there is no substantive research evidence that firm discontinuance is associated singularly with gender. As this chapter helps to clarify, fear of failure is not the full story. There are other influences that motivate venture creation and growth.

We have described how being female is associated with entrepreneurial identity and success. Being female is also associated with intention in a multitude of other ways: in attitudes about startup and growth; perceptions about securing resources; and assigning importance to the views of spouses, friends, business partners, and investors. For example, our studies found significant gender differences with respect to factors that influence entrepreneurial intention, including the following:[43]

- *Knowledge accumulation*: A perceived threshold of management knowledge is associated with owner's growth expectations, a threshold that many women do not attain prior to startup.
- *Access to resources*: Many women assume that they are unable to access resources necessary for growth. This includes financial capital. This leads

to self-fulfilling outcomes in which "discouraged borrowers" are less likely to ask for capital.

- *Deference*: Female entrepreneurs are more likely to defer to others, such as spouse, with respect to the decision (or not) to grow the firms. This is not the case for males.
- *Control*: Women are more likely to voice concerns that enterprise growth is associated with the loss of control of employees. Conversely, men were more likely to seek growth in order to gain more control of their time and other resources, such as employees.
- *Education*: Being female influences entrepreneurial aspiration early in the lifecycle, as early as post-secondary education. Within our entrepreneurship classrooms that comprise engineers and senior business students, female students are more likely to seek corporate employment than business ownership compared to male colleagues.

Multicountry studies also report gender differences with respect to factors that influence entrepreneurial aspirations. For example, university education appears to play a role in students' entrepreneurial intentions—in a gendered way. Even when a team of researchers *controlled* for influences (that is, the analysis held constant *individual-level* factors such as students' perceptions about the availability of entrepreneurial role models, social network support, experience, and opportunity perception) to examine *organizational-level effects on entrepreneurial propensity* (effects such as entrepreneurship courses, business support programs, and industry ties), entrepreneurship course work and institutional support did not increase desirability of self-employment among female students to the same extent as among male students.[44] Entrepreneurship training did make a difference on entrepreneurial intention, but more so for males than females. Other research findings include the following:

- Entrepreneurial institutional support did not have an equivalent impact on men and women (for example, public seminars, technology transfer offices, startup incubators). Industry ties, such as professionals in the classroom, or formal connections that facilitate commercialization of technology, inspired male students. This was not nearly the case for female students.
- Among males, need for independence, risk-taking, and social network support were positively related to self-employment intention. Among female students, only need for achievement was associated with self-employment intention. Again, risk-taking behavior was less likely to be seen as an attribute associated with female student career aspirations.

- Most important, females were less likely to intend to pursue self-employment, holding all individual and institutional influences constant.

It is not clear why entrepreneurship training affects male and female students differently. We advance three potential explanations: an absence of female connections and role models, gender bias in who receives institutional support, and masculine entrepreneurship curriculum.

Gendering of entrepreneurial intention is not only associated with startup and growth aspirations. It is evidenced in how men and women perceive enterprise growth. Far from being a product of fear and risk-taking, intention comprises multilayers of external and internal influences. The next section provides another set of tools to help you to recognize decision trade-offs. These are helpful because they are based on current research. We contend that many popularized startup diagnostics are dated and gendered. Outdated diagnostics can get you on the wrong path.

The Entrepreneurial Identity Framework

The Entrepreneurial Identity Framework (Figure 2.1) ties together the determinants of entrepreneurial identity: intention and perceptions of success. These, in turn, influence opportunity recognition or how one sees possibilities. For demonstration purposes, the framework lists precursors of intention and success. The model indicates that entrepreneurial identity is a function of intention (composed of attitudes, influences of others, and resources) and the components of perceived success.

Let's review the *components* of entrepreneurial intentions, as defined by Maria Guidi. As the owner of a small construction firm, she is considering the prospect of enterprise growth (intention) through the decision to join WEConnect International. We also learned in Chapter 1 that Maria likes the idea of keeping her business small. For some time, she has assumed that enterprise growth is associated with increased workload and stress (attitude to growth). She likes to run a tight operation and to oversee the work of her employees. She wonders how she will be able to monitor performance, should she expand the firm. At the same time, she appreciates that market expansion may allow her to better serve clients and that new employees are often a source of new ideas. She is not alone in making this decision. Others, such as investors, clients, bankers, and a domestic partner influence this decision (influence of others). Growth may enable Maria to attract quality blue chip clients and to develop more innovative services. Maria's larger

Figure 2.1: The entrepreneurial identity framework

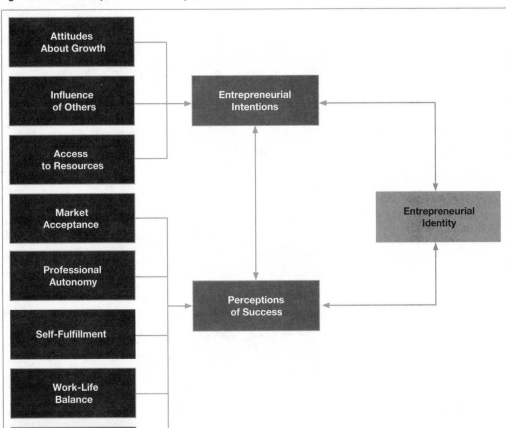

Entrepreneurial Intentions

Attitudes about growth: Creating wealth, ability to maintain control (surveillance), employment for others, industry recognition, stress, time, employment for others, workload, employee well-being, atmosphere, independence, quality of products and services

Influence of others: Clients, advisors, domestic partner or spouse, banker

Access to resources: Administrative support, staff, time, financial and social capital

Perceptions of Success

Market acceptance: Product and service quality, client feedback, and customer relations

Professional autonomy: Engaging in community such as maintaining community relations

Self-fulfillment: Spiritual well-being, pursuit of intellectual activities, self-determination

Work-life balance: Relational interactions between professional and personal relationships

Financial performance: Reflecting organizational performance, productivity, personal income, and profitability

clients favor growth, as they hope to use the firm's services in other regions. Maria's domestic partner also likes the idea of growth, but has voiced concerns that the decision may imply travel and time away from the office (influence of others). So far, growth appears to be an obvious choice. But with the firm's credit line already stretched, the decision will require Maria to seek external investors, renegotiate her line of credit, or both. Staff can barely meet existing demand. And Maria retains a limited professional network outside the region (access to resources). The growth decision implies trade-offs and careful consideration of all these factors. As she thinks about her decision, she reflects on what she values most in her life: self-fulfillment, work-life balance, autonomy, or wealth accumulation (perceptions of success).

Building from such a scenario, how do you view enterprise growth? What factors influence your perspective? Who influences this view? Do you have access to the resources required to fuel enterprise growth? These questions are rarely straightforward, given that less than half of all business owners seek to grow the size and scope of their enterprise.

To answer this question, complete Learning Aid 2.3. This tool is designed to help you understand what factors influence *your* entrepreneurial intentions. To do so, complete the diagnostic by scoring on the left-hand side the *importance* of the growth impacts, including anticipated growth outcomes, access to resources, personal dimensions of growth, influencers, and control. Having done so, complete the right-hand column indicating the *likelihood* of each of the growth impacts. Again, what response patterns do you observe? If gaps exist, how can you move closer to achieving likely *and* important outcomes?

Linking Intention, Success, and Identity

We hope that, having completed this chapter, you have a better sense of how *you* define success and how your intentions link to entrepreneurial identity and enterprise performance. We also hope that you have learned about some of the underlying cognitive influences that motivate entrepreneurial intentions. For example, the entrepreneurial identity gap challenged notions about what it is to be entrepreneurial and successful. The paradox of the optimistic entrepreneur challenged more assumptions about success and how one's perceptions can influence intentions and outcomes. With gender filters firmly in place, we turn the focus, in the next chapter, to the nature of feminine capital, opportunity recognition, and the venture creation process.

Learning Aid 2.3: Building blocks of entrepreneurial intention

Instructions: To complete the exercise, circle the number that represents how you feel, where 1 = not important or not likely, 3 = somewhat important or somewhat likely, and 5 = very important or very likely. Add your scores for each section to determine the relative importance and likelihood of each. Where are the gaps? What patterns do you observe in your responses?

Importance of Impacts						Likelihood of Impacts					
Outcomes of Growth						**Outcomes of Growth**					
Generating wealth	1	2	3	4	5	Generating wealth	1	2	3	4	5
Creating employment	1	2	3	4	5	Creating employment	1	2	3	4	5
Contributing to my community	1	2	3	4	5	Contributing to my community	1	2	3	4	5
Market recognition	1	2	3	4	5	Market recognition	1	2	3	4	5
Score						**Score**					
Access to Resources						**Access to Resources**					
Spousal or partner support	1	2	3	4	5	Spousal or partner support	1	2	3	4	5
Administrative support	1	2	3	4	5	Administrative support	1	2	3	4	5
Financial capital	1	2	3	4	5	Financial capital	1	2	3	4	5
Accounting or financial reporting	1	2	3	4	5	Accounting or financial reporting	1	2	3	4	5
Score						**Score**					
Personal Dimensions						**Personal Dimensions**					
Family demands	1	2	3	4	5	Family demands	1	2	3	4	5
Work-life balance	1	2	3	4	5	Work-life balance	1	2	3	4	5
Stress	1	2	3	4	5	Stress	1	2	3	4	5
Time availability	1	2	3	4	5	Time availability	1	2	3	4	5
Score						**Score**					
Influencers						**Influencers**					
Spouse or partner	1	2	3	4	5	Spouse or partner	1	2	3	4	5
Business partner[s], employees, advisors	1	2	3	4	5	Business partner[s], employees, advisors	1	2	3	4	5
Clients, suppliers	1	2	3	4	5	Clients, suppliers	1	2	3	4	5
Investors	1	2	3	4	5	Investors	1	2	3	4	5
Score						**Score**					
Control						**Control**					
Retain ownership	1	2	3	4	5	Retain ownership	1	2	3	4	5
Control of quality	1	2	3	4	5	Control of quality	1	2	3	4	5
Manage employee output	1	2	3	4	5	Manage employee output	1	2	3	4	5
Time management	1	2	3	4	5	Time management	1	2	3	4	5
Score						**Score**					

Getting to Go

3

How can you leverage your insight and knowledge in an entrepreneurial way? If you are thinking of venture creation, how do you spot opportunities? In Chapter 2 we focused on entrepreneurial identity—the convergence of intention, perceived success, and ideas amid possibility. In this chapter, we consider how women entrepreneurs are "getting to go," how opportunity recognition is realized through venture creation. Along the way, we share inspirational stories of women following different pathways and creating different types of enterprises.

To understand more about getting to go and the practicalities of venture creation, we asked female entrepreneurs to describe their visions and how they went about developing their ideas. We learned that gender and the venture creation process are inseparable. Among the women we interviewed, we found that recognizing need is one starting point for venture creation. Opportunity recognition was reflected through a unique view of the market, a view that inspired ideas about new products, processes, and service opportunities. Dissatisfaction with the status quo spurred others: insufficiency equated to opportunity as products or services were deemed to be lacking. Sometimes, personal changes such as motherhood or job loss triggered ideas and action. For some, opportunity reflected the desire to build communities of like-minded individuals. These entrepreneurs spoke about their ability to connect with other women and to learn through others' experiences in similar circumstances.

Getting to go is a creative process that entails structure and systematic thinking: left-brain logic (analysis, research) meets right-brain creativity (inspiration, insight, imagination).[1] Researchers have attempted to capture this dynamic decision process, and in this chapter, we highlight four models of the venture creation process. As always, our focus is to marry current entrepreneurial thinking with a gendered perspective. We invite you to reflect on each of these models. Think about which ones speak to your experience or to that of entrepreneurs whom you know and admire. We then present a figure that illustrates the outcomes of enterprise creation and summarizes different perspectives on entrepreneurial action.

This matrix also captures how personal values and managerial practice shape business ventures.

Think back to Chapter 1 and recall how neoclassical economic theory has been used to explain entrepreneurial behavior. Also, recall social feminist theory as a rationale for women's subordination. These well-trodden explanations do not adequately reflect women's entrepreneurial experiences. We believe that for many women, entrepreneurial feminism bridges that gap. For this reason, we begin and close the chapter with snapshots of inspirational female business owners (feminist entrepreneurs) who illustrate how feminine capital is embedded within venture creation and how they are infusing feminist values in business practice.

Opportunity Identification

Inspiration 1: A Unique Market View

Moxie Traders specializes in the design, sourcing, wholesale, and retail sale of work and safety wear for women. In the words of founder Marissa McTasney, "Our target market is women who wear work boots. Customers include women factory and construction workers, farmers, tradeswomen, and the do-it-yourself market. And they're all now wearing work boots made specifically for them." Marissa McTasney's inspiration came from a love of working with her hands. Her motive was to build a house. A first step was enrolling in a course for women in construction. With no women's work boots to equip her for training, her startup idea became wrapped in color and contours. She knew what she needed; she could visualize the end product because, in her own words, "I am my market." McTasney has built a global enterprise by responding to the growing demand for female-friendly products and the desire to support other women with interests akin to her own. Through her entrepreneurial actions, she is "making change for women" by forging new ground in nontraditional fields and changing attitudes about women's participation.

Inspiration 2: Building Community

For Pamela Jeffery, recipient of *Fast Company*'s League of Extraordinary Women award, her startup ideas grew out of the desire for connection and community. Her vision was to connect women, to share or validate experiences with others, and to enhance learning through community. Today, Pamela Jeffery is the president of a transatlantic enterprise that is creating communities of successful, like-minded professionals across public, private, and nonprofit sectors. On a given day, Women's Executive Network touches over ten thousand women. Her inspiration stemmed from a client assignment. "I put together a room full of really smart women that I had assembled using my contact list, and I loved the event. Many said that they have never been in a room full of women just like themselves. I thought, wow, there's a need for peer groups, as all my clients were male. I created something that is important to me, and when I started talking to prospective clients, they saw that there was a gap as well. That morning the event evolved into a business." Pamela is a relationship builder. Her message to others is "never say never." From Pamela's perspective, women's inclination to share stories and talk to each other is a natural advantage that can be leveraged to support a community of business leaders.

Inspiration 3: Cut Out the Middle Man

Pam Strand has built a different sort of community. A geologist by occupation, Pamela established a female board of directors to help hunt for gold and other metals. In 2009, Pam launched Takara Resources Inc. with "a whole bunch of women that I know in the industry. In geological exploration, women who have been successful are still in the shadows of men. We decided it was time to create a company where women owned the lion's share." Pam Strand saw her enterprise as capitalizing on a license to prospect, while working with Aboriginal Indigenous communities and the environment. A primary challenge was accessing investment for speculative projects. "Investors measure you against the market and every other investment opportunity. You can't take decisions personally, as potential backers are just making a business decision. You've got to remain positive. Fortunately, everyone will give you their two cents—especially if you're a woman." Her message? Seize all opportunities.

Inspiration 4: Opportunity Knocked

For the founding president of Unique Solutions Design, Tanya Shaw, "opportunity knocked," and she opened the door. The timing was perfect for her to use her experience as a former designer and wardrobe planner to build a new consumer-oriented company. Unique Solutions Design measures and monitors consumers' body mass and body measurements, the information used to match consumers to products that fit them best. The firm's three-dimensional scanner and measurement technologies enable consumers to monitor their fitness, find out what clothing size will fit them best, and assist in ordering custom-made apparel from a growing list of retailers. Like the other three, Tanya is combining her business savvy with an opportunity to make positive change for women. In filling a market need, she is promoting a healthy lifestyle and positive self-image for women. This desire for social change is being enabled through entrepreneurial action.

· · ·

These cases differ from those typically described in studies in which women are positioned as disadvantaged due to lack of experience and resource constraints.[2] Here, being female has created opportunity. These entrepreneurs have leveraged knowledge about consumers and buyers in idea generation and innovation.[3] They are also aware of commercial opportunities that consumer needs present. Feminine capital is then employed in marketing, including product design and delivery. Targeting female customers responds to evidence that females control most household spending and domestic investment decisions.[4] Furthermore, women's asset portfolios are continuing to grow, assets such as earnings and investments as well as educational credentials and industry experience.

The stories illustrate that women are approaching venture creation in many different ways. The path depends on your own creative, problem-solving skills. To scope out the journey, here are four routes and several learning aids to guide the way. When reading about these different paths to venture creation, think about the many ways in which you have created opportunities in your life.

Paths to Venture Creation

Planned Strategy

Planned strategy is a linear approach to enterprise creation. It is predicated on the mantra "failing to plan is planning to fail." First, you identify a product or service: the right product at the right place and right time. Then you build an enterprise around the idea. A founding assumption is that opportunities (products and markets) exist, to be discovered and exploited by knowledgeable entrepreneurs. Opportunities stem from social, technological, ecological, and political influences, including changing consumer needs and preferences, and innovative processes, services, and products. Opportunities are then recognized by those who possess the requisite skills and experience to appreciate their unique value proposition. "[E]ntrepreneurial opportunities are like lost luggage in a train station: they exist, just waiting to be claimed by alert individuals who know of their existence."[5]

Planned strategy therefore assumes the existence of opportunities that are then realized through the process of idea generation → idea gestation → idea evaluation → product, market, or enterprise development → initial sales → customer feedback → product or service modifications. According to most how-to publications, crossing the chasm from idea to sales entails writing a business plan, a document targeted at potential investors, advisors, employees, and customers. This document is intended to validate the business concept or idea by spelling out the firm's unique selling proposition. Entrants vie for investment and customer dollars.

The vast majority of startup ideas are refinements of existing products or me-too products. If you have a startup idea, ask yourself the following questions:

- Why the product or service?
- What is the value proposition?
- Who is the target market or niche?
- How do you differ from the competition?

You should be able to answer these questions for yourself, but also for others! Having a clear and confident answer to these questions demonstrates your expertise and implies a threshold of knowledge,[6] sensitivity to customer needs (commonly referred to as their "pain point"), and understanding of competitors' strengths and weaknesses. Yet knowledge alone does not create value. Entrepreneurs also need to acquire reputational, social, financial, and sometimes political capital to overcome the barriers to starting up. The resources required differ depending on the nature of the service or product. For example, service ideas require entrepreneurs to create a credible promise,[7] credibility that is generated through relational[8] and reputational capital.[9] Knowledge-intensive products or services often require considerable financial capital, more than other types of products or services. Advocacy and nonprofit enterprises favor entrepreneurs with established social networks and political capital.[10] Learning Aid 3.1 lists some of the startup activities associated with planned strategy, moving from idea refinement to customer and market development and enterprise structure. The social and financial implications of each are noted.[11] If you are a nascent entrepreneur considering venture creation, this learning aid presents an initial list of expenses that should be considered in your financial plan. But financial capital is not the only investment required to build an enterprise. Listed in the right-hand column are social activities associated with a startup. These are particularly important for consideration by readers who have limited professional networks and contacts.

A key message that interview respondents voiced is that too often female entrepreneurs sell products and services for less than market worth, responses that reflect the paradox of the optimistic entrepreneur (Chapter 2). While this is hard to believe, remember that many women are motivated by other factors such as work-life balance, social change, and connecting with or empowering others. Feeling pulled in many directions can be a challenge. The second tool, "Managing Startup Ideas" (Learning Aid 3.2), is targeted to those in the initial phase of business development or expansion. This learning aid captures lessons shared by female entrepreneurs—in their own words—about managing ideas in the planned approach to the venture creation process.[12] You can use this checklist of ideas to ensure that you maximize all opportunities and stay focused as you "get to go"!

Learning Aid 3.1: Planned strategy

Instructions: This checklist of startup activities is not complete. Add activities, ensuring that you consider the expected financial costs and how each activity contributes to building reputation and networks (social capital). How well do your social and financial assets balance?

Activities	Financial Capital	Social Capital
Idea Refinement		
☐ Scale: size of idea or concept and markets	Research expenses: field or market studies to identify competitors and customers	Communicate with business owners and opinion leaders for advice about startup ideas
☐ Service or product development	Engineering expenses: prototypes, modeling, tooling, production, testing	Establish relationships with initial customers; bring potential buyers into the development process
☐ Advertising and product impact	Up-front expenses: media purchase, creative production, samples	Develop "credible promise" for potential clients, suppliers, and investors
☐ Building inventory	Parts, services, materials, staff	Determine service delivery model and customer service "scripts"
☐ Information reporting	Software purchase and development; order and reporting systems	Establish systems for client ordering, reporting, and information management
☐ Legal	Incorporation, patent filing and licensing agreements, insurance, protection of intellectual property	Document commercial expectations to avoid misunderstanding down the road
Customer and Market Development		
☐ Customer paying methods	Cash flow planning: capital to offset the lag between sale and payment	Negotiate terms of sale: delivery schedules, mode and frequency of service interactions
☐ Market entry	Promotional entry pricing, which can erode margins	Create agreements with salesforce and customers
☐ Geographic expansion	Travel and communication expenses, association fees	Network; have a presence at industry trade (buyer) shows, association meetings, newsletters
Enterprise Structure		
☐ Secure premises, equip office	Leases, rental expenses, computer and filing system setup, invoicing, and supplies such as furniture and computers	Determine professional services required (such as accountant, lawyer) and other relationships that support firm
☐ Human resources	Fees associated with contracting relationships with employees and suppliers	Train employees and contract workers
☐ Governance	Allocation of ownership for investors	Establish an advisory board, performance and reward systems
☐ Business model	Investment in processes such as workflow, customer interface, and information processing	Create an environment to build trusting relationships with clients, employees, suppliers

Learning Aid 3.2: Managing startup ideas

Instructions: Read through this list of startup tips from experienced female entrepreneurs. Check those that you think you already do well. Where do you think you could improve? Do you have a business partner or mentor with whom you can discuss these lessons? How can you put each of these into action?

Startup Tips
☐ **Structure your ideas:** "Ideas require structure and structure requires paperwork. We tend to put the cart before the horse. You have an idea and you want to go for it instead of thinking out systems and processes and an infrastructure to support it."
☐ **Stay focused:** "Focus on what you're trying to achieve. Check in with yourself frequently to make sure that you're still on board and passionate about the mission. Then allow time to replenish your energy so that you have the personal resources that you need to address your mandate with conviction."
☐ **Don't capitulate:** "Second-guessing yourself on a regular basis is not helpful. Have a belief in your own capabilities."
☐ **Manage your time:** "Time management means prioritizing--determine which ideas to focus on. Don't get blind-sided by bright shiny objects."
☐ **Understand the rules:** "Be very clear about all expenses and costs and make sure you are working with the best people possible. Do your homework. Walk before you run or leap. And make sure you know the country's rules."
☐ **Don't sell service short:** "It's all right to charge for your services. It's all right to market them. It's all right to hustle and make money."
☐ **Be ready with plan B:** "There are different ways to achieve an objective. Sometimes the route that you think is going to work doesn't. It doesn't mean that what you thought is not valid; it means you need to find a different way to get there."
☐ **Believe that you have something to offer:** "I used to think, 'Someone is going to catch me out. I'm not nearly as great as everybody thinks.' How do you overcome that? It's by believing that you have something to offer."
☐ **Don't expect perfection:** "You can't wait for the right circumstances to come along. Get moving before the next person fills in. We didn't have a photocopier, so we started without a photocopier. When we made money, the next step was to get a photocopier. These are the 'principles of next.'"
☐ **Build relationships that fit your needs:** "We've learned some very expensive lessons about how important it is to choose suppliers wisely. I'm much less patient with suppliers who don't meet our needs."
☐ **Leverage contacts:** "I should have called on people that I knew, not necessarily to seek work from them but just to seek advice."
☐ **Build a cheerleading team:** "When you are starting out, it is isolating. You'll have all sorts of questions: 'What am I doing? Why am I doing this? Can I really do this?' Your family may be less supportive than expected. Build your own cheerleading team."
☐ **Network with purpose:** "Networking is not just meeting people. Networking is meeting people for a purpose. Don't walk out of a business event with nothing. Go for a purpose, something that is action and results-oriented."
☐ **Share your vision:** "Keep looking for people who share your vision and motivation. This is particularly true when moving from a founding into mature stage of development."
☐ **Enlist others:** "Solicit input and advice from as many sources as possible: clients, suppliers, trade commissioners, foreign tax revenue services. Keep asking questions until you get the answer that feels right."

Planned strategy is an individualistic view of the venture creation process. It does not recognize the social context in which enterprise creation occurs. In particular, planned strategy is mute with respect to gender. Our research found that gender is infused within all phases of startup: idea discovery and generation, sector engagement, governance, and enterprise structures. For example, while almost all business owners need more time and capital than anticipated before entering the market, females invest significantly more time crafting business plans compared to males.[13] This is notable. Time lags carry risks and costs: too much analysis can cause paralysis. While one entrepreneur is refining ideas, another is in the market, creating sales and building relationships. Here are two evidence-based explanations for this behavior:

- Research shows that women report lower entrepreneurial self-efficacy than males.[14] Entrepreneurial self-efficacy is defined as the confidence to engage in entrepreneurial activities. So taking more time enables female entrepreneurs to build their confidence prior to pitching their business ideas.
- Female entrepreneurs need to amass knowledge in preparation for launching an enterprise. This is because, on average, female entrepreneurs bring less industry experience to a startup. And human capital (skills, competencies, and other knowledge) links to performance factors such as firm size, survival, and longevity. Experience is also associated with the ability to acquire resources and to address common business plan deficiencies: unrealistic assumptions and lack of owner credibility. Therefore, taking the appropriate amount of time to build a knowledge base early in the venture creation process can be a wise investment.

Planned strategy assumes that entrepreneurial decisions, such as idea discovery or sector engagement, are rational and individualistic. But the assumption that sector engagement is a function of choice does not stand up to feminist criticism. Decisions are influenced by social context. Gendered norms, cultural expectations, and economic structures allow biases in choice to occur, regardless of abilities and self-efficacy.[15] Persuasion, in the form of positive or negative commentary among family, friends, potential clients, and investors, also signals to the founder (and others) whether she has the skills and talent to pursue venture creation in nontraditional fields.[16] Odds are that if you are female, you work or own a firm in a traditional female-dominated sector, such as retail, real estate, health care, education, personal or professional services, and communications. This is because occupational roles and career expectations are socially constructed.

Table 3.1 presents rationales, other than free choice, to explain why female-owned enterprises cluster in services[17] and why few operate enterprises in male-dominated

Table 3.1: Gender dimensions of sector "choice"

Rationales	Implications for Women in Female-Dominated Sectors
Occupational Crowding	**Disadvantaged groups, such as female business owners and self-employed workers, crowd certain sectors and occupational roles** (for example, females in administration, education, and health care; males in executive roles, resource extraction, and construction). This creates an excess supply of female-owned firms or self-employed workers relative to those sectors or occupations that are not so designated. This produces two distinct labor markets. A primary market is typified by healthy margins (for example, knowledge-intensive firms, technology-based enterprises), and a secondary market is disorganized, crowded, highly competitive, unstable, and subordinated. Primary markets are predominantly male dominated while secondary markets are predominantly female dominated.
Role Delineation	**Most females enter the workforce in service or support roles.** Even in nontraditional female sectors, women are more likely to be employed in "soft" occupational service roles such as marketing or customer and public relations. Males are significantly more likely to retain bottom-line responsibilities and critical strategic portfolios. Females are less likely to retain the transferable skills and experience required to start enterprises in primary markets (such as higher gross margins, knowledge-intensive, and advanced technology sectors).
Invisibility	**Lack of research, media, and government engagement** lend to the invisibility of women in nontraditional (primarily service) sectors and occupational roles. The absence of heroines, role models, and inspirational female entrepreneurs is a consequence.
Discrimination	**Females are less welcomed in certain sectors and professions,** even though they bring equivalent abilities and qualifications. Such behavior reflects predetermined assumptions about ability.
Myths	**I can't:** Girls and boys assume socially differentiated roles, role expectations that spill into business practices, including sector choice. Myths about women's lack of aptitude for the technical trades and nerd stereotypes further deter many girls and women from engaging in technology, engineering and computer sciences.

sectors such as construction, wholesale, manufacturing, telecommunications, and the trades. Decision parameters reflect historical patterns that have defined women's work and women's abilities. Contemporary expectations continue to create subtle pressures that influence vocational decisions.[18]

Reinforcing these points are studies that examine career decisions and entrepreneurial expectations of women in female- versus male-dominated sectors.[19] What this means is that there is a relationship between what women *expect* to gain from doing business in a particular sector and what they actually end up doing. For example, a team of American scholars reports that women entrepreneurs in female-dominated sectors have higher career expectations regarding work-life balance and security. This observation is in line with the stereotyping of female entrepreneurs. However, women business owners in male-dominated sectors have comparatively higher career expectations of earning money or wealth.

Not all business owners pursue venture creation in such a linear way. Many women describe the process as iterative: learning by doing, thinking through talking, and assessing resources through interactions with emerging networks.[20] It may be that venture creation is not as prescriptive as it is described in some textbooks. Iteration is characteristic of the effectuation process, a second approach to creating market value that we describe next.

The Effectuation Process

An idea is one starting point. But ideas can emerge over time, an approach referred to as the effectuation process: ready, fire, aim.[21] In contrast to the linear approach to planned strategy, scholar Saras Sarasvathy contends that ideas—the operationalization of human aspiration—do not create one single effect.[22] There are multiple effects and hence multiple possible outcomes to venture creation, regardless of the initial idea or goal. Enterprises are therefore outcomes of actions such as listening to customers, building networks, and responding to serendipitous events. Actions create opportunities. Saras Sarasvathy also articulates guiding principles for the effectuation process. Aspiring entrepreneurs can follow these principles, reflecting on how their business might take shape as they move forward (and backward) with an idea.

- *Determination of affordable loss.* What is at stake? The effectuation process positions decisions within parameters rather than assuming that an individual can foresee outcomes. Entrepreneurs ask, "How much loss is affordable?" and "How much can I lose?" This perspective differs from planned strategy, in which entrepreneurs, often through a written business plan, predetermine expected return on investment and sales projections and worst-case scenarios at the outset of the planning process.
- *Forging of alliances and collaborations.* Within the effectuation process, network relationships are used as a means to reduce risk and uncertainty; alliances build reputational capital and trust. Planned strategy assumes that market interactions are competitive.
- *Exploitation of contingencies.* Entrepreneurs seek to control an unpredictable future rather than assume outcomes are predictable. Hence, they respond to contingencies. A critical issue is the entrepreneur's willingness to change when confronted with new information, opportunities, or surprises.

Rather than writing predefined plans, effectuation theory recognizes that venture creation is fluid. Little is predetermined at the outset. As entrepreneurs acquire information, they change course.[23] Decisions are based on new knowledge, new experiences, and a sense of loss—of affordability, flexibility, and experimentation.[24] Prospective entrepreneurs acquire knowledge and skills in the field. Some jump into the market early in the process, building relationships, garnering initial sales, and acquiring feedback to secure other resources, such as investment capital and credibility. Enterprises are created through alliances and cooperative strategies. These are powerful assets to overcome the liabilities of newness when competing with established firms.

Sarasvathy suggests that entrepreneurs *construct* rather that *recognize* opportunity by asking questions. They do so by thinking about entrepreneurial identity; experience, or human capital; and social capital.[25]

- Who am I?   [Identity]
- What do I know?   [Experience or human capital]
- Whom do I know?   [Social capital]

Different business models reflect different answers to these questions, and differences are reflected in the ways in which entrepreneurs view similar opportunities.[26]

The question of "Who am I?" speaks to identity, which overlaps with "What do I know" and "Whom do I know?" In other words, the key components of feminine capital. So female business owners must assess their own assets in constructing a business venture and draw upon their feminine capital to determine their value and how to build upon these strengths. Of course, such decisions are not easy. As mentioned earlier, entrepreneurs sometimes grapple with potentially conflicting decision parameters such as the need to earn an income and generate wealth, the passion to create, recognition and achievement, and the desire for security or independence.[27] Decisions are not made in isolation, just as firms are not autonomous.[28] For example, how others see you determines the extent to which you are about to gain initial legitimacy in the market and establish reciprocal and cooperative relationships.[29] Alliances, rather than autonomous or competitive behaviors, help to reduce uncertainty. For these reasons, successful entrepreneurs listen to customers, build networks and strategic partnerships, and demonstrate the ability to respond to serendipitous events. These values are also evidenced in the choice of resource providers that support the venture, as well as governance structures that regulate and control behavior.[30]

The effectuation process is also predicated on the assumption that entrepreneurs create the means to accomplish their emerging goals through the very process of venture creation. The theory challenges the notion of "requisite inaugural capability," defined as the entrepreneur's ability to assemble her assets before launching an enterprise. Effectuation theory argues, instead, that key assets are not always required prior to starting up. Rather, capabilities are acquired along the way. These ideas complement observations that women bring different experiences and other assets to venture creation, resources that sometimes enable and sometimes constrain venture creation. "Who am I?" respects the fact that organizations are the aggregate of the founding team members and employees' individual contributions—contributions such as capital and other fiscal assets and managerial, social, and technolog-ical capabilities. A large-scale literature review of empirical studies that have tested the validity of the effectuation process and firm performance concludes that many heuristics, such as locus of control, need for achievement, tolerance of ambiguity, risk propensity, and personality, are "irrelevant."[31] These are the same entrepreneur-ial constructs that presuppose women are disadvantaged entrepreneurs.

The theoretical alignment of the effectuation process and feminist theory is stronger than that of planned strategy and feminism. Effectuation suggests that entrepreneurship is transformational, not prescriptive. Outcomes are never pre-determined or predictable. Entrepreneurs shape the future through services and products, their firms, and collaborative partnerships.[32] Similarly, entrepreneurial feminism focuses on *effecting change*, with and for others. Feminists seek to better control influences that have enabled women's subordination. The effectuation pro-cess explicitly considers how values are reflected in the mutuality of relationships, economic interdependence, social actions, and synthesis of opposites. These are hallmarks of feminist workplaces.[33]

We challenge you to reflect on the lessons learned about planned strategy and the effectuation process and how these paths to venture creation are relevant to your business practices. Learning Aid 3.3 consolidates and compares the four main elements of these two approaches. Use this tool to identify your own prefer-ences.[34] Review, score, and tally your responses to estimate your own way of doing business—how you would describe your own style? This information is useful in discussing with others, such as employees and investors, how you exploit opportu-nities. You can also use this information to map out development strategies. For ex-ample, you may prefer to use formal planning processes when entering new markets (planned strategy). Alternatively, you or members of your team may prefer to enter new markets serendipitously, jumping in to feel the water when the opportunity presents itself. You might have observed that, in the past, certain phases of business or product development followed one approach while different phases followed the other. As this section illustrates, neither approach is correct, particularly given that many successful small enterprises undertake little formal planning. This learning aid affirms that highly structured planning, processes used in large organizational settings and described in many textbooks, is less relevant to many small businesses.

Family Embeddedness

A key element of the social context of business ownership is family.[35] The family embeddedness perspective acknowledges that decisions occur within family sys-tems and that family and entrepreneurship are intertwined.[36] Several forces are at play: one's position within the family (for example, child, single or married adult,

Learning Aid 3.3: Effectuation process versus planned strategy

Instructions: To complete the exercise, circle the number that corresponds to your preferred way of doing business, where 1 = not preferred, 3 = somewhat preferred, and 5 = very preferred. Add your scores for each approach to venture creation. What patterns do you observe?

Effectuation Process						Planned Strategy					
Focus on Resources						**Focus on Goal Setting**					
The starting point is available means or resources of the startup team.	1	2	3	4	5	I have targets and understand the value proposition.	1	2	3	4	5
Score						Score					
Affordable Loss						**Expected Returns**					
Decisions are based on worst-case scenarios, minimizing risk and costs.	1	2	3	4	5	My decisions are based on an expected return on investment.	1	2	3	4	5
Score						Score					
Collaboration						**Market-Based Analysis**					
At the outset, I established partnerships and alliances with external stakeholders.	1	2	3	4	5	At the outset, I undertook market and competitive analysis.	1	2	3	4	5
Score						Score					
Contingencies						**Overcome the Unexpected**					
I am flexible and adjust easily with new information. I take advantage of new opportunities.	1	2	3	4	5	I avoid potential threats and surprises through up-front market analysis.	1	2	3	4	5
Score						Score					

parent or step-parent, caregiver), stage of family lifecycle (for example, young adult, married with children, empty nester), and the social context in which one's family is situated. Family dynamics are also influenced by

- *Politics*: availability of affordable day care, education, health care
- *Economics*: disposable income, employment, social safety nets and family benefits including paid parental leave
- *Religion*: communities of faith and prescribed gender roles[37]
- *Geography*: presence of role models; local economy; access to markets, suppliers, and other business partners.

Family embeddedness is evidenced in entrepreneurial decisions and actions: startup motives such as the desire to better balance work and family responsibilities;[38] degree of spousal support for economic engagement;[39] time invested in household versus commercial activities; and how women manage the work-family interface.[40]

Family influences venture creation just as venture creation influences family.[41] And entrepreneurship is embedded within reciprocal economic and social associations—for many women, associations with family. For some, family triggers recognition of opportunity.[42] In our research, we listened to women who described how divorce resulted in the need to become economically self-sufficient. Lack of products for daughters created opportunities to customize sporting goods equipment for girls. Women who followed a spouse or partner's career to new countries created "born global" enterprises to sell products in their countries of origin.

Other studies report that for some entrepreneurs, discussions with family and friends bridge the chasm between intentions and venture creation. Friends and family help to verify nascent ideas and affirm role legitimacy.[43] Talking through the entrepreneurial possibilities enables some to practice persuasion and to refine language that will be used to shape their enterprises.

One reason why women tend to rely on "closer ties" is comparatively less small-business and managerial experience. Two more reasons are the tendencies to negotiate for spousal (or partner) support and to monitor their commercial and domestic roles.[44] For instance, in an in-depth study of fifteen Irish female entrepreneurs, the research team of Pauric McGowan compared the women's startup motives and "the reality" of business ownership. Participants identified many issues associated with time management and their need to juggle a myriad of work-family responsibilities. Thirteen of the fifteen women expressed frustration that they were expected to fulfill most caregiving roles despite running a burgeoning business (for example, "I am constantly firefighting"). Most received little or no support for domestic tasks from a husband or partner (for example, "If you pushed him, there would be times where he would definitely help out, but it would be a favor"). All played the central caregiving role in their families. Overall, this study captured a vivid picture of the strong tension between entrepreneurial affirmation and the challenges of business ownership, in the context of family.[45]

Some writers have referred to family relationships, expectations, and norms as yet another type of capital that is required for entrepreneurial action, *family capital*.[46] For instance, in a study of Turkish entrepreneurs, Dilek Cetindamar and colleagues reported that family capital, measured by the number of family members living in a residence, was positively associated with entry into entrepreneurship.[47] That is, women with larger families were slightly more likely to become entrepreneurs. Such observations do not explain the complex sociocultural pressures and mechanisms behind family capital. For instance, does larger family size grant permission for one of the female members to break free of domestic responsibilities or does it just provide more mouths to feed and therefore stronger economic pressure to promote female entrepreneurship? These studies reinforce the notion that many women entrepreneurs construct decisions on the basis of family context and are vulnerable to differential power relationships that exist therein.[48] Women are still held accountable for the welfare of the family but are not expected to make more money than their partners or husbands.[49]

Gender and Organizational Creation

Researchers Barbara Bird and Candida Brush provide the fourth lens through which to view opportunity identification.[50] This perspective differs from the preceding three by situating gender in the center of venture creation. They describe five dimensions of the organizational creation process: concept of reality, orientation of time, actions and interactions, power, and feminine ethic.[51] Masculine and feminine qualities of each dimension are listed in Table 3.2.

- *Concept of reality* is associated with entrepreneurial vision. The authors describe feminine reality as reflective, diffuse, vague, and ambivalent. In contrast, a traditional or masculine concept of reality is typically qualified as analytical and futuristic, in which agents seek to control.

- *Orientation of time* describes the evolution of startup ideas. Within a feminine process, promising ideas are nonlinear and lacking direction; multiple concept iterations are common. In contrast, the masculine startup process is characterized as linear and fast-paced.

- *Actions and interactions* reflect the idiosyncrasies of founders. Feminine founder actions and interactions are emotional, cooperative, harmonizing, and empathetic. Traditional masculine actions and interactions are described as rational, strategic, competitive, aggressive, and distant.

- *Power* is identified as a differentiating motive for launching a startup. Founders of feminine organizations are motivated by the desire to seek self-mastery or contribute to the social good. Traditional or masculine motives reflect behavior that seeks mastery over others, as power is centralized and used for personal gain or self-benefit.

- A *feminine ethic* is described as being responsive to others. Founders are open to negotiation and conciliation with aggressors. Conflict is mediated. Management of masculine ventures is characterized as aggressive and controlling through rights and laws.

This perspective challenges commonly held assumptions about enterprise creation, by highlighting the masculine and feminine dimensions of both opportunity recognition and the venture creation process. This conceptual model helped to stimulate our thinking about how gender is embedded within opportunity identification. For example, two of the dimensions explicitly reflect elements of

Table 3.2: Gender perspectives on venture creation

Dimensions	Traditional (Masculine)	Personal (Feminine)
Concept of Reality	Focused consciousness Analysis Separable nature Knowledge as control	Diffuse awareness Appreciation Interconnected nature Knowledge as caring
Orientation of Time	Future Faster pace Linear	Present Slower pace Circular or spiral
Actions and Interactions	Rational Strategic Grounded in goals, reason Competitive Aggressive, violent Distant	Emotional Personal Influenced by family history, biology Cooperative, caring Harmonizing Empathetic
Power	Mastery of others Used for self Centralized	Self-mastery Used for others Shared
Feminine Ethic	Responsibility as control over self Restrain aggression or limit behavior Rights and law	Responsibility as a response to others Preserve relationships or repair harm Caring and fairness

Source: B. Bird and C. Brush, "A Gendered Perspective on Organizational Creation," *Entrepreneurship Theory and Practice* 26, no. 3 (2002): 41–65.

women's subordination—power and ethics. These dimensions are not typically acknowledged by the media or included in entrepreneurship research; however they are fundamental principles of feminist criticism.[52] These ideas also provoked our thinking about how feminist theory and entrepreneurship are interconnected, at a theoretical level, but potentially at a practical level as well. And this prompted us to investigate further—to determine how, in everyday activities, masculine and feminine qualities are evidenced in leadership practice and how feminist values are enacted within entrepreneurship.

Gendered Matrix of Venture Creation

Through our research, we found that, in practice, gender is multidimensional. It is not dichotomous (masculine and feminine). In this way, it does not follow Bird and Brush's typology of venture creation process. For example, we asked female business owners about how they identified opportunities and set up their ventures, including strategic planning, performance management, governance, and control mechanisms. Some described vision and ideas using feminine qualities. Others described feminine ideas and masculine managerial practices. Performance metrics were sometimes predicated on financial objectives, such as profit maximization and revenue growth, and other times on nonmonetary outcomes such as building networks and contributing to community.[53] Our conclusion is that gender is enacted along *continuums*—across different inputs and, hence, outcomes. To summarize the study results, we have constructed a matrix to depict gendered associations in entrepreneurial processes and outcomes (Figure 3.1).

Along the horizontal axis, we position *entrepreneurial process*. On the vertical, we position *enterprise outcomes*. You can use the matrix to reflect on your own vision of the enterprise creation process and outcomes. Does the vision land squarely inside one quadrant or straddle a continuum? Having done so, place those enterprises that you admire in the matrix. Where do they best fit?

- The upper left quadrant reflects enterprises with a purely for-profit mandate. *Neoclassical enterprises* are defined in classic economic theory as those that operate within the market for the purpose of profit maximization and wealth creation.
- The lower left quadrant captures *social enterprises*. Countering neoclassical values, social enterprises are values-based, focusing on social rather than economic opportunity to address social, economic, or environmental challenges that are not served by existing markets or institutions.[54]
- In the upper right quadrant are enterprises that exemplify feminine leadership with for-profit outcomes. *Relational enterprises* emphasize both financial and relational outcomes. The culture is typified as feminine: cooperative, relationship-oriented, creative, empathic, and sensitive to the needs of multiple stakeholders (not necessarily women).[55]
- In the lower right quadrant, feminist enterprises are motivated by humanitarian or feminist outcomes such as improving the quality of life and well-being of others, particularly making change for the betterment of girls and women.

To illustrate how women enact opportunities in each of these different quadrants, we introduce you, once again, to four inspirational female entrepreneurs. Each of these women is consciously leveraging feminine capital in a different way. Two are expressly seeking feminist outcomes—social change for girls and women.

Inspiration 5: Neoclassical Enterprise

Teri Kirk is the founder of a neoclassical enterprise. Through her business, the Funding Portal,[56] she has accomplished what the Canadian government could not. The Funding Portal has successfully mapped $30 billion worth of government funding

Figure 3.1: Gendered matrix of venture creation

	Entrepreneurial Process	
	Dominantly Masculine →	→ Dominantly Feminine
Neo-Classical Enterprises		**Relational Enterprises**
Performance measures: profit maximization, revenue growth		Performance measures: process-based, financial and nonfinancial
Governance: owner or private shareholders		Governance: shared leadership
Control: formal, centralized, clear boundaries, hierarchical		Control: informal, participative, cooperative
Social Enterprises		**Feminist Enterprises**
Performance measures: self-sufficiency; ability to respond to social and community needs (such as community development, assembly)		Performance measures: impact to address women's subordination to men, to improve quality of life and well-being of girls and women
Governance: leverage social assets, community leaders, volunteers; typically nonprofit		Governance: typically collective and cooperative versus competitive
Control: community-based, depending on social needs		Control: shared, empowered, ethic of care

Enterprise Outcomes — High Financial ↔ — High Social ↔

for business, executives, chief financial officers, entrepreneurs, venture capitalists, nonprofits, and universities. Its search engine enables users to query and access Canada's public and private financing marketplace. The Funding Portal is a private venture corporation that provides efficient, fee-based services to assist small- and medium-sized enterprises to prepare for financing rounds. This unique and rapidly growing firm provides small companies with access similar to large firms to lucrative government funding. The focus of the Funding Portal is to grow revenues and maximize return on investment. As the president, Teri reports to an investor board and has built a national advisory council of government and industry leaders.[57]

Inspiration 6: Relational Enterprise

Relational enterprises that embrace the Internet not only challenge the status quo but introduce collaboration by employing new ways in which business owners can combine invention and commerce to engage in social change. For example, visit TED Talks and search for "Robin Chase on Zipcar and her next big idea." A serial entrepreneur, Robin Chase is one of the founders of Zipcar, an international on-demand, car-sharing club. Her current vision is a global network of owner-to-user rental vehicles. Rental drivers can enjoy just-in-time access to vehicles when owners don't need them. Online matchmaking systems reverse work out to renters and owners. Peer-to-peer relationships are built; the environment, owners, and consumers win.

Inspiration 7: Social Enterprise

The women's health center founded by Elaine Jolly[58] illustrates the delineation between traditional "feminine" opportunity recognition and "masculine" opportunity exploitation.[59] Elaine Jolly's vision for a women's health care center stemmed from knowledge about patient need. While Dr. Jolly might be considered a "feminist entrepreneur", building and operationalizing the center reflected a stereotypical masculine model of governance. An advisory council, a network of prominent women that operated outside of the medical community, was established to support her vision for the health care center. The council enabled Elaine Jolly to gain access to senior bureaucrats, politicians, and donors and offered reputational capital and project legitimacy. Group cohesiveness was fostered by trust and respect for the founder. Without the council's social influence, political and bureaucratic support was unlikely.

Inspiration 8: Feminist Enterprise

President Amy Millman is also a feminist entrepreneur. She co-founded Springboard Enterprise[60] with Kay Koplovitz (then, chair of the National Women's Business Council) to support and empower women by facilitating access to resources such as capital, professional development, and role models. The not-for-profit organization grew from their observations that women remain underrepresented among rapid growth technology firms. Springboard Enterprise is focused on scaling up women-led technology businesses. Capital is important because most firms need financing to grow before technology changes the window in the market. The founders saw a disconnect between investors and female entrepreneurs. Research confirmed that the gap was a function of women lacking familiarity with equity markets while investors lacked familiarity with women as leaders. Springboard Enterprises fills a gap in access to financing, sources, and business resources by providing workshops and accelerator programs for aspiring female entrepreneurs.

Springboard Enterprises is not unique. Among the feminist entrepreneurs whom we interviewed, there were several who cited inequality as a motivation for entrepreneurial action. We learned that many women consciously draw on feminist values to inform their business practices as well as their enterprise structures. The last section captures findings from our studies that focused specifically on how feminist values are enacted within entrepreneurship. We zoom in on feminist entrepreneurs because they exemplify emergent entrepreneurial feminist theory. More important, these women provide insights into communities of like-minded entrepreneurs, women who are creating wealth and social change.[61]

Feminist Entrepreneurs

To better understand the nature of entrepreneurial feminism, we conducted a series of studies with women who explicitly defined themselves as "feminist entrepreneurs." They answered our call for business owners who identified themselves as "change agents who seek to improve women's quality of life and well-being through innovative services, products and processes."[62] Table 3.3 lists the lessons learned. Like Amy Millman and Kay Koplovitz (Springboard Enterprises), they see themselves as enablers—facilitating access to many types of resources. These entrepreneurs view the marketplace as cooperative, one in which all relationships are built through collaboration and respect for mutual gain. They used words such as *team approach*, *win-win* and *open and honest* when talking about competitors. Interactions are practical and action-oriented. Leadership is participatory. Enterprise structures are nonhierarchical. Governance is relational and process-focused. For these women, entrepreneurship and feminist values are interwoven within the value creation process.

These behaviors and attitudes counter feminist criticism of capitalism and business ownership. While doing public and academic presentations about our work, we learned that not all women think wealth creation is worthy of celebration. Rather than seeing venture creation as a means to affect change and enable others, some perceive women's economic success with suspicion. Suspicion is

Table 3.3: Lessons learned from feminist entrepreneurs

Actions and Interactions	
Cooperative	"I try to establish a relationship with them [employees] and have a good rapport and make sure they understand what my company goals are, what I'm all about. . . . I don't have to follow a lot of policies like bigger companies. . . . I'm more flexible to either supplier needs or my customers' needs."
Team Approach	"I do try to respect and listen to what customers have to say. . . . With my suppliers, we have a team approach. . . . competitors, if possible I try to form an alliance with them. . . ."
Polite Yet Persistent	"I am easy on people, hard on the issue."
Win-Win, Nurturing	"I like to try to identify how we can work together, and usually there's some sort of win-win situation that can come out. . . . you have to nurture over time. . . ."
Fair	"I'm fair, I ensure that people get the service that they deserve, both inside and outside the role of being the owner . . . knowing that giving the best advice and counseling and excellent example will deliver what I feel inside."
Friendly, Sharing	"With competitors, I always try to be very friendly and keep the door open, and sometimes we sit down. . . . When two people sit down in a room great things can happen. . . . You can share about practices, you can learn from each other. . . ."
Kindred Spirits	"I could say that I only work with people that I like, period, point blank. And over the years . . . I have become very good friends with the people that have hired me because there's a kindred spirit that develops."
Positive, Respectful	" [Looking] at clients, I think the style is positive and constructive, and if we look at suppliers, I think we're straightforward and not demanding. . . . We are focused on what we have to achieve, and I like to look for common ground with competitors, and to, rather than trying to compete head on, I try very hard to find complementary roles. . . ."
Enterprise Structures	
Diverse Workforce	"In terms of representation, we look at geography . . . cultural and racial background . . . and select the most balanced board. . . ."
Community Building	"It's going to be about building communities and having local people be able to connect with each other. . . ."
Flat and Flexible	"There's no rigidity. There's very little hierarchy. . . . It's very flat."
Loose Structure	"It's a very loose structure. . . . I have a business partner . . . and she works from home and has a very flexible schedule. . . ."
Lots of Communication	"It is a very open door policy. . . . I'm always encouraging people to throw in their ideas to contribute."
Community	"It becomes our community because most everybody has remained involved."
Nonhierarchical	"I think it's fairly relaxed. It's not very hierarchical; you know I think it's a pleasant work environment."

Source: Adapted from B. Orser, C. Elliott, and J. Leck, "Entrepreneurial Feminists: Perspectives About Opportunity Recognition and Governance," *Journal of Business Ethics* 26, no. 8 (2012): 561–589.

echoed in arguments that wealthy women do not contribute to community and coalition building.[63]

Feminist entrepreneurs counter negative stereotypes about feminists (for example, feminists are unhappy, bra burners, male haters, radical), stereotypes that are unappealing to many people. These attitudes can lead to comments such as, "I'm not a feminist but . . . " and they may cause opportunities to effect change to be lost. Such biases are in sharp contrast to what we observed through our research with feminist entrepreneurs. Most focused on "win-win" collaborative attitudes and their abilities to solve problems in the face of limited resources. Given that resource constraint is characteristic of most social enterprise initiatives, there is much to learn from how these women "get the job done."

REFLECTIONS

Table 3.3 captures the actions, interactions, and enterprise structures described by entrepreneurial feminists. How, if at all, are these characteristics reflected in the way you do business? Use the table as a starting point to stimulate discussion among colleagues, including employees or classmates, about your leadership practices. How, if at all, are these characteristics reflected in corporate culture? In what ways might such actions support or detract from business development? What are the risks associated with such actions? Consider how you and your colleagues can enhance organizational culture and firm performance using the governance practices described.

• • •

This chapter centered opportunity recognition within four pathways to venture creation. We discussed how gender is enacted along a continuum that reflects entrepreneurial process and outcomes. Feminist entrepreneurs typify feminine processes and feminine outcomes. However, other female entrepreneurs leverage their feminine capital in a variety of ways along the axis, creating a multitude of different enterprise combinations.

So far, we have focused primarily on the entrepreneurial process, but process in and of itself does not create financial value. Financial (market) value is created through growth—growth in relational or social capital, revenues, market share expansion, investment in research and development, new product or service introductions, and retained earnings. In Chapter 4, we change gears by exploring feminine capital within the context of enterprise growth and innovation.

Enterprise Growth

4

"Don't waddle, waltz! I'm always going forward, instead of back and forth." We loved this advice shared by an entrepreneur. Her words imply positive energy and momentum, confidence, and creativity. In this way, women are leading new dances, moving beyond venture creation and building innovative enterprises. Waltzing embodies the ebbs and flows of enterprise growth and change, no matter how one defines success: commercializing a product or service idea, revenue growth, community development, employment for others, or creating change in other meaningful ways. Understanding growth and innovation is important because innovative enterprises grow twice as quickly as noninnovative firms, regardless of sector.[1] Size lends viability to the enterprise and the associated efficiencies of scale. It is also a powerful strategy to increase wealth and social impact. Growth offsets the high risk of failure by

- Generating additional sources of revenue
- Sourcing new customers, products, and suppliers
- Acquiring investment capital
- Attracting quality advisors, employees, and suppliers.

Our research on female entrepreneurs has identified gender differences in the growth patterns of small- and medium-sized enterprises (SMEs). For example,

- Compared to male counterparts, female business owners perceive growth to be less likely, important, and feasible[2]
- After controlling for factors associated with growth, such as firm and owner attributes, female-owned young firms do not grow to the same extent as those that are jointly owned by males and females, nor those that are majority male-owned.[3]

In this chapter, we explain the growth trajectories of small- and medium-sized enterprises and present learning aids to help you visualize what growth might look like for your own enterprise. In the first section, we provide four explanations as to why some firms grow and others do not. We also describe typical gender influences that are linked to growth performance. We again present a series of learning aids to assist you in designing business models that are sustainable, generate wealth, and create social change. In the second section we change tactics. To illustrate the diverse nature of growth and innovation, we share the experiences of three more feminist entrepreneurs. Each is growing her enterprise using very different business models. We describe the value proposition for customers, streams of revenue, plans for growth, and ways in which each owner mitigates risk.[4] These detailed case descriptions present an opportunity to talk about the "how to" of business ownership, including strategy, business models, and operating philosophies.

A business model is the business concept put into practice,[5] the story that explains how an enterprise works.[6] The business model is the center of business strategy.[7] Innovative business models are dynamic, reflecting continuous experimentation and adjustments to changing market conditions.[8] When reading the three cases, position yourself in the role of founder. Consider different solutions to the challenges presented. In this way, you can put theory into practice and use your own ideas to solve problems that create market value. The learning aids will then help you to define a growth strategy. Before doing so, we encourage you to test your assumptions about enterprise growth. Start by answering the following three questions:

1. Why do some enterprises grow and others do not?
2. Picture a growth-oriented enterprise. What owner and firm attributes come to mind?
3. Now, picture a lifestyle enterprise, one in which the founder's objective is to earn a living. How does this enterprise differ from the enterprise pictured above?

Once you have read the chapter and completed the learning aids, answer these questions again. Compare your responses to see how your thoughts about enterprise growth and innovation may have changed.

Why Some Enterprises Grow and Others Don't

Small enterprises grow in one of two ways: organically or through mergers and acquisitions. Most expand organically. Growth-oriented entrepreneurs seek new opportunities, as existing markets become less profitable and new market opportunities become attractive.[9] Those entrepreneurs who assemble resources in an effective, cost-efficient manner are best able to respond to market opportunities and, hence, to grow. Organic growth strategies can differ depending on one's perspective. Here are four alternative views.

Resource Exchange

Enterprises need resources in order to grow. Resource exchange theory suggests that growth is associated with the ability to gain access to resources, including financial and social capital, knowledge, technology, and management skills.[10] Enterprises enter into transactional relationships because they cannot generate all of the necessary resources internally. For example, a company may lack the human capital required to spark innovation within the firm. They will then seek to acquire resources through recruitment, strategic alliances, or other means. Acquiring these skills, in the right combination, is critical and is reflected in innovative business models, products, services, and processes,[11] where *innovation* is defined as the commercialization of new ideas.[12]

Growth-oriented entrepreneurs perceive innovation as a strategic asset. A 2013 EY global survey of entrepreneurs reports that 88 percent viewed innovation as a key differentiator.[13] Competitive advantage is most often gained by institutionalizing innovation throughout the firm, as part of product and service processes and corporate culture, rather than through one-off projects and experimentation. The focus on innovation is also seen as a change from the tendency of small firms to gain market entry and growth through discount pricing. Therefore, from a resource exchange perspective, growth-oriented entrepreneurs are motivated to acquire resources that fuel innovation. Where can these be found?

Innovative ideas, concepts, and designs are drawn externally from customers and suppliers and internally through marketing, product development, and technology. Even among rapid-growth, technology-driven enterprises, most innovations are created through *informal* rather than formal research and development processes.[14] When innovative activity (defined as "the number of innovations per employee") of small firms was compared to that of large firms, small firms were found to be more innovative.[15] But fewer small firms engage in *formal* innovation, when innovation is defined as inventions, designs, and patents.[16] Among small firms, the impact of informal innovation is significant. Small firms that innovate are more likely to value top talent.[17] As a result, such enterprises not only employ more workers, they are attractive employers. While demanding higher skills, they pay higher wages.[18]

Many of the entrepreneurs profiled throughout this book illustrate the gendered nature of resource exchange and innovation. Gender is evidenced in the design of female-targeted products and services (such as hockey equipment and construction gear), in the introduction of new ways of doing business (for example, win-win relationships), through enterprise structures (collaborative governance), and by the creation of businesses whose beneficiaries are other women.[19] These stories are not typically what we hear about or see in the media or in management textbooks, particularly when the topic is innovation.

There are several reasons for the failure to report on the gendered nature of resource exchange and innovation. Innovation is usually associated with technological capacity—the traditional research and development capability of a company, as measured by the number of engineers, scientists, or mathematicians (and the associated scientific inventions, patents, and research-based discoveries). However, this definition of innovation is exclusionary, and it tends to discount many of the innovative activities in which women are involved. A broader definition of innovation refers to other types of creative processes, such as the production of new products and services, the opening of new markets, and accessing new sources of raw materials.[20] Innovation can range from the commercialization of small-scale ideas (such as product modifications to meet female customer needs) to the reorganization of an industry (for example, women's enterprise networks) or the introduction of radical products and services (for instance, the Internet: women leveraging social media to challenge masculine norms).

In the context of innovation, academics have focused almost exclusively on technology, losing sight of who participates in the broader spectrum of innovative activities.[21] Doing so favors male-owned enterprises and industries, making invisible the innovative (resourceful) contributions of female-dominated sectors (professional, administrative, and creative fields). A consequence is that men are seen to be more innovative.[22] This is reinforced through policy. For example, a Swedish study about "innovation policies and programs" revealed that most public funding defaults to male-dominated sectors: 80 percent of funded programs were in new technology, basic science, and manufacturing; 20 percent supported services and creative industries, sectors in which women are overrepresented.[23] The authors conclude that masculine discourse is placed at the center of public funding; feminine policy discourse is relegated to the sidelines.[24]

There are also relatively few female founders of small, high-tech firms. There are many reasons why. Women are less likely to obtain engineering credentials. Women have shown less desire to work in technology-based firms, in part because of perceptions of a macho industry culture. Those women who do work in high-tech firms are less likely to consider venture creation as a means to leverage their intellectual capital (that is, apply for patents, create spin-off firms).[25] And when women have founded technology firms, they report gender-related barriers to enterprise growth.[26]

The evidence suggests that resource exchange processes are not gender-neutral. Gender is embedded in the allocation and acquisition of resources that are linked to enterprise growth.

Reputation and Legitimacy

For a firm to grow, the owner and enterprise must also establish a positive reputa-tion in the marketplace.[27] While difficult to measure, reputation is one of the most valuable, intangible assets an enterprise possesses. *Reputation* is a set of beliefs and evaluations about the enterprise held by an external group of stakeholders such as investors, clients, and suppliers.[28] A good reputation is associated with competitive advantage achieved through access to customers, financing, and quality employees and cost advantages such as favorable pricing on supplies. A poor reputation, often created by a breach of trust, is difficult to change.

How does gender influence the assessment of reputation? Investors, customers, and other stakeholders respond to social cues. Cues conform to predetermined role expectations, in which, typically,

- Males retain key decision-making and investment roles
- Females predominate support and relational-oriented roles.[29]

In processing reputational signals, market players can fall back on gendered ste-reotypes. They do so by benchmarking one firm against a comparable firm. If the comparator is a stigmatized or stereotyped enterprise, such as a female-owned firm, such an association can reduce the firm's reputational capital. The impact is the discounting of a company's status and, hence, the anticipated financial value of the enterprises.[30] The link between reputation and financial valuation is illustrated in the following scenario.

Firm A is a micro, nanotechnology enterprise that is developing a suite of lead-ing-edge products to enhance the analysis of proteins, DNA, and RNA. Firm B is a micro, service-based enterprise that is developing a suite of leading-edge as-sessment tools to enhance organizational effectiveness. Which description reflects your perception about a prototypical female-owned enterprise? Chances are you would choose firm B. Others will too. Why? Because the majority of female-owned firms are small and operate in the services sector. Let's take this point a couple of steps further.

Assume that founders A and B attend a trade show. When both nascent en-trepreneurs walk onto the showroom floor, what is the stereotype that a potential client retains? In some likelihood, if both are women, that both own firm B. What is the implication? In establishing reputations, entrepreneurs must overcome the liabilities of newness, as well as potential stereotypes about founder competencies or firm capacity. The prospective client, assuming that these nascent entrepreneurs adhere to prototypical attributes of a female-owned firm (such as very small, ser-vices-based, lifestyle-oriented), is less motivated to understand the nature of their firms or products. When potential purchasers lack the motivation to acquire and process new information, they are less likely to change initial judgments, unless the credibility of signals conveying new information is very high.[31]

Eileen Fischer and Becky Reuber call this phenomena "reputational stickiness."[32] Reputational stickiness refers to the fact that initial assessments of a company become very quickly entrenched (sticky) and difficult to change. In the case of the female-owned firms just described, perceptions can be biased or negative, on the basis of preexisting, gendered stereotypes and on little information. Even when more knowledge about the firm or owner is available, an observer may ignore it, if it does not conform to his or her first initial impression. Similarly, reputations may be discounted if the credibility of the initial source of information is not perceived as extremely high. In other words, biases can have a negative effect on the reputational capital of women-led firms. Such biases are difficult to change, and can have lasting impacts on success.

Gender stereotypes, reinforced by reputational stickiness, are reproduced at the firm and industry levels.[33] For example, industry-wide constraints and barriers to entry for women entrepreneurs are documented in the advanced technology sectors. Many women attribute startup challenges directly to gender.[34] In North America, women attributed a proportion of the challenges they encountered to gender. Challenges are reflected through

- *Capability*: assumptions that women are not technically competent
- *Industry culture*: attitudes that technology is a man's world
- *Social capital*: limited access to social networks
- *Occupational roles*: the tendency to value certain occupational roles and skills (engineering, technicians, software developers) more highly than occupations that rely on prototypical female roles such as research, consulting, education, public relations, and other services.[35]

As we will discuss in Chapter 5, broadly speaking, reputational bias can also translate into gender stereotyping within social networks and sectors.

Thresholds of Growth

This explanation of growth suggests that some enterprises exhibit continuous change over time, including change in the maturation of the leadership team as well as changes such as in the number of employees.[36] Changes can be small, slow and steady, or sudden, such as the influx of substantial capital or the entry of a major competitor. Over time, particular growth "thresholds" are reached, and these stages are critical for progressing to the next growth trajectory. For illustration, we present two types of change that demonstrate the link between theory and practice: size and psychological thresholds.

Size Thresholds

One means of exploring size thresholds and resultant enterprise growth is to study strategic changes in the evolution of microfirms (that is, firms that have fewer than five employees). One such inflection is the decision to enter international markets. For illustrative purposes, we draw on the decision to enter international markets by means of export. Here are some facts that motivate owners' decisions to export as a market development strategy and, hence, surmount this growth threshold:

- Ninety-five percent of the world's population lives outside the United States.
- In 2010, the U.S. Chamber of Commerce reported that women business owners who engage in international trade grew at a rate of 57 percent, while domestic-based firms grew at less than half that rate.[37]
- International trade is a key strategy for growth-oriented enterprises. This is also true for the European Union—the world's largest trading block leads all nations in gross domestic product.[38]
- Yet, less than 10 percent of North American small firms export their products or services.[39]

The likelihood of engaging in export has been described as an S-shaped relationship between export propensity and firm size. The S-shaped relationship assumes that internationalization is a staged process and that a threshold size is reached before exporting occurs. Revenue growth and associated employment growth are initially sourced through transactions in local, then regional, then national, and then, finally, international markets.

We tested the concept of size thresholds and export by drawing on the experiences of sixteen hundred small businesses.[40] The study found that, as predicted in resource exchange theory, years of management experience is a dominant indicator of exporting. However, size thresholds differed depending on the nature of the enterprise and sector. Figure 4.1 illustrates the results.

For goods producers, a significant shift—or threshold—was observed in the size-export propensity continuum, particularly at the twenty-five-employee mark. The S-curve is observed as the likelihood of export increases substantially once a firm has more than thirty employees.[41] This was not the case for services firms, for which no minimum size threshold was observed. We learned that services exporters rely, to a significantly greater extent than goods producers, on management experience rather than on number of employees. Hence, you will notice on Figure 4.1 that the "S" is less pronounced. What is also telling about the results is that enterprises, of all size, do engage in international trade. Some are born global, exporting since inception.

Figure 4.1: Export thresholds: Association between firm size and export propensity

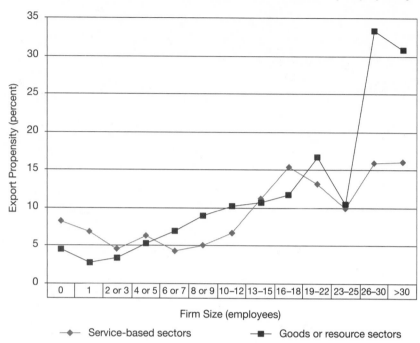

Source: B. Orser, A. Riding, and M. Spence, *Canadian SME Exporters* (Ottawa: Industry Canada, Small Business and Tourism Branch, 2007).

What our export study also found was that, even after we controlled for owner and firm characteristics associated with exporting (that is, factors such as growth intention, management experience, firm size, and industry sector), female-owned businesses still were less likely to export.[42] It may be that for women, the threshold is higher. The bar is higher. This explanation aligns with our studies that report on gender-related barriers to exporting.[43]

In another Canadian study of female exporters, gender was seen to influence the business practices of most respondents. For some, it did not.[44] Among fifty-four female respondents, four explicitly described being female as advantageous. Advantages included

- The ability to speak with and better understand other businesswomen
- Being able to capitalize on the novelty of being a woman
- The ability to obtain a response to cold calls. (This point is likely related to the two previous.)

About one third suggested that there were no gender influences, but then went on to articulate one or more issues. We labeled such statements "No, but . . ." because they qualified their responses with gendered examples. Here are two sample statements:

- "I don't think in my business there really are. I mean there probably are, but I don't see them. I think I'm too old. Been there. Done that."
- "I haven't had any problem because I must say that when you start talking to people that work in science, gender is not really an issue. It's more when you're working in the finance and the business part. That's when it becomes an issue. They have a harder time in taking you seriously sometimes."

Among those exporters who cited gender challenges, principal issues were cultural and experiential differences, lack of respect by foreign business owners, businessmen who explicitly refused to do business with women, bravado, physical gestures, and chauvinism. Digging deeper, we found that gender barriers were prevalent across sectors and degree of export readiness as well as size and age of firms. Conversely, in another qualitative study of seven "award winning" Scottish female business owners who export, none reported that being female created challenges for them, either in international trade or in maintaining work-life balance.[45]

What conclusions can we draw from these studies? If a female entrepreneur perceives that her enterprise will be deemed less credible, or that she will encounter gender-specific barriers in export, she will be less attracted to international expansion. We refer to this phenomenon as "discouraged exporters." As the term implies, these perceptions can dissuade entrepreneurs from entering new markets. This creates a disadvantage, given that international trade facilitates growth through the cross-pollination of knowledge, management practice, and innovation.[46]

Psychological Thresholds

Psychological factors affect enterprise growth in other ways. A psychological threshold, for example, reflects an optimum or ideal size that an entrepreneur deems to be comfortable to manage—a size that allows her to maintain control over the enterprise and a size that requires expending reasonable time or energy. In a study that examined attitudes and behaviors of entrepreneurs, scholar Jennifer Jennings has reported that compared to males, females are more likely to express the desire to stop growing upon attaining a maximum business size threshold pre-established for the enterprise.[47] The study concludes that some women may have different psychological thresholds and comfort levels than men when it comes to growing their firms.

Similarly, we undertook a study of female business owners and asked each to indicate if they intended to grow the scope and size of their enterprise. Among those who had no growth intentions, we asked respondents to explain the reasons why. Responses fell into three categories: perceived feasibility of growth, resource constraints, and personal or lifestyle decisions. Issues of feasibility were most frequently cited. Feasibility reflected concerns about levels of risk and debt, operational expenses such as taxes, and market opportunities and profits. Resource constraints included lack of growth capital, difficulty securing qualified labor, and lack of credibility or management skills. Lifestyle and personal reasons were secondary (for example, being content with the way things are, family obligations, a desire to maintain control). Psychological thresholds of growth were evidenced in personal and lifestyle rationales. Some also perceived growth or the decision to not grow to be associated with the ability to control the enterprise and work-life balance.

Exogenous Influences

Economists point the enterprise growth compass to factors outside the firm.[48] In cross-national studies, researchers found that the birth and growth rates of enterprises were two to four times higher in strong economic regions than those labeled as being weak.[49] Stable political and banking systems, monetary and fiscal policies, low levels of corruption, and recognition of property rights are associated with higher levels of economic prosperity. Enterprise stagnation is associated with turbulent exchange rates, excessive government regulation, high personal and commercial taxes, labor costs, limited availability of qualified and skilled workers, and monetary instability.[50] In response, governments have established frameworks to develop policy support for small businesses. Frameworks typically reflect two agendas:

- Ensuring that the business environment is conducive to the growth of small businesses
- Distributing limited government resources more effectively to enhance competitiveness and encourage small-firm growth.

Yet most economic frameworks lack women-focused policies. This has created macro-economic policy constraints for many women business owners. Constraint-driven performance gaps reflect challenges that some women may face in obtaining the resources required to grow their firms.[51] For example, the constraint of time availability is directly associated with the acquisition of other resources requisite to growth. Constraint-driven performance gaps have been the focus of several women in enterprise taskforces.[52] The reports point out that policies that are of particular importance to women remain housed in social versus economic development agencies and that few governments have established metrics to estimate the economic benefits of women-focused policies such as maternity, day care, and health insurance provisions. Many female business owners are not eligible for sickness and compassionate care benefits, private short- or long-term disability insurance, or health or dental plans. Such policy support has a disproportionate impact on women's abilities to grow their enterprises.

REFLECTIONS

Drawing on these four explanations of enterprise growth (resource exchange, reputation and legitimacy, thresholds of growth, and exogenous influences), determine how each perspective is reflected in your business practices. Do you find that one speaks to you more than another? For growth-oriented entrepreneurs, can you list one or more response strategies that you might take to address a related hurdle of growth? For example, experience in a large packaged goods company has provided Susan Ross with a robust international network. She wonders how she can leverage such contacts (resource exchange theory). Lack of employees may be an obstacle to growth for Susan, however, given that export trade often implies incremental operating expenses to create and support foreign clients (for example, 24/7 client service, travel). Psychologically, she is prepared to do business with international clients. She is therefore thinking about a business model that reflects Internet-based strategic alliances with foreign professionals (resource exchange theory). Fortunately, the local Chamber of Commerce encourages small firms to export (exogenous influences). Part of Susan's planning is to estimate financial and network support to determine the viability of launching a born global professional services firm (resource exchange theory).

Remember Maria Guidi? She operates a growing construction business, yet is reluctant to enter another state or to go international, a psychological threshold. While her advisors have encouraged her "to go for it," she remains concerned about regional differences in industry regulations (exogenous influences). She hopes that contacts made through WEConnect International will help her to identify trade association or government personnel who can assist her in unearthing often difficult-to-locate regulatory standards (resource exchange theory). This can be a very effective response strategy in the case of exogenous influences.

The third entrepreneurial heroine, Cynthia Goh, works in a different sector, advanced technology. In this domain, one possible approach is to access the resources of a business incubation center. Like university technology transfer offices, incubation centers often operate in affiliation with research-intensive universities. In her case, Cynthia Goh sought the support of MaRS. The mission of MaRS, an urban business development hub, is to help create successful global businesses from science, technology, and social innovation. The center "provides resources—

Learning Aid 4.1 Explanations of enterprise growth

Theory	Explanation	Potential Gender Influences	Strategies
Resource Exchange	Enterprises enter transactional relationships because they cannot generate all necessary resources internally. Growth is associated with the ability to gain access to a predictable and uninterrupted supply of resources. Those entrepreneurs who cannot secure "essential resources" are more likely to fail than those founders that do.	Growth is the outcome of accumulated wisdom, knowledge, financial capital, and other essential resources. Women bring fewer inaugural resources to venture creation, creating disadvantages in securing "essential resources" necessary for growth.	Participate in small-firm training that is sensitive to gender differences in inaugural knowledge and resources. Seek out mentors and role advisors with experience and knowledge about enterprise growth.
Legitimacy and Reputation	Legitimacy is the perception that the actions of one entity (founder, firm) are desirable, proper, or appropriate within the socially constructed system of norms, values, and beliefs. Reputation is a set of beliefs held by an external group of stakeholders, such as investors, clients, and suppliers. It is an assessment or measure of favorability (competitive advantage).	Market players fall back on stereotypes. The impact is evidenced through discounting of female entrepreneurs' reputation, legitimacy, status, and the anticipated financial value of female-owned enterprises.	Build credibility by managing professional introductions (for example, acquire testimonials and endorsements from lead clients, establish alliances with established firms, populate the advisory board with prominent entrepreneurs and industry leaders). Participate in industry meetings. Access support offered by trade commissions, financiers, and other intermediaries charged with facilitating trade.
Psychological Thresholds	Growth follows abrupt changes or thresholds, including asset accumulation, employment, revenue, and psychological thresholds. Thresholds can reflect continuous, step-wise or catastrophic jumps.	Compared to males, female entrepreneurs perceive growth to be less likely, feasible, or attainable.	Seek mentors who are experienced with managing specific or incremental phases of enterprise growth (such as startup versus maturation, early versus late-stage financing). Visualize and socialize with growth-oriented entrepreneurs. For example, seek out women exporters through export trade associations.
Exogenous Influences	Enterprises located in regions characterized by high economic prosperity and human capital (education, training), are more likely to grow.	Most economic development frameworks lack women-focused policies, creating macro-economic policy constraints. Constraint-driven performance gaps reflect challenges that women may face in obtaining the resources requisite to growth.	Advocate for public policies that explicitly support women's entrepreneurship. Demand equitable access to public investment in monetary or fiscal programs in sectors in which women predominately operate enterprises.

people, programs, physical facilities, funding and networks—to ensure that critical innovation happens." They "stimulate, identify and harness great ideas, nurture their development and guide the transformation of those ideas into reality." Such centers help nascent entrepreneurs and microbusiness owners traverse barriers associated with resource exchange, reputation and legitimacy, and thresholds of growth. In reality, however, few females access or benefit from such support. Many fail to meet selection criteria of technology incubation centers. For example, only 10 percent of MaRS clients are female entrepreneurs, a phenomenon that is indicative of other centers, including those in Silicon Valley.[53]

Learning Aid 4.1 summarizes the four explanations of growth, potential gender influences, and more remedial strategies. Work your way through the learning aid to help generate more response strategies for each explanation of enterprise growth.

Case Studies of Enterprise Growth

In this next section we shift gears. We move from a theoretical perspective to one in which theory meets practice. We introduce you to three feminist entrepreneurs who are applying some of the growth strategies described earlier. Each of these cases applies a unique business model to venture creation. Through their stories, you will see how their business models are designed to leverage innovation and generate growth. We describe how owners operationalize strategy within the firm's value proposition, streams of revenue, and plans for growth. Toward the end of each case, we highlight their perceptions about gender and how feminine capital has influenced their business practices. We also present a series of questions to help you integrate case-based insights into your decision making. To pique your interest, here is a preview of what is to come.

Just Us! Coffee exemplifies a hybrid and emergent venture. This fair trade, wholesale-retail cooperative grew from the passion of Debra and Jeff Moore for social justice in Latin America. Through Just Us! the dynamic duo has reinvented the cooperative business model, helped to establish fair trade standards, and founded one of Canada's first organizations to capitalize on impact investing.[54] This case touches on strategy, governance, and branding.

The next case is that of Womenable, a firm founded by Julie Weeks. Julie had a vision that drove her to business startup: to enable women's entrepreneurship worldwide. This for-profit, home-based global consultancy is a knowledge repository for women's entrepreneurship. With clients around the world, Julie advises corporations, governments, and academic institutions about policies to support women entrepreneurs. Her definition of growth is defined as social impact, change through policy interventions that create ripple effects. In this case, we present strategies to build and grow an international, home-based venture and outline trends in women's entrepreneurship.

The mantra of Janet Longmore, founder and chief executive officer of Digital Opportunity Trust (DOT) is "leading for change—empowering youth and women with technology." DOT is harnessing the power of youth to facilitate technology, business, and entrepreneurial learning experiences for people in disadvantaged and stressed communities. This nonprofit global enterprise showcases how to effect change by embracing technology.

Case 1: Just Us! Coffee—People and the Planet Before Profits

Launched in 1995, Just Us! Coffee Roasters is Canada's first fair trade coffee roaster.[55] Operations consist of twin cooperatives: Just Us! Coffee Roasters, a production-wholesale-retail cooperative, and Just Us! Fair Trade Investors Co-operative. Co-founders Debra and Jeff Moore have also initiated alliances and collaborations that extend the Just Us! mission to new consumer and supplier markets, including municipal government.[56] Hybrid enterprises such as Just Us! are characterized as organizations that seek to simultaneously create private and public wealth by pooling social, financial, green, and community-based values. Entrepreneurial success reflects

- The ability of founders to adapt in uncertain environments
- Structural elements of for-profit and nonprofit enterprises
- Innovative business models.[57]

We asked Debra Moore to share the story of how she helped to build a successful hybrid enterprise with global outreach and impact. In Debra's words, "The Just Us! mission is to support small-scale, sustainable agriculture through promotion and education about fair trade and awareness of development and trade issues. We are always looking for ways to be a vehicle for change, working towards healthy communities and a healthy world. We have grown our revenue at 35 percent a year. So balancing the demands of a commercial and social enterprise is a struggle."

Ability to Adapt to Uncertain Environments

In the early 1990s, Debra and Jeff Moore sensed that fair trade practices were a means to improve the livelihood of coffee producers in Latin America. An initial support network of like-minded friends who shared a passion for social justice got together to talk about how they could make a difference. Having validated their startup concept for a fair trade coffee operation, the team was missing a key ingredient of the business plan.

"We called ourselves Just Us! because we were a small group of friends who had very little business experience and few resources, but we shared a belief that we could do our bit for social justice. We were in the right place at the right time. The province of Nova Scotia was supporting small business startups, so there was money and resources. Organic food and fair trade were just beginning. Fair trade grew as a charity model through the churches. But churches were not growing the business, and that's what the coffee producers needed. So we saw a need and invited three friends to join us. The missing piece was beans.

"We met with a few roasters, and everybody said, 'You can't do it. Coffee is a cartel. You can't get beans.' But the idea of fair trade was growing in Europe, and we knew there was a framework there. We saw an article in a magazine that featured coffee. So Jeff jumped on a plane to Mexico and met with a group that was featured. It was pure luck. He went into this cafe. He doesn't speak Spanish, but one person spoke English. So he talks to her for a bit, and she says, 'I know Geronimo, the guy who is doing the development work for this organization, so why don't I give him a call?' Geronimo was difficult to meet with because he was so busy, but he thought Jeff was a friend of this woman's, so he agreed to meet. They clicked and a great relationship formed. Canada was a market they had targeted. So it all fit together. Jeff phoned to tell me, 'The good news is, I found beans. The bad news is we have to put our house up for collateral to purchase the container of beans.'"

In June 1996, a year after writing their initial business plan, Debra and Jeff pledged their home to finance the first shipment of coffee beans. The co-op was under way, with more unexpected developments. Debra and Jeff had not anticipated municipal by-laws that prohibited certain types of home-based businesses. "We thought that we would produce and wholesale out of our house for a while, but the city said, 'The minute we get a complaint, you're out.' So we purchased a smaller house in a different community. With the purchase for business purposes, we then learned that the bank required a down payment of 40 percent, not 25 percent, the norm in Canada at the time. Just things you learn. Luckily, the guy who sold us the house held the mortgage. So we didn't have to put very much down. It was a good place to start, but not a good place to grow.

"We invested another $10,000 into the basement, because green coffee beans are particular in the way they need to be stored. Then the roaster arrived. It was like the first washing machine in town. People were fascinated by it. Everything came together at that point. We've never done a cold calls call since we started. We've grown through word of mouth. After purchasing the house, we were informed that the county had rules about what you could and could not do in a commercial district. We were told that we needed to have a retail operation. So we built a cafe upstairs. I baked the cookies and muffins."

Over time, their cafe expanded. Debra and Jeff needed to restructure the operation to support their ambitious plans and growing demand. In doing so, they sought to keep their values at the center of the planning process. They accomplished this by evolving from a traditional financing model to a model that emphasizes employee empowerment, social justice, and community development and engagement. They set up a worker cooperative structure to capitalize on their social enterprise goals.

Innovative Structure

Debra and Jeff Moore attribute enterprise growth to constantly focusing on community needs. Under the cooperative agreement, Just Us! is controlled by employee-workers and, more recently, indirectly through the investor cooperative. Regardless of investment, it is one member, one vote. To qualify, employees must work for the company for two years and contribute a nominal investment to receive an equal share of profits or losses. Members elect the board of directors and have input into company operations and product development.

Initially, the venture creation process was emergent and organic. On reflection, Debra believes that change is the heart of Just Us! Today, success reflects continuous innovation through strategic planning. To motivate change, the leadership team sets performance targets. Growth is monitored through an innovative scorecard. The scorecard process enables the founders to continuously improve their performance by gauging the social, financial, and environmental impacts of Just Us!

"Throughout all periods of Just Us! history, growth has come from need. We regroup about every three years. We have had strategic plans since the beginning, and this is what has helped us to survive all the changes. In the first two years after the planning, things would move along smoothly. But because we were such a high-growth firm, by the time we entered year three, life would become quite challenging. This would bring us back into another strategic planning process."

The expansion of brand-name coffee houses and, more recently, adoption of fair trade product by competitors have created new challenges for Just Us! Coffee Roasters' value proposition. Latin American and other offshore cooperative coffee producers have matured and are better positioned to negotiate price. To offset flattening coffee sales, Debra's marketing team has engaged in product and other brand extensions, focusing on worker and leader competencies and securing expansion capital through an innovative cooperative financing fund.

The Just Us! product line has expanded significantly. At the beginning, Just Us! Coffee Roasters focused exclusively on processing and wholesaling coffee beans. Today, Just Us! wholesales and retails 100 percent fair trade sugar, cocoa, and organic or local produce such as milk in four retail locations. They have also listened intensely to their customers. "People would say, we want to support fair trade but we don't drink coffee. So we brought in tea. We work with a women's co-op in Ecuador to bring in herbal teas. Sri Lankan tea is grown differently in fair trade. There are a number of small tea producers banding together to form co-ops. In the last forty years, the offshore Latin American producers have also found their voice and are more organized. So now we are focusing on producing a small producer's symbol. It has been a five-year project, of telling the story of small producers and explaining the differences between minimum fair trade and truly supporting small producers."

Investing in Skills and Competencies

Debra has learned two other important lessons: rapid growth requires people who are willing to embrace change, and this in turn requires a significant investment in training. "You can't assume that because employees support social justice, everyone understands business. This was a problem for those who did not understand what needed to change. We were disappointed that Just Us! was unable to bring everyone along with growth. Now when we are hiring, we discuss the nature of the business. We also heavily invest in training staff. Training includes business, communication, and management skill development. We are training around sustainability, cooperative management, and governance. It is training that has propelled us into radical restructuring because the team feels like they now have the skills to take significant change on.

"We brought in experts. Just Us! has had a number of skilled consultants working on different aspects of capacity building along the way. We are now at a point that we have capacity in house. We have internal people to take on training and to mentor new staff. We also established the Centre for Small Farms. One of the objectives of the center is facilitation and skills development. We will use the center to help us to continue to build capacity. We also align Just Us! with larger cooperatives. We are learning that these organizations have gone through similar changes and that we are not unusual. We own this environment. It is a healthier way of looking at change. We shifted mind-set and realized that change is what our company is about."

Social Impact Investment

Like most founders, Debra struggled initially to pay the bills. It was not long, however, before the firm had more interested investors than employee-owners. Just Us! was able to secure $1.6 million in financing through a provincial Community Economic Development Investment Fund (CEDIF). Funds are not secured, hence investors are like employee-workers and ownership is retained. The fund has helped to finance continued growth and provide investors with a return on investment. The investment fund is structured to provide tax relief on contributions.

Debra described the advantages and disadvantages of the Just Us! CEDIF-supported investment fund. "With investors, they want to know the story. They are invested emotionally and financially. They want to see change, regular reporting, and understand the struggles. They provide new expertise through the investment board. We feel like we now have 450 salespeople who are looking out for us. They are our eyes and ears. They tell us about shelf presence. They tell us about a cafe that has done well. Investors hold you accountable and, due to their interest, we have created monthly newsletters to share stories.

"As the market has matured, revenue growth has slowed down. So we struggle to find concrete projects. We are now constantly looking for good investments. First, we invested in staff training. We are now looking at different types of ideas."

These investments have paid off. Just Us! enjoys market visibility, brand loyalty, and sustained growth.

Extending the Mission

The Just Us! mission to create healthy communities and a healthy world extends beyond consumer and wholesale markets. Jeff and Debra Moore were champions of a local initiative to certify Wolfville, Nova Scotia, as the first fair-trade-designated municipality in North America. We asked Debra to describe how she parlayed the Just Us! fair trade mission into practice.[58]

She recalled, "It happened quickly. Wolfville had it all in place, so it was easy for them to do it. Most people on the town council drank Just Us! coffee. So we said, you clearly support fair trade in your personal lives. Why wouldn't you take that to the next step? You just had to offer people the opportunity. They were like, 'Oh! I hadn't thought about it.' There was a poll taken. The majority of people in Wolfville were prepared to pay a higher price for fair trade goods. The decision put Wolfville on the map." Large cities are only now becoming fair trade certified.

As Debra explains, "Over the past two years, Just Us! has become more active in helping to lead the food movement. We are engaged with small and local producers in food production, focusing on rural development. This has brought new passion. We founded the Centre for Small Farms, and now have the leading specialist of the province working with us. We are working with three hundred small farmers from around the province."

Feminine Capital

Toward the end of the interviews, we asked Debra, "How, if at all, does gender influence Just Us! practices?" She was quick to respond that the Just Us! team is very conscious about the ways in which feminine capital shapes the company—through decision-making processes and corporate culture. "For many years, Just

Us! was primarily a group of women. There was storytelling and lots of interactions. Customers talk about the sense of caring. I have no doubt that this comes from strong feminine leadership. Most leaders are women. This is part of who we are. Jeff has dealt more with producers, working with farmers, and the international work. I lead the local work. Our structures come from a feminine side. Our working partners are aware of this. We are actually talking about this with partners and are conscious about what this means to Just Us! We use a feminine approach to decision making. We see people holistically. We are sensitive to what is happening in their lives.

"Sometimes this is good and sometimes bad. There are lots of meetings and discussion. We work hard to make everyone feel valued and important. The struggle is that this is not always that efficient, but we have come to a balance. We have good male and female presence. And the males whom we attract to Just Us! are in touch with their feminine side. That's why it works. They bring a balance to conversations. We are talking more about this as it is in the fabric of Just Us! The approach that many businesses have today is being inclusive. It is about wanting to include others. We talk about family and teams. At the heart of everything that we do is respect and dignity. We have created a business of equals."

REFLECTIONS

For Just Us! Coffee, social justice is the product. The co-op is among a growing number of enterprises that market products and services tagged with a social message.[59] For example, Blake Mycoskie is a social innovator who helped introduce the world to one-for-one selling of TOMS Shoes.[60] TOMS Shoes donates one pair of shoes for every pair purchased. Other sample enterprises are Sir Richard's Condom Company[61] and the New York–based eyewear company Warby Parker.[62] Here are some other questions for you to consider in reflecting on the implications of adopting a hybrid, emergent model such as Just Us! to address social justice goals.

1. What are the opportunities and challenges of adopting a business model in which the product is the message?
2. How might this philosophy and marketing concept affect your firm?
3. Social enterprises are faced with paradoxes. How would you resolve each of the following dilemmas?[63]
   - *Inputs*: Using inputs that generate local versus foreign employment that support free trade among disadvantaged farmers. How can you reconcile the incremental environmental impact of shipping?
   - *Manufacturing*: Incurring higher production costs by promoting small producers versus purchasing from large firms operating in Asia.

- *Distribution*: Using central warehouses for staffing efficiencies and consolidation of goods, at the expense of transportation costs and carbon footprint.
- *Human resources*: Avoiding staffing cuts during economic or seasonal downturns and stagnating sales.
- *Labor*: Resolving ideological differences between cooperative and union values.

The next three questions link the Just Us! case to insights presented earlier in the book:

- In what ways does Just Us! exemplify the emergent process of venture creation?
- Which of the four explanations of enterprise growth are exemplified in this case study?
- How is innovation evidenced in this particular case?

Case 2: Womenable—Enabling Women's Entrepreneurship

Collaborating with stewards of the business community, private bankers, academe, and media, Julie Weeks is accelerating women's entrepreneurship through her consultancy and publication services.[64] Julie is the founding president of the for-profit enterprise Womenable (http://www.womenable.com/). A global connector with an impressive research dossier and active social media platform, Julie undertakes and manages a portfolio of small to million dollar projects. She does so by collaborating with experienced subcontractors and vendors. We asked Julie to share her observations about trends in women's enterprise support, making the transition to business ownership, and managing a born global, micro-enterprise.

Opportunity Identification

Julie recognized the need for women-focused research, programs, and policy shortly after arriving in Washington in the early 1990s. In the role of deputy chief counsel for statistics and research at the U.S. Small Business Administration (SBA), among Julie's first questions was, "What kind of research do we have on women entrepreneurs?" She chuckled as she recounted the response. "The answer came through blank stares. A room, full of male economists, fell silent . . . but not for long. Gender analysis became a focal point in all contracted studies."

Over the next decade, Julie amassed knowledge about women entrepreneurs, as managing director and director of research at the Center for Women's Business Research and executive director, National Women's Business Council. We asked Julie to explain why she journeyed from the public and nonprofit sectors to venture creation. Her response aligned with a rationale described in Chapter 3, "I recognized a need in the market."

Time in Washington taught Julie how the public sector works. One lesson was that changes on Capitol Hill happen slowly. By the mid-1990s, Julie was ready to pick up the pace of change. Micro-enterprise was a perfect place to do so. The career transition afforded her freedom to move ideas into international markets and to plant more seeds for change. "As knowledge about women's entrepreneurship emerged, I began to see that many studies were missing links to policy and practice. The lessons learned were not being deployed. Working with international colleagues, I saw a need for national infrastructure to support women entrepreneurs."

Globally, Womenable is now recognized as a key source of information about women's entrepreneurship. The firm specializes in working with governments and market intermediaries to craft policy and program frameworks for enterprise development. Julie provides expert analysis about the economic growth of women-owned firms. The firm's reference library is free to use and houses a repository of must-have reports for leaders in entrepreneurship programming. Publication services include

- Articles, including opinion pieces
- Research briefs and reports
- Quarterly newsletters
- Annual membership surveys for the National Association of Women Business Owners
- Trends in U.S. Federal small business contracting
- Consultancy in the creation of gender assessment tools.

Julie's blog is read by thousands in ninety-nine countries, from the United States to Bahrain, Brazil, Ghana, Myanmar, Mongolia, and Senegal.

An Accelerating Pace of Change

Julie described how, around the world, circumstances are converging to accelerate support for women entrepreneurs. With ownership tenure, women are leveraging wealth and influence to advocate on behalf of other women. Governments are recognizing that the traditional economic policy focus does not necessarily help small business, particularly groups such as minority, disadvantaged, and women business owners. Budgetary pressures remain. These factors are pushing governments into more public-private partnerships. Julie sees this evolution as good news for women. Corporations are also working to bring women-owned firms into their customer and supplier bases. And governments are slowly recognizing the economic impacts of women-focused policies. All this is leading to a trickle-down effect, in which municipalities and regional development agencies are rolling out women's entrepreneurship programs and policies. "I see a shift in corporations supporting women's entrepreneurship as a charitable expense to it being a marketing endeavor. Corporations are also helping to underwrite large-scale studies and networking events. Nonprofit funders of women's programs are recognizing impacts."

Generic "one size fits all" small-business training programs, introduced by governments in the 1990s and 2000s, are now well tested. While many have been shown to be successful in some areas, not all address the specific needs of women. As a result, women-focused initiatives are being supported. Programming is increasingly sophisticated and specialized. Each new program, center, company, and online community refines women's enterprise infrastructure. Many service providers now tailor programming to match sector needs with clients' expectations, including perceptions of success and professional experience.

From Julie's viewpoint, "Women learn and lead differently. It is not so much about 'the what' women-focused programs offer clients, but *how* programs are delivered. Programs are more collaborative and relationship-oriented. They are less transactional, relying on peer or one-on-one mentoring. All this is in addition to delivering technical knowledge. This builds a sense of community, support that goes well beyond the technical assistance that is offered. These are the things that make women's business education different. Many governments still do not consider 'the how' to be as important as 'the what.'"

Microcredit

Julie views increasing market recognition of the paybacks of investment in women's enterprise programming as parallel to the history of microcredit. In her experience, process can make all the difference. Rather than the traditional lending model, one that entails assessment of clients' credit histories and collateral requirements, pioneers in microcredit financing replaced individual assessments and loans with group lending. These lenders learned quickly that women are more likely to repay microloans than men, that such lending has ripple effects on family and community. Women are more likely to reinvest earnings close to home. BRAC (Bangladesh Rehabilitation Assistance Committee) and the Grameen Bank (India) have capitalized on community pressures and values of small rural villages. BRAC is the world's largest nongovernment organization.[65]

According to Julie Weeks, "Research, when it has been done, shows that reinvesting in women business owners in developing economies has a higher return on investment than many other development strategies." Yet it took years for this realization to be acted upon globally and over fifteen years for the Grameen Bank to reach a million customers. In comparison, Equitas, an Indian microfinance firm that entered the market in 2007, successfully reached its first million customers in less than five years.[66]

Today, the Grameen Bank lends to millions of women.[67] Women are also shareholders. And governments have moved into microcredit financing. In 2013, India's finance minister pledged $185 million to establish another rural cooperative specializing in microfinance loans to poor women, a bank run by women and for women.[68] Government and the private sector are institutionalizing microcredit financing to poor women. Fiscal policy support for women entrepreneurs has gained traction. And slowly and persistently, Julie is helping to facilitate such change. She is doing so by operating Womenable within a niche market of global micro-enterprises.

International New Ventures

Like Womenable, our own research about international new ventures counter common assumptions held by many people about born global micro-enterprises. We discovered, for example, that exporting is as common among young firms as among older established firms.[69] And like Womenable, export-intensive new ventures tend to be born global, exporting at or near founding. The prototypical founder is urban-based, older, experienced, growth-oriented and more likely to be an immigrant, compared to domestic firm owners. We also learned that there is little variation in the proportion of export intensity of ventures over time (intensity is defined as percentage of export versus domestic sales revenue).[70] That is, contrary to the media stories, international new ventures are *not* predominantly technology-based. They are, however, concentrated in particular sectors—professional services, manufacturing, and technology—yet they still operate across all sectors.

What Womenable reports and other studies about international new ventures are teaching us is that there is little need to establish local, regional, and then national operations. Entrepreneurs are benefiting from export revenue early in the life of the firm. Social entrepreneurs, such as Julie Weeks, bring global mind-sets, international resourcefulness, and new business models to the marketplace.[71] Julie shared with us her strategies to keep pace with the tidal wave of change. Here are five that she has used to build a born global, home-based enterprise:

- *Partnerships build scale*: You can expand revenues, build scale, and be a global business without growing your payroll. If you are leveraging partnerships, you can be a multimillion dollar company.
- *Success entails teamwork*: Global growth is not "do it yourself" entrepreneurship. Julie understands the value of delegation and surrounds her firm with

a team of professional contractors, what she calls plug-and-play relation-ships. She avoids time-consuming, low-margin tasks. For her, these include webpage design and desktop publishing, tasks that require specialized ex-pertise. Whenever possible, she downloads production costs to clients. This avoids having to invest in internal publication infrastructure. As a result, Julie has more time to grow the business, rather than manage projects.

- *Create community*: "Network, network, network! Find like-minded souls, and create a Silicon Valley wherever you are. Get out of your comfort zone. Attend matchmaking sessions. Make a speech at your Chamber of Commerce. It all helps to build reputation, investments that pay off."

- *Manage visibility*: Julie consciously manages the firm's brand equity to build legitimacy. This includes attending key conferences and meetings, and generating visibility through a quarterly newsletter. Twitter has grown, and it lets others "re-tweet." Tweeting does not necessarily increase busi-ness revenue, but being known as a thought leader adds value to clients.

- *Be mindful of place*: "Be place-based. Be mindful that this is where you want to be." Prior to launching Womenable, Julie moved to the midwestern United States, away from Washington and the center of U.S. policy. She wondered what impact the move would have on revenue. She is now con-vinced that it has made no difference. "While travel cuts into profitability, the lifestyle decision was the right one. Where I work and live enhance my well-being. Working with an international clientele means that it does not matter where I am living. With an airport close by, high-speed Internet, Skype, and other tools, I do just as well as if I were living in a city center."

REFLECTIONS

Having described strategies that enable Julie Weeks to lead her home-based global consultancy, this reflection focuses on skills and competencies. To learn more about the skills and entrepreneurial acumen of women business owners, we asked over a thousand women to identify their most important entrepreneur-ial competencies.[72] The ability to maintain customer relationships ranked number one, a soft skill that in today's marketplace is facilitated by information communi-cation technology (ICT).[73] When we asked them to share key challenges, lack of financial acumen topped this list. Many cited concerns such as lack of fiscal confi-dence, confusion about terms and jargon, and the need to utilize financial informa-tion and understand types of capital to better structure deals.[74] This makes sense given that weak financial management is directly associated with venture failure, including setting prices that are too low to be profitable, poor invoicing processes, and weak bookkeeping practices.

We identified three more key knowledge domains.[75] Small-business know-how includes functional knowledge about regulations, knowing how to work with the rules, and managing supplier-client relationships. Operational capability reflects competencies such as project management, managing people, and professional networks and the ability to delegate. Marketing fitness is the ability to develop new products, use market research, set prices, and launch advertising and promotion campaigns.

Our studies produced more insights. Years of industry experience did not translate into entrepreneurial competencies, particularly experience associated with operational capacity, financial acumen, and technological proficiency. While many of the women we surveyed had been in the labor force for decades, their breadth or diversity of experience was, on average, far narrower than matched cohorts of male entrepreneurs. The women then replicated the same tactics in current practices (such as lack of research, financial diagnostics) even though they had owned their firms for an extended period of time, sometimes years. Entrepreneurial tenure, or how long the entrepreneur was in business, did not supersede lack of experience prior to venture startup. And regardless of entrepreneurial tenure, most perceived that they retained limited technological and financial proficiency. The lesson learned is that conscious effort is needed to develop essential entrepreneurial skills and competencies.

Given these study insights, here are three questions for your consideration:

1. What are Julie's strengths (skills, competencies, knowledge) that enable her to manage a home-based global enterprise?
2. What are your entrepreneurial strengths: skills, competencies, and knowledge that you bring to venture creation?
3. Given these strengths, what are your areas of improvement?

Now that you have reflected on your entrepreneurial skills, competencies, and knowledge, hopefully you have a better understanding of your personal assets. Reflecting on growth strategies that build on these skills is one way to further boost confidence. And as with Julie Weeks, one strategy to increase sales is exporting.[76] But what are the specific skills needed to build an international enterprise? When is the best time to start exporting? How do you go about finding global contacts and markets? And what export strategies can fuel the growth engine of your enterprise?

Our studies among women exporters found that most initiate international trade during the early phase of enterprise development. Over half took their first steps within two years of starting up. The most common method of market entry was direct export and the hiring of agents and distributors. Which of the following market entry strategies might be appropriate for you and your firm?

- *Exporting directly to foreign markets*: defined as the transferring of goods and services to foreign clients.
- *Indirect exporting*: defined as shopping goods and services to foreign customers through hired agents or distributors (intermediaries) who do not take title of the goods but who earn revenue through commissions.
- *Establishing a joint venture:* in which two or more companies pool resources and create a new entity with equity provisions.
- *Exporting indirectly*: in which goods are shipped through a customer.
- *Servicing foreign clients in your own domestic market*: for example, offering services online.
- *Licensing agreements*: agreements that grant the legal rights, production methods, or both to a foreign business in return for a fee or a royalty.
- *A consignment agreement*: a contract relationship in which the business owner transfers goods and services to another party while retaining ownership until the product is sold.
- *Foreign direct investment*: investment by an individual, firm, or public agency in another country; investment that can reflect investment in production, brands, or firm acquisition.

Exporting is not, however without challenge. The challenges most often cited were associated with limited knowledge of foreign markets and customers, including costs of developing new markets, regulatory concerns such as tax and legal issues, and setting up effective distribution channels. Contrary to stereotypes, only the minority (two in ten) active women exporters cited family responsibilities as a barrier to conducting business abroad.

Complete the following three questions, before moving on to the next section:

1. What is your preferred strategy of market entry? Why?
2. What are the barriers associated with each of the entry strategies?
3. How can you overcome some of these market entry barriers?

Overcoming the Challenges of Exporting

We asked the women, "If you could give one piece of advice to another business owner who was considering exporting, what would you say?" The importance of doing homework prior to market entry is the key success factor cited by active women exporters. The right-hand column in Figure 4.2 summarizes their advice. Again, a lesson learned is that success requires knowledge of cultural differences,

Figure 4.2: Lessons learned and advice about exporting

Export Challenge (% citing challenge)	Women Business Owners' Advice
Cost of developing new markets (56%)	Understand the international market in order to differentiate your products, meet customer expectations, and understand the long-term viability of your products in international markets.
Setting up distribution channels (39%)	Purchasing labor and materials from foreign nationals is one way to learn about markets. Solicit advice, referrals, and introductions from suppliers, consultants, and foreign tax advisors.
Finding local partners (32%)	Contacts are key. Market intelligence can be gathered through secondary market analysis and follow-on leads from trade shows or personal visits.
Obtaining foreign market information (31%)	Gathering information is the first step toward exporting, and can help to establish rapport with regulators and increase firm visibility. This entails understanding trade regulations, tariff barriers, labeling requirements, brokerage fees, and certification. Government and trade associations are useful sources of information.
Cost and supply of labor and materials (24%)	To avoid inventory and cash flow problems, understand your financial and production capabilities. Be ready for clients' questions about your firm's capacity.
Foreign exchange risk (21%)	Strong financial management is needed. Exporting is a long-term investment that requires a healthy cash flow to finance transactions that may be held up during production. Receipt of foreign receivables can also be delayed.
Being taken seriously (21%)	Present yourself as an authority with respect to your product or service. This may include introductions from trade agencies and industry partners.
Lack of networks (20%)	Be persistent. Don't do it yourself. Ask for help. Find those who have done it before.
Language and cultural differences (19%)	Language skills are not a dominant problem. However, you need to understand cultural differences in consumer taste and how business is conducted. The elements that are most frequently adopted in international markets are pricing and promotion.
Personal safety (12%)	Solicit introductions from suppliers and trade commissioners. Stay in name-brand hotels.

Source: Adapted from B. Orser, E. Fischer, S. Hooper, R. Reuber, and A. Riding, *Beyond Borders: Canadian Businesswomen in International Trade* (Ottawa: Department of Foreign Affairs and International Trade, 1999).

customers' buying habits and tastes, customs and related trade regulations, and a clear strategy to weigh the financial risks and rewards of exporting. To acquire advice, women sought information from experienced individuals, including suppliers and government agencies. Another theme is to define an export strategy. This includes establishing clear export objectives.

Case 3: Janet Longmore — Empowering Women with Technology

Positioned at the intersection of youth and technology, Digital Opportunity Trust, or DOT, is focused on the economic empowerment of marginalized communities. Janet Longmore's vision is to eradicate inequality, poverty, and vulnerability by giving people the skills and knowledge to use technology to achieve educational, social, and economic opportunities. In a sector that is dominated by men, DOT is accelerating technology adoption by employing a disproportionate number of female interns and managers. This is another example of how entrepreneurs are leveraging feminine capital to improve women's quality of life and well-being.

Launched in 2001 as a registered nonprofit agency and headquartered within walking distance from their Ottawa offices, DOT's youth-led education and leadership programs are delivered all over the world. We asked Janet, founder, president, and chief executive officer of DOT, to tell us how she has built an international social enterprise that operates in ten countries, with over 4,500 "DOT Interns" (see description further on) and close to one million community members. DOT's annual revenues, including subsidiaries, exceed $10 million.

Opportunity Identification

The idea for DOT came to Janet while she was riding in a taxi in New York City, a world away from the communities in which DOT works. She was advising a United Nations organization on youth unemployment and the growing digital divide. "It was focused on the excess capacity and talent that underemployed and jobless youth represent throughout the world," she recalls. "The prevailing view expressed at the meeting was that adults needed to be sent to the developing world to 'help' the locals. It hit me—my personal moment of inspiration—we had to turn the model upside down. We had to build the capacity of youth to lead change in their countries, mold the role models in their own communities, and embed change-makers in society. We had to move away from the old model of importing the leaders of change. Eureka!"[77]

DOT was born from a need to create a social media platform to link young leaders in cross-cultural, transnational collaboration. Janet's epiphany was generated from her unique lens on youth. Prior to founding DOT, Janet was the CEO of the U.S.-based Communities in Schools, the largest American youth-at-risk organization. She understood the passion of youth, the opportunities that technology offers, and the strength of her relationships as a leader in the nonprofit sector. Janet recognized and acted upon an opportunity that others missed—the hallmarks of entrepreneurship.

Over half of DOT Interns, program participants, and the majority of local DOT enterprise leaders are women who share a passion for technology and change. DOT Interns deliver technology and business training in their local communities, while gaining workforce readiness skills for themselves. Recruited from local universities and colleges in the communities where DOT works, each is equipped with facilitation, coaching, mentoring, technology, and communication skills and then placed in communities with which they are familiar. After completing their nine-month placement, DOT Interns enter the workforce as talented, experienced, and in-demand professionals.

Entrepreneurial Competencies

Janet described two personal attributes that are reflected in her transformational leadership: having a clear message and staying focused. This simple yet powerful perspective guided Janet's decisions during the two years of prelaunch planning, and they remain the core of DOT's operating philosophy. What Janet did not mention was a leadership style that reflects a spirit of generosity, evidenced before our interview started. Enroute to a family cottage, Janet fit our 8:30 A.M. telephone interview into her holiday, before heading onto the highway. Doing so, she shared insights about the strategies that underlie DOT's rapid growth.

Be Aware That Lead Investors Can Enhance Legitimacy

To refine the DOT business model and launch the enterprise, Janet Longmore was able to call on long-standing relationships in her network of prominent advisors, foundations, corporations, and government agencies. "They understood the need to close the gap between digital technologies and human capacity, and to use technology to improve the livelihood of marginalized people." Their endorsements provided legitimacy for the startup concept.[78] During idea inception, Janet reached out to the Honorable Dr. David Johnston, then president of the University of Waterloo, and asked him to chair DOT's inaugural board of directors. Dr. Johnston, now Governor General of Canada, was the perfect fit. The University of Waterloo—referred to as the MIT of the north—was a perfect location. It is a recruitment target for many high-tech giants, including Google, Blackberry, Microsoft, and Apple. As a result of extensive expertise and affiliation with the University of Waterloo, David Johnston understood the power of education, digital networks, and other technologies that enable women. Today, DOT partners such as Cisco Systems, IBM, The MasterCard Foundation, and the Canadian government are lending brand legitimacy and funding to DOT. Blue chip partners not only enhance DOT's brand equity, they signal the importance of youth, including women, as a focal point for high-impact economic and social development.

Focus on Market-Based Solutions

DOT belongs to a new generation of enterprises, designed around business models that employ market-based solutions and entrepreneurship to solve social problems.[79] Best-in-class social enterprises such as DOT challenge conventional thinking about economic development. And like most rapidly expanding enterprises, DOT's business model is constantly reconfigured. An early challenge for Janet's team was to design a model that mobilized local teams, respected ethnocultural differences, and was supported by a lean mothership. A decentralized, network organizational structure was selected. Across the globe, a network of locally staffed DOT enterprises supports a suite of services, including economic, educational, research, volunteer, and executive development programs. DOT executives are also working with technology leaders, such as CISCO and IBM, to understand how young adults are creating, producing, and contributing as consumer-producers to Web 2.0 technologies and social media applications.[80] Research in African countries such as Ethiopia, Kenya, Rwanda, Uganda, and Tanzania is used to inform the redesign of curricula.

The DOT funding model has also made the transition from a more restrictive donor model of revenue generation to a service-delivery model. For example, DOT now works directly with private sector partners to generate alternative sources of revenue. This enables DOT to contribute and hence to capitalize on retained knowledge with partner agencies. Private partnerships and services also generate margins that are reinvested into DOT's expanding operations. DOT continues to attract social impact investment.

Social impact investment is a relatively new and growing field of finance.[81] The purpose is to mobilize capital, in order to scale up best-in-class social enterprises and to create operational efficiencies. In principal, investors support high rates of social transformative change, forgoing traditional rates of return. There are billions of dollars at stake.[82]

Looking ahead, DOT executives are currently exploring strategies to retain DOT interns, and to deploy their knowledge to social service agencies, at a price. DOT has also learned that just because an individual adopts digital technologies for personal use, it does not mean that he or she knows how to modify these tools for value-added, venture creation. DOT digital literacy curricula therefore include legal, ethical, and responsible use of the Internet, intellectual property, privacy, data security, and data ownership training.[83]

Understand That Board Members Are Key Assets

With a changing business model, the competencies of DOT Enterprise leaders have also evolved, from entrepreneurial staff with development expertise to tech savvy professionals, many of whom have founded technology firms. As Janet described, "Being a visionary and having passion was one thing. But as the business model changed, we needed experts with the ability to manage a network of hundreds of

DOT Interns. We needed financial acumen, management, and social media skills. Today, our vice-president of innovation is pushing us forward. What does not change is a consistency in language, message about the DOT mission, and the presence of young people at the forefront of the organization."

Janet's extensive leadership experience has also taught her the importance of governance and board oversight. "We are trying to determine an international governance structure, one that will allow us to maintain control of the DOT mission and programs, while at the same time fostering strong local operations." She expects that in time, country operations will support stand-alone boards of directors. In terms of managing boards, Janet offered these suggestions:

- Keep the board small.
- Ensure there is synergy between the executive and board members.
- Be clear in communicating responsibilities: members must understand their respective roles and fiduciary responsibilities. This includes the role of the CEO and founder.
- Maintain open communication about strategic direction.
- Inform your board members on an ongoing basis. Ensure there are no surprises.

Embrace Technology

DOT's cost effectiveness is achieved through technological proficiency, including the early adoption of social media and online education or training and communication platforms. Janet walks the talk. Janet understands what studies confirm, that technology adoption improves business processes and communications among customers and trade partners.[84] Technology is a means to gain competitive advantage and to overcome challenges inherent in venture development.[85] Compared to larger firms, however, small enterprises are disadvantaged in the adoption of information and communication technologies due to limited inaugural capacity, including quality and availability of skilled personnel.[86] Yet, in many instances, small enterprises in emerging economies are leading the technology adoption.[87] This is due to the fact that the decision to adopt technology is rarely predicated solely on enterprise scale. Many tools are available online, in the cloud, and on free-trial basis. Gone are the days when entrepreneurs must be technologists to adopt information, communication, and technology (ICT) tools. Nontechnical founders can also thrive in the advanced technology sector.[88] Operational efficiencies and productivity are not the only reasons to adopt ICT. The survival rates of technology-focused enterprise far exceed those of all other types of new ventures.[89]

Be as Innovative in Financing as in the Design of Products

The startup hurdles and risks of pioneering enterprises that operate in emerging economies and stressed communities are daunting.[90] We need only think about the challenges of launching a venture in more established markets, with infrastructures, supply chains, and customers with disposable income. And without track records of demonstrable results, most foundations and social investors shy away from nascent social enterprises. This was not the case for DOT. Janet's relationship with Cisco Systems led to a generous, three-year investment. Along with sweat equity, the grant was the turning point that enabled Janet to kickstart DOT.

Impacts

A glance at the DOT website tells visitors that DOT is results driven.

While many students worldwide are graduating into unemployment, the impact of DOT programming is impressive. Over 90 percent of DOT Interns start businesses or find jobs. Sixty percent of program participants double their use of technology and the Internet; eight in ten DOT participants report increased self-esteem and self-confidence. DOT is helping to redress what critics of traditional development policies have known for some time, that too often women and youth are ignored in development practices.[91] DOT demonstrates the value of empowering women through access to and control of technological resources.[92] Such empowerment is rapidly changing the architecture of power,[93] trickle-up changes that are helping to dismantle male-centric political and institutional authority.[94]

To learn more about social impact investment, we encourage you to follow Janet's advice to us. Visit McKinsey & Company's website on learning for social impact (lsi.mckinsey.com). The site hosts a database of tools, workbooks, and other practical resources. Information on emerging nonprofit investment funds can be found at Nonprofit Finance Fund (NFF), "Pay for Success Learning Hub" (payforsuccess.org). This site offers checklists and scorecards for constructing performance benchmarks and conducting due diligence (the assessment of a social enterprise's capabilities).[95]

REFLECTIONS

The objective of this reflection is to provide you with an opportunity to think strategically about technology adoption within your enterprise.

1. What steps can you take to increase your technological proficiency (for example, seek assistance from knowledgeable business associate or association, colleague, or staff member; attend technical seminars offered by entrepreneurship centers; use student consulting services)?

2. When evaluating a technology, do you follow a systematic process? What criteria do you use? It might be helpful to capture those criteria in a reusable format, for quick comparisons. Seeking input from other stakeholders is another best practice to consider (for example, criteria such as complexity, ease of use, cost, restrictive vendor lock-ins, total sunk costs, service support availability).

3. Does your enterprise monitor "system security" against internal or third-party sabotage, cyberattack, and other security breaches? If not, who can you contact to discuss technical support?

Weaving a Pattern

There is a multitude of ways in which firms innovate and grow. This chapter has presented multiple models of enterprise growth, insights into why some firms grow revenue more than others, and examples of how gender can potentially influence growth performance. We shared stories about enterprise growth and constructed a series of reflections and learning aids to help you to personalize the information shared.

Just Us! Coffee Roasters exemplifies what we described in Chapter 3 as an "emergent enterprise." Growth has been attained through incremental acquisition of resources, such as a reputation, extensive product line, supplier network, and community investment. Simultaneously, the enterprise has been the catalyst of market change. Today, growth is partially defined as building the legitimacy of sister organizations that share Just Us! fair trade, environmental, cooperative, and community-based values. Feminine capital continues to be reflected through a mission of equity and social justice and Debra and Jeff Moore's collaborative leadership. Julie Weeks personifies feminine capital through her consultancy's products and services—her desire to make positive change for women entrepreneurs. Firm growth can, in part, be credited to exogenous market forces such as the desire of governments to acquire expert advice about women's entrepreneurship. The growth of DOT, from Janet Longmore's idea to a multicountry, multiservice operation, captures feminine capital in the organization's founding mission to educate women about ICT, engagement of women as ICT trainers (a sector that is not typically populated by females), collaborative service delivery models, and team-based leadership. Janet's understanding of the impact of reputation and legitimacy in the growth process was evidenced since inception, through the role and composition of DOT's inaugural advisory board membership. Growth thresholds are reflected in a changing service portfolio, including the current strategy to work with global corporate clients to profitably leverage DOT's multicountry and cultural knowledge. No one explanation or growth trajectory is best. All are contributing to economic and social change.

Another key message of the chapter is that, while only half of all business owners seek to expand the size and scope of their enterprise, there are unexpected costs of managing a stagnant or lifestyle firm. These include limited opportunities to recruit top talent; to attract quality customers, suppliers, and investment capital; and to earn a good living. Given that many business owners work in excess of forty hours per week, remuneration is an important product of hard work. There are a multitude of innovative models, just as the rewards of enterprise growth are infinite. Remuneration is just one. Just Us! provides an example of economic and environmental outcomes. DOT exemplifies the impact of harnessing technology to affect social change. Womenable demonstrates the power of one person to create global change networks. All three—Debra Moore, Julie Weeks, and Janet Longmore—are testaments to the power of feminine capital to create wealth and social change.

Social Capital

5

Texts, blogs, podcasts, wikis, and tools such as Facebook and Twitter are fostering billions of global dialogues.[1] For entrepreneurs, these social media platforms are launching pads for participating in online communities and creating innovative enterprises. While social media enable these types of conversations, we believe that *social capital*—the collective knowledge, connections, and relationships developed through these tools—is the most important outcome. Social capital is a powerful resource, an asset that empowers women through the sharing of information. Social capital fosters wealth and social change, by increasing access to proprietary information, markets, and economic resources such as financial capital.[2] Social capital is linked to the performance of small firms.[3]

Female entrepreneurs recognize the power of the web in building social capital. Sites such as WomeninBizNetwork, Boss Network, Youthbiz, YoungFemaleEntrepreneurs, and StartUpPrincess have been created by women to bring like-minded entrepreneurs together to share ideas, build community, and enhance learning and professional development.[4] Companies such as Google, through their Women Entrepreneurs on the Web (WeOW) program, are assisting female entrepreneurs in developing online presence and connecting with leaders in their global community. Perhaps the clearest indication of the increasing clout of the World Wide Web for women's entrepreneurship comes from popular media. For example, *Forbes* magazine now publishes an annual survey titled *Top 10 Entrepreneurial Websites for Women*, launched in 2011.[5] Female entrepreneurs are visibly onboard and online.

In this chapter, we explore the who, what, and why of social capital. We also share research-based insights about the gendered nature of social capital. This is to help you to build a specific type of knowledge: *know-who*, the ability to develop meaningful business relationships. Information is presented in three sections. The first focuses on the elements of social capital. Our framework is predicated on the notion that *trust* is the critical element upon which to build social assets. Social assets include psychosocial support, information and advice, and access to resources. The second section describes the configuration of social networks, including the characteristics of value-added relationships. The third section delves into the spheres of influence, sources of knowledge such as friends and family, informal networks, mentors, boards, and associations. Special attention is devoted to mentors, because mentoring is a highly effective source of entrepreneurial *know-how*.[6]

Elements of Social Capital

The foundation of social capital is *trust*, the glue that binds all relationships. Trust implies a willingness to be vulnerable to another, an expectation that the individual will perform particular actions that are important to the trustor.[7] We like to think of trust as an emotional bank account.[8] Just as with a financial bank account, we make deposits and withdrawals. Rather than exchanging units of monetary value, however, emotional bank accounts deal with "trust units." Over time, you earn trust by making deposits. However, the balance can be quickly depleted with just one big withdrawal. Trust is hard to earn and easy to lose.

How then, can you build trusting relationships with colleagues, new business partners, customers, and suppliers? Research shows that trust is heightened when perceptions of integrity, ability, and respect are maximized, particularly at the outset of a new relationship.[9] Self-disclosure and perceived similarities also increase interpersonal comfort and, hence, trust.[10] This is one reason why nascent female entrepreneurs tend to gravitate toward other female entrepreneurs.[11] Perceived similarities and mutual interests can create competitive advantage. Women acquire tips and strategies, and gain confidence from others who, like themselves, may have encountered entrepreneurial or gender-related challenges.[12]

Integrity refers to the belief that one adheres to principles that others find acceptable. Integrity is associated, in part, with a clear message of intention. This is why exaggeration and overpromising are deal-killers during initial client and investor discussions. Integrity is enhanced by honesty, consistency, and conscientiousness in messaging and actions. In these ways, one shows respect for relationships, as one recognizes the importance of others' time and knowledge.

Perceptions of ability can also affect trust formulation. Ability is signaled through credentials, accreditations, a track record, and familiarity with industry standards. Ability is communicated through willingness to learn, openness, setting realistic goals, and being able to take criticism.[13] For this reason, it is suggested that entrepreneurs think about how they can best showcase their talents and abilities when establishing new relationships. Within promotional materials, on websites, and as part of the investment prospectus, for instance, think about how you can best communicate your experience and credentials. How can social media be leveraged effectively? Given the wide variety of media now available, entrepreneurs are getting increasingly creative in expressing themselves and their services in a trust-inspiring way.

Self-disclosure is the final element that contributes to trust building. As we build trust, we share ideas, thoughts, and feelings with others. In so doing, we make ourselves vulnerable. But self-disclosure can feel precarious, particularly for novice entrepreneurs who may feel exposed, given their lack of track record and other liabilities of newness. Most nascent entrepreneurs prefer a polished image when pitching themselves and their enterprise.[14] The challenge, then, is to maintain the balance between being forthright, to enhance trust, and to expose vulnerabilities that, at times, can be perceived as unprofessional.[15] Practicing introductions and presentations with trusted colleagues can help in this regard.

Consider the following scenarios about building trust with your clients and business partners.

Scenario 1: Initial Trust

You are the founder and owner of a small, web-based company, and you have just acquired a new client. This client is key to your growth plans, strategically located within a sector that you hope to develop. At first, the firm's vice president seems pleased with your work and congratulates you on your ideas for an innovative social media strategy. This represents a deposit in your newly opened mutual trust account. You have established credit with your creative, high-quality work and she with her positive feedback. Two months later, however, your account balance takes a hit. In preparation for a test launch of the newly designed webpage and social media accounts (Facebook, LinkedIn, and Twitter) one of her employees discovers a technical glitch on Facebook and a critical error in the company logo. Your client expresses public shock and disappointment. She is distressed about the impending delay and serious branding error. From the client perspective, you have let her down. You have made a large withdrawal from her trust account. At the same time, you too, are affected. Your faith in her judgment is somewhat eroded. While you clearly understand her displeasure, you do not appreciate the public manner in which it was communicated. Feeling embarrassed and worried about the repercussions, you feel that she has also made a small withdrawal.

As a supplier with a disgruntled client, you must now salvage the relationship and regain trust; however, you are vulnerable given that the balance is getting precariously low.

REFLECTIONS

In this scenario, what actions would you take to regain and build trust? Are there any special considerations because of the newness of the relationship? Would you employ different strategies if this scenario took place in a virtual or online relationship, across different cultures, or both? What are the implications for building trust when you cannot meet face to face?

Scenario 2: Speed to Trust

During a networking event, a prospective client approaches you to chat. It turns out that she has received a glowing reference about your work from a mutual friend. Because of this connection, you both have a sense of ready-made trust. Your trust account already has a balance. Mutual trust is so high that she discloses information to you about a potential business opportunity and suggests that you meet for lunch. At your lunch meeting, she shares proprietary information with you about a competitor. Because she is willing to take such personal risks, you feel that she has made a large deposit in your trust account.

REFLECTIONS

Introductions or referrals from respected clients and colleagues lend trust when building relationships. Speed to trust creates competitive advantage through accelerated access to protected information, resources, and decision makers. What are other factors that influence speed to trust? How can you leverage these factors in all of your business relationships?

Scenario 3: Breach of Trust

You decide to join a peer-mentoring group for entrepreneurs. Members agree to maintain confidentiality at all times. Feeling comfortable with the group, you disclose information about an upcoming event that you are organizing and to which you have invited a high-profile speaker. You subsequently discover, from the guest speaker's office, that confidentiality has been breached. Much to your surprise, one of the peer group members has contacted the speaker's office with a competing request to host the speaker herself when she comes to town. You feel angry, betrayed, and vulnerable. How could she use this confidential information to further her own interests? At this point, you wonder if the trust account has been overdrawn.

REFLECTIONS

Is the relationship salvageable? How would you deal with this breach of trust? Would you continue with the peer-mentoring group? What are some conflict resolution strategies that you might consider? How might these strategies differ when approaching an individual versus a group?

· · ·

Learning Aid 5.1 provides additional strategies for building trust. This checklist is based on a series of mentoring studies in which we examined gender influences in building trust. Refer to this learning aid to determine which tactics you are already using and which you might consider adding to your repertoire. For instance, you may notice that you have not checked off the box "Communicate Clearly" under "Ability." This provides an opportunity to think about how you can develop your communication skills with prospective clients. Here are three ideas to boost your competence in this area:

- Prepare an elevator pitch. This is a thirty-second explanation of your enterprise and startup concept. Imagine you are stuck in an elevator with a prospective client or investor. Can you clearly and concisely describe yourself and your value proposition? In preparation, draft a set of speaking points and responses to questions others might ask.
- Do your homework before meeting with a client. Are there any perceived similarities that can help you to establish rapport (for example, common personal or business interests)?
- Remember speed to trust? Think about how you can overcome the hurdles of establishing initial trust with clients by seeking referrals from friends, colleagues, or associates. Be specific in making this request. Ask if he or she will endorse your firm or product. Establishing trust will be much easier.

Framework of Social Capital

On a foundation of trust, entrepreneurs build social networks, accumulating social capital over time. Social capital is an important set of assets that has strategic value in the marketplace. These assets include psychosocial support, information and advice, and access to resources.[16] Together, they help entrepreneurs remain competitive and create economic value.[17] Refer to Figure 5.1 for a graphic representation of these assets. Each is now described.

Psychosocial Support

Psychosocial support refers to emotional and moral support that is reflected in friendship, acceptance, and having someone to confide in and trust.[18] Such support can boost *self-efficacy*: the belief in oneself and ability to perform tasks well.[19] *Entrepreneurial self-efficacy* refers to confidence and a positive assessment of competencies and knowledge domains essential to creating new ventures.[20] Psychosocial support is also important, as entrepreneurial self-efficacy influences intention to pursue self-employment or a business startup, particularly for women. Gender differences in

Learning Aid 5.1: Strategies to build trust in relationships

Instructions: Review the following trust-building strategies for working with new clients, business partners, mentors, or colleagues. Identify those practices that you consistently use. Are there any new strategies that you could consider adopting?

Ability: Present Yourself Clearly and Authentically	
Reflect and Research	☐ Before getting involved in a business relationship, reflect on the following questions: "Why do I seek this relationship? What value will it add?" Do your research as well (for example, check references and credentials) before getting involved. It pays to be strategic.
Communicate Clearly	☐ Clear communication sets up the relationship up for success. It prevents misunderstandings and establishes the psychological contract. Communicate your experience, abilities, and expectations clearly. Think carefully about your choice of communication media. Face to face is the richest form of communication, and a meeting in person may be warranted to set things off on the right foot.
Set Realistic Goals	☐ Goals should be established at the beginning of the relationship. Having reasonable expectations encourages both partners to discuss and agree upon where they want to go.
Be Open	☐ Show that you are open to feedback. Our research on mentor-protégé relationships found that trust-building was facilitated with protégés who are keen and demonstrated a willingness to learn.
Integrity: Adhere to Principles That Others Find Acceptable	
Keep a Confidence	☐ The ability of trustees and trustors to keep a confidence is the foundation upon which trusting relationships are built.
Work Through a Crisis	☐ Surviving a major event or crisis together can further strengthen the relationship.
Recognize Gender	☐ Recognize that gender can influence relationships. Whereas perceived similarity can help build trust, cross-gender relationships can sometimes create discomfort. If getting into a cross-gender mentoring relationship, for example, it may be advisable to discuss how to maximize interpersonal comfort and minimize any misconceptions that may arise from colleagues, partners, and so on.
Follow Up	☐ If you are seeking advice, be sure to follow up. If you make promises, do the same!
Declare Conflicts of Interest	☐ Any potential conflict of interest should be addressed as soon as the situation arises. In fact, our research has shown that declaring a potential conflict of interest can solidify trust and help to further entrench confidence.
Respect: Recognize the Contribution of Others—Their Time, Knowledge, and Experience	
Be Succinct	☐ Communicating succinctly demonstrates respect for your trustor's time. Establish early that you will use their time efficiently. Plan your main messages before picking up the phone or sending an email.
Stay Organized	☐ Being organized ensures that you optimize the relationship. Establish a meeting schedule (regularity, mode[s] of communication, meeting length, length of mentoring commitment). Prepare questions or subjects of discussion before meetings.
Express Admiration Through Action	☐ Demonstrate your respect by following up on advice or recommendations received. Your trustor has taken risks and invested in you. Follow-up builds mutual trust.
Exit Elegantly	☐ In certain types of relationships, it is important to set a timeframe for reassessment (for example, in formal mentoring programs you might suggest, "I think that we need to assess how we are doing" or "We've reached the one-month mark, how are we doing?"). Upon exit, clarify appreciation (for example, "I am grateful for . . ."; "I have received and learned . . .").

Source: J. Leck and B. Orser, "Fostering Trust in Mentoring Relationships: An Exploratory Study," *Equality, Diversity and Inclusions: An International Journal* 32, no. 4 (2013): 410–425.

Figure 5.1: Framework of social capital

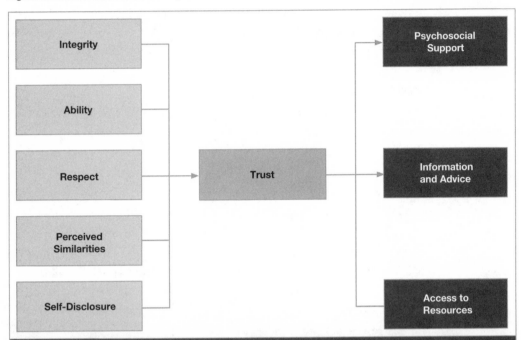

Trust

Integrity: Adherence to a set of principles
Ability: Skills, competencies, other characteristics that enable influence
Respect: Admiration through action, follow-up, adherence
Perceived similarities: Common or shared attributes such as gender
Self-disclosure: Transparency, sharing, becoming vulnerable

Psychosocial Support

Goal-setting: Clarifying or setting realistic performance expectations
Self-efficacy: Belief in oneself, ability to perform tasks
Moral support: Acceptance, someone to confide in and trust
Role modeling: Learning consequences of decisions, observational learning

Information and Advice

Industry culture: Norms of behavior, underlying values and attitudes
Sounding board: Expert guidance, complementary knowledge
Ideas: Seeking opportunities or prompt action
Intellectual capital: Technical competencies, know-what, know-who

Access to Resources

Financial capital: Initial and expansion investment
Reputational capital: Enhanced judgment by outsiders, favorability
Tangible assets: Labor, materials, space
Networks: Access to key contacts

self-efficacy are also reported.[21] Compared to males, females are more likely to retain preconceptions about having a lack of entrepreneurial skills.[22] The good news is that entrepreneurship training can have a positive impact on entrepreneurial self-efficacy and entrepreneurial career intentions.[23]

Information and Advice

Information and advice are invaluable, in a variety of ways, throughout all phases of venture creation. Advisors help novice entrepreneurs navigate sector politics and gain access to networks and other tangible and intangible resources.[24] Even seasoned business owners can benefit from mentors who provide feedback about ideas and opportunities.[25] Such feedback can motivate protégés to undertake critical self-reflection and constructive confrontation that lead to the development of better problem-solving skills.[26] Information and advice are critical, given that entrepreneurial skills and competencies are not typically taught in formal education environments. Much entrepreneurial learning is achieved on the job and just in time, typically through mentorships or social networks.

Access to Resources

Through social networks entrepreneurs access tangible resources such as labor, materials, and financing, more building blocks for venture creation. For example, securing early stage investment is difficult at the best of times. But for female entrepreneurs, the challenge is exacerbated by the fact that early stage equity investors, known as "business angels," are not listed in directories. Many prefer to remain obscure. As women are less involved in wealth management, they generally have fewer contacts in investment networks.[27]

Women entrepreneurs may be disadvantaged for another reason. As discussed in Chapter 4, some investors have perceptual biases about women entrepreneurs. When processing signals about social capital, some fall back on stereotypes: "women are less capable," "women lack confidence in the cut-throat world of business," "a woman's place is in the home."[28] Such attitudes have a serious and dramatic impact on reputational capital. They can lead to a discounting of the legitimacy, status, and assessed financial value of female-owned enterprises.[29] Building social capital can go a long way to overcoming such biases.

Spheres of Social Capital

We characterize social capital as spheres of influence, relationships that develop over time. Sources of social capital differ in proximity to the entrepreneur and the underlying degree of trust. During early stages of venture creation, for example, *family and friends* are often a primary source of social capital. Psychological proximity is close. As entrepreneurs mature within the venture creation process, they typically reach further afield to build their networks. Many then begin by reaching out to *informal networks*, including business associates; trusted colleagues (often from previous jobs); and experts for specialized resources, information, and advice. These relationships often generate referrals. At this point, most novice entrepreneurs become less reliant on family and kinship ties.[30] Many also seek *mentors*. Mentors are experienced individuals or sometimes corporations that are willing to help less experienced founders or protégés.[31]

As entrepreneurs become established, distal sources of social capital are developed, relationships that are typically more formal. These include *advisory boards* and *boards of directors*, structured committees that provide founders with guidance on goal setting, governance, and strategy. *Industry and professional associations* are organizations that span commercial sectors or functions of the enterprise (such as sector producers, professional governing bodies, accreditors), or both.[32]

REFLECTIONS

When managed, each sphere of influence plays a role, to varying degrees, in providing psychosocial support, offering advice and information and increasing access to resources. Figure 5.2 illustrates these spheres. Take a few minutes to reflect on your social capital. Where does your social capital lie within these spheres? Is

Figure 5.2: Spheres of social capital

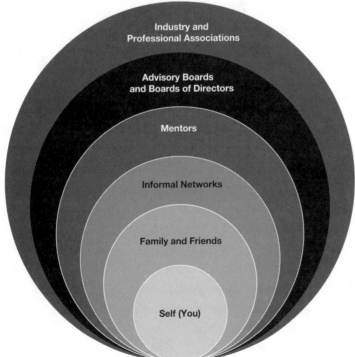

it densely clustered, predominantly focused around family and friends? Do you have access to each of the spheres? Who are the primary influencers within each sphere? Who contributes the largest deposits to your trust account?

Managing Your Social Networks

Not all social networks are created equal. In addition to thinking about the spheres of influence, it is important to understand how your networks are configured and how feminine capital contributes to their strength and structure. Only then are you best able to actively manage your social networks.

Much research has been undertaken to determine the ideal characteristics of entrepreneurial networks. Using mapping methodologies, scholars have sought to identify those attributes of networks that are critical in supporting venture creation, including enterprise growth. More recently, gender influences have been thrown into the research mix. While study results are not conclusive, here are several important observations.[33]

- *Network size*: the number of contacts in an individual's social network is positively related to early stage growth and innovation.[34] While women often report having larger or denser networks than men, the quality of the network may be lower. Within their networks, women are found to retain more family and friends,[35] with fewer entrepreneurs and business associates, particularly at early stages of enterprise growth.[36] This can create challenges associated with securing financing, finding role models, and accessing resources such as practical advice from seasoned entrepreneurs.

- *Network strength* refers to the number of strong ties in one's network, individuals who are closely connected—emotionally, geographically, and in terms of trust and reciprocity. Strong networks are associated with reliable and timely information. Compared to males, on average, female entrepreneurs' networks are disproportionately populated by family and friends. This may be advantageous for emotional support, but not for objective business advice, particularly in later stages of business growth.

- *Centrality* refers to the most important person in a network. Often this person provides multiple types of information, such as a friend who provides financial advice, technical expertise, and emotional support. For many women, this is typically a spouse or partner, or other family member. While such a contact may be an efficient means to acquire information and other resources, studies tell us that it is best to obtain multiple points of view. Family members may not provide the best quality or most objective advice and information.

- *Direct versus indirect ties* refers to the degree of separation between network contacts. Direct ties (one-to-one contacts) generally offer faster responses and more emotional support; however, they may offer fewer novel ideas and access to information and resources outside the existing network. Women are seen to maintain more direct versus indirect ties.

As an enterprise evolves, so do relationships. Learning Aid 5.2 provides an opportunity to analyze the configuration of your social capital. Use it to assess your network configuration, including the quality, depth, and breadth of social capital. This is important because the composition of a network affects one's ability to obtain the right kind of resources, at different stages of the enterprise lifecycle. As well, certain individuals might be particularly powerful in the network, and it is important to recognize this fact.[37] Such individuals can create risk when they are not reliable or do not fully support your entrepreneurial aspirations.

REFLECTIONS

Because of the tendency for female entrepreneurs to retain dense, closely tied networks (that is, a high percentage of kin) it is useful to think about reaching out. How can you build other relationships in your portfolio of networks? How can you identify seasoned advisors who can provide objective advice in key strategic areas of your enterprise? Is there one particular individual in your network that you consider to be indispensable? If so, can you prepare a backup plan to mitigate risk in the event that he or she is not available?

· · ·

In the next section, we return to Figure 5.2, to further illuminate the power and potential of each sphere of influence. By understanding the elements that constitute each sphere, you can better manage these assets for business success. It is our belief that many women are naturally oriented toward forming collaborative relationships, across all of these spheres of influence. This is a key component of feminine capital. Recall that, in our research with feminist entrepreneurs, women overwhelmingly described themselves as relational and participative. They consistently talked about achieving business results through partnerships, collaborations, or cooperation with others. They led by empowering and inspiring.

As you read through the next section, continue to think about how you can leverage feminine capital, your unique skills and attributes, across all the spheres of influence. Keep in mind that not all contacts are of equal value to your venture. You also will have different needs at various stages of the enterprise creation process.

Learning Aid 5.2: Sources and configuration of social capital

Instructions: Referring back to Figure 5.2, identify individuals (in each of the spheres) with whom you discuss your venture creation ideas or enterprise. Think about the types of resources that each provides (psychosocial support, advice, information, other resources). With these thoughts in mind, document your reflections.

Questions	Reflections
In which sphere(s) do most of your contacts lie? If your contacts are mostly family and friends, then you have a *dense network with strong ties*. This is unusually very high in connectedness— high trust and emotional support. Communication is typically frequent and fast. However, you may need to seek out new contacts in order to bring in new ideas. Are most of your business contacts similar to you (for example, gender, ethnicity, age, stage of firm maturity, sector)? If your answer is yes, it may be time to add variation in your contacts.	
Do you know many entrepreneurs? Having entrepreneurs in your network has been shown to be beneficial, particularly for women who are in the earlier stages of venture creation. If you don't have many in your network, think about strategies to meet more.	
Who is central to your network? Do you have one or more contacts that provide multiple social capital assets (psychosocial support, advice and information, and resources)? Such individuals likely retain key strategic roles in your networks. Do you have a backup plan if the individual(s) is no longer available for support? Who else might fulfill these roles?	
Are key relationships formal or informal? If you have few formal sources of social capital, then this may be an area in which you could add a new network tie, such as a formal networking organization or professional association. Think about areas in which this might help you.	
Who provides functional expertise? Who in your network supports functional needs such as marketing, legal issues, communications, finance and accounting, information systems, and so on? Are you lacking social capital in these areas?	
Are your relationships value-added? It is useful to review your relationships from time to time to determine if they are still adding value to you or your business. Sometimes it makes business sense to discard certain relationships that do not contribute positively to your needs.	

Family and Friends

The influence of family and friends can be positive and negative. They often help to assemble initial resources for aspiring female entrepreneurs. Conversations with them can bridge the chasm between entrepreneurial intention and enterprise startup, build self-efficacy, verify ideas, and affirm role legitimacy.[38] Talking through possibilities with family members and friends enables women to practice persuasion and refine language that will be used to shape the enterprise. This is particularly useful when nascent entrepreneurs lack experience and contacts.

For most, family and friends are critical to emotional well-being. However, within those cultures and communities with strongly prescribed gender roles, many women continue to face pressure to conform to the occupational and behavioral expectations of family and friends.[39] And while family and friends may provide psychosocial and financial support, their feedback on an entrepreneurial venture is typically less effective than that received from experienced business associates.[40]

Informal Networks

All of us are connected to others through informal relationships with family and friends, community and business organizations, and volunteer activities. The composition of informal social networks is seen to differ by gender. As men traditionally have occupied the public domain, they historically have accumulated more informal business relationships, relationships that are laden with economic value. Women have resided in the private sphere, in which networks tended to revolve around domestic concerns.[41] While this is rapidly changing, the pattern persists. Informal networks continue to be sex segregated. Studies report that male business owners identify their most important network supporters to be accountants, lawyers, and other professionals. Spouses come second. Conversely, female business owners are more likely to name spouses or partners followed by close friends as their most important network supporters.[42] A similar pattern is found with advice-seeking behavior. Males tend to name professional acquaintances; women name family and friends.[43]

In constructing informal networks, attitude appears to play a significant role. A study of growth-oriented women entrepreneurs in Norway and Sweden found that "willingness" was a key feature of network diversity. Those women entrepreneurs who had a positive attitude toward new networks had a more diverse network. Securing a mentor is one response strategy for women who are eager to expand their informal networks.[44]

Mentors

Mentors are a proven source of value-added social capital. A survey of over one thousand successful businesswomen in nine countries found that 80 percent had been mentored. In the span of their careers, most had benefited from an average of 2.6 mentors. This makes sense, given that the right mentor can provide advice and feedback, help entrepreneurs navigate sector politics, digest market information, and make introductions.[45] Studies suggest that women business owners prefer female role models. Same-gender matches are seen to increase interpersonal comfort, facilitate the development of trust, reduce social distance, and hence improve the quality of the mentoring relationship.[46] But this can create a catch-22. Finding a suitable female mentor is not always straightforward, as women entrepreneurs have reported that such mentors can be hard to find.[47] We conjecture that these dynamics help to explain why, compared to nascent male entrepreneurs, females also tend to draw on family and friends as mentors.

Studies also illuminate the complexities of trust in mixed- versus same-gender mentorships. In building trust, relationships that appear to work best are those in which the mentor and protégé perceive similarities in their values and interests.[48] Perhaps this is why same-gender relationships are seen to offer relatively more psychosocial support.[49] Our studies of mentoring with mixed-gender dyads found another insight with respect to trust. When we asked male mentors who they would select for an important organizational project, the majority choose male protégés over equally qualified female protégés. When asked why, a common response was, "I trust him more."[50] How male and female mentors viewed their roles also differed. Female mentors viewed mentoring as an opportunity to colearn through two-way communication; male mentors were more likely to view relationships as one-way advice giving.[51] When we asked respondents to tell us about how they formulate trust, female mentors were inclined to rely on "chemistry" while men relied more on "past successes."[52] These insights alert mentors and protégés to the importance of formalizing expectations at the outset of all mentoring relationships. They also illustrate the merit of having male and female mentors.

Informal mentorships occur spontaneously, often through mutual attraction. A strategy to address the absence of a mentor is to enroll in a formalized mentorship program. Formal mentorship provides third-party matchmaking. Service providers can include trade associations, entrepreneurship and innovation training agencies, private firms, and government. The largest such program is the U.S. Small Business Administration SCORE program. Introduced in the 1970s, this program provides online matchmaking that is supported by over thirteen thousand volunteer mentors with over three hundred chapters across the United States. Women-focused programs are also available. Both types of programs remove a key obstacle: finding a mentor. And while some think that mentorship is primarily about face-to-face dialogues, there are an increasing number of alternative models to consider. Here are four scenarios to illustrate the options of classic, peer, reverse, and e-mentoring. We invite you to reflect on each.

Scenario 4: Creating a Portfolio of Mentors

Susan Ross has made the difficult decision to launch her entrepreneurial venture. Having worked in a corporate environment, she has a healthy professional network in the packaged goods industry from which to draw. However, none of these contacts has established a business. Ideally, she wants to find a female entrepreneur to mentor her, someone who is in a similar stage of life. Unfortunately, Susan cannot locate another female entrepreneur who is willing to mentor her through a business startup. Not to be deterred, she decides to create a portfolio of mentors. Each expert can help her to achieve a specific outcome. She locates a specialist on financing issues. She turns to her brother to identify a potential entrepreneur from his client base. He recommends Paul, a client with an impressive list of credentials. During their initial conversation, Paul mentions that he prefers to focus on career-related questions and not Susan's personal concerns. This frankness is helpful and best to know at the outset of the relationship. Paul's approach is consistent with our research that male mentors are more likely to provide technical and hands-on knowledge, rather than psychosocial support.[53] Susan feels that her portfolio of mentors is not yet complete. She contacts a women's entrepreneurship center to inquire about finding a female mentor to discuss work-life balance issues, from a woman's perspective.

REFLECTIONS

Are you currently in a mentoring relationship? If yes, what functions does it provide: psychosocial, career, role modeling, and learning? If not, how would you go about finding a mentor(s)? Does the gender of a prospective mentor matter? If so, why? What areas of expertise would round out your portfolio?

Now, complete Learning Aid 5.3. This tool lists learning outcomes that can help guide conversations between prospective mentors or protégés. It can also be used to avoid misunderstanding, or worse, disappointment with your mentoring relationship.

Scenario 5: Reciprocal Mentoring

Early in the relationship with Paul, Susan realizes that her mentor knows little about social media and online networking tools. She, however, considers herself to

Learning Aid 5.3: Learning expectations of mentoring

Instructions: Check off those list items that apply to you. If any other outcomes or expectations are missing, add them to the list. You can then refer to this checklist to guide your search for a mentor(s) and your initial discussions to clarify expectations and priorities.

A mentor could help me to:
☐ Set the strategic direction of the enterprise
☐ Refine my business model or business concept
☐ Understand the challenges of enterprise growth
☐ Develop the enterprise's human capital
☐ Procure new sources of revenue
☐ Avoid a cash flow crisis
☐ Improve my operational skills
☐ Better understand the financial risks of growth
☐ Build my business contacts
☐ Identify strategic areas of weakness
☐ Access financing or loans
☐ Learn about new market opportunities
☐ Position my products or services
☐ Manage my financial welfare
☐ Build my self-confidence
☐ Understand my skills as an entrepreneur
☐ Learn to identify and better leverage my feminine capital
☐ Learn strategies to better achieve work-life balance
☐ Other:

be an expert. She recently read an article about Jack Welch, former general manager of General Electric, who recommended reciprocal peer mentoring, particularly for boosting technological competencies.[54] She suggests reframing her relationship with Paul to create a similar arrangement. A reciprocal mentoring relationship fits her collaborative approach to doing business. She also believes that such a relationship will be mutually beneficial.[55]

REFLECTIONS

If you have a protégé or mentor, how can you encourage colearning? List five specific skills and competencies that you would like to share or learn.

Scenario 6: E-Mentoring

The local women's entrepreneurship center supports an online mentoring program. Susan thinks that the digital approach might offer advantages: convenient, flexible, available as needed, and anonymous. The e-mentoring platform might also increase the pool of potential mentors from which she can draw. Of course, e-mentoring is not for everyone. For those who prioritize psychosocial support or prefer face-to-face dialogues, e-mentoring may not be an option.

REFLECTIONS

Is this the kind of mentorship group that you could see yourself joining? In any mentoring relationship, what ground rules should be discussed?

Scenario 7: Peer Mentoring

About a year later, Susan's firm is operational. As a sole proprietor, she realizes that she would like the camaraderie of more like-minded women entrepreneurs. This prompts her to establish a peer-to-peer mentoring group, what she calls her "circle of wisdom." The group meets monthly in a member's home. Participants act as mentors, protégés, or both, depending upon the issue at hand. They decide to establish a circle of wisdom "charter," a document that spells out guiding principles for the group, their objectives, and membership expectations. Learning Aid 5.4 provides tips for establishing your own peer-to-peer mentoring circle.

Learning Aid 5.4: Tips for establishing a peer-to-peer mentoring group

Start-up
☑ Determine objectives and anticipate learning outcomes for the group.
☑ Determine criteria for membership before assembling the group.
☑ Clarify and discuss members' roles and responsibilities.
☑ Be conscious of member compatibility and potential conflicts (such as competitors, individuals who may dominate conversations).
Governance
☑ Consider having leadership as a rotating responsibility.
☑ Choose an administrative leader who will schedule meetings and draft agendas.
☑ Plan a recruitment strategy to maintain the group when turnover occurs.
☑ Remind members, "What is discussed in the circle stays in the circle."
☑ Appreciate differences: listen and seek to understand.
☑ Plan a roster of topics for each meeting.
☑ Encourage frank communication to create a more trusting environment.
☑ Set up a mechanism and timeframe for review of membership, objectives, and so on.

REFLECTIONS

Would you consider engaging in a virtual mentoring relationship? If so, check out the following sample e-mentoring programs. When doing so, explore and compare the program features. What are the potential advantages and disadvantages of each?

- Mentor Net offers e-mentoring for individuals who are pursuing careers in science, technology, engineering, and mathematics, especially women and underrepresented minorities.
- Initiative France, Eget Foretag (Sweden), and Mentorsme (United Kingdom) support online gateways for entrepreneurs who are seeking a mentor.
- Private firms and national governments are increasingly targeting women entrepreneurs. See the Moroccan Women's Network for Mentoring (assisted by the IBM Corporate Service Corps); WEMentorUK in the United Kingdom (The National Network of Mentors for Women Entrepreneurs); and the Women's Executive Network, operating in Canada and Ireland.

Advisory Boards

Advisory boards are another source of social capital. They come in various forms: one time, ad hoc, ongoing, and, increasingly, virtual communities comprising individuals with skills and knowledge that complement those of the founder. Advisory boards may be active or on paper only. If your firm is incorporated, in many countries a particular type of advisory board is legally required: a *board of directors*. A McKinsey study on the role of directors found that many are preoccupied with fiduciary matters (such as reporting, audits, compliance, and budgeting), rather than on planning for the future. The report recommends that directors "act as effective coaches and sparring partners for the top [ownership] team."[56]

Our research found that only a small percentage of female-owned enterprises retain advisory boards. When we asked women entrepreneurs why they did not have an advisory board, the most common response was lack of understanding about the role and benefits.[57] Yet among those firms that retained advisory boards, most business owners acquired much-needed expertise and experience. Learning Aid 5.5 provides tips for setting up an advisory board and the duties of board members.[58] It is not as difficult as you might think.

Industry and Professional Associations

Industry and professional associations are the most formalized source of social capital. Many are mandated to meet members' functional needs, such as professional development or group purchasing. Some reflect distal network ties, com-

Learning Aid 5.5: Tips for building an advisory board

Who should be on your advisory board?

A good place to start is small. Start to work with two to three initial members. Designated members might include
- A legal representative
- A financial representative to provide accounting, insurance, and banking advice
- A technical or market expert who is familiar with your product or service sector.

Where do you find advisors?

- Use your network: contact colleagues, friends, and family for referrals.
- Talk to other entrepreneurs, suppliers, and potential clients.
- Sometimes retired executives are interested in helping nascent entrepreneurs in their community.
- If available, talk to a women's enterprise center or the municipal small-business center.
- Think about people whom you admire and trust. They may be your initial advisors and confidants.

What should you ask them to do?

- Map out a set of expectations.
- Establish specific terms of office, including frequency of meetings, duration, compensation, and length of term (for example twelve to twenty-four months).
- Your legal representative should help select the governance structure and file all paperwork.
- If you are an incorporated firm, the board oversees the company according to its bylaws.*
- Typical functions include
  - Establishing and managing the objectives of the company
  - Appointing or selecting the chief executive officer and other senior executives
  - Seeking out financial resources
  - Approving the company's annual budget
  - Setting salaries and other compensation
  - Making sure all the interests of the shareholders are protected
  - Creating, approving, and supporting the company's corporate bylaws
  - Approving the sale of stock
  - Recording board minutes.

How do you compensate board members for their services?

- Compensation can be made either directly or indirectly.
- Some may not expect to be paid. Simply being an active part of your business may be payment enough. However, a gesture of appreciation is usually warranted (for example, host an upscale lunch each meeting, pay a modest per-meeting honorarium). Others, however, will expect compensation. For example, you may pay your legal advisor or accountant on an hourly basis. An insurance representative, however, would make a commission from the products or services that you purchase.

How do you best communicate with the board?

- Communicate frequently, clearly, and professionally.
- Prepare well in advance for meetings by soliciting input for the agenda.
- Select a venue for your meeting that is private, quiet, and nice.
- Summarize each meeting with minutes or an action plan.
- Distribute your business plan to all members.
- Keep in touch between meetings.

*For example, in the United States, if the company is publicly held, the board members must adhere to the rules and regulations stipulated in the Sarbanes-Oxley Act.

Source: Adapted from *How to Create and Manage a Corporate Board of Directors, All Business*, accessed at http://www.allbusiness.com/corporate-governance/2532-1.html.

prising people who may not know each other, but with whom one shares common issues or concerns. For example, industry associations tend to focus on sector issues such as advocacy, group and bulk purchasing, and establishing industry standards. Joining is often dependent upon aggregate benefits, such as

- Cooperative marketing to gain visibility
- Competitive intelligence: access to industry information and research
- Education and training
- Member benefits such as group insurance programs
- Advocacy: a common voice to government
- Creating a community of like-minded entrepreneurs.

Women business owners cite formal networking as another benefit of belonging to industry and professional associations. And research shows that such networking works. A recent study by EY reports a clear link between networking and improved business outcomes for female entrepreneurs.[59] Women involved in association workshops and support meetings realized greater improvement in access to growth and expansion capital.

Scenario 8: Maximizing the Power of Networking

You have joined a professional organization and are attending the first formal networking event. Within the first ten minutes, you notice that one of your male colleagues has handed out five business cards. In the same time, you have spoken to only one person, another female colleague. You have complimented her, shared a few personal stories, and commiserated about finding time to sneak away from the office to attend the event. You have forgotten to exchange names, but you will do so before moving on. This is a prototypical example of the "networking gender gap."[60]

Research has shown that, for men, association networking is all about selling themselves and their firms, and trading information. They expect conversations to lead to tangible business results. Typically, conversations are shorter, more direct, and to the point. In contrast, women look for opportunities to help others. They discuss a broader range of subjects, regardless of the professional benefits. According to one LinkedIn networking commentator, "Men start with a statement about their status. Women create community."[61] This observation mirrors our research on women entrepreneurs and feminine capital. Women are natural relationship builders. They seek to achieve results in collaborative ways.

So how can you leverage your feminine capital to network most efficiently and effectively? Here are some suggestions. Investing in social capital is a critical entrepreneurial task.[62] Remember that men and women can differ in their approaches. Men are typically more direct. So, there is no need to provide lots of personal information. Get to the point. Don't feel apologetic about your accomplishments. Present your firm's value proposition clearly and don't feel guilty about taking time to network. Business is all about relationships. Networking needs to be a business priority. When business owners stay heads down "in" the business, opportunities are lost.

Experience has also taught us, however, that not all associations are alike. To maximize the power of networking, we encourage you to critically assess the value of your association affiliations. Learning Aid 5.6 highlights decision criteria that you can use to estimate the social and economic value of joining or retaining memberships.

Learning Aid 5.6: Should I add this association to my social capital portfolio?

Instructions: Answer each of the following questions about associations in which you are considering membership. General decision criteria will help you assess whether membership would be beneficial. If, however, you are having difficulty finding an association, ask yourself the second set of questions.

General Decision Criteria	Comments
☐ Does the association promote commercial benefits in its membership material? Can you access or achieve these benefits, at a comparable time and cost, on your own?	
☐ What can you contribute to the association? How will these contributions benefit you? What "in kind" contributions of your time are expected?	
☐ What does participation entail? For example, what are the initiation or membership fees?	
☐ Does the association have bylaws and transparent governance and reporting structure? Are board members and the executive directly accountable to members?	
☐ What is the tenure and what are the successes of the association?	
☐ Other:	

Finding the Right Association to Join	Comments
☐ Do you have a mentor or trusted advisor with whom you can consult?	
☐ Have you spoken to association members or clients of the organization about their experiences or for references?	
☐ Do you have a women's entrepreneurship center where you can go for suggestions?	
☐ Do you go to trade shows where you could gather information and observe association presentations and presence? If yes, which ones have you noticed?	
☐ Who sits on the executive board? Remember that some of your competitors may be active members.	
☐ Other:	

Women's Networks and Associations

An increasing number of associations support subcommittees or forums for women entrepreneurs. There is also a growing number of small-business, sector, and professional networks targeted explicitly at women, providing a recognizable and collective market presence. The importance of women-only organizations and networks has gained visibility through the publication of Sheryl Sandberg's book *Lean In: Women, Work and the Will to Lead*. Sandberg views women-only spaces, what she refers to as "lean in circles," as forums for collective support and spheres to teach indispensable business skills.[63] Her views are supported by research on women's networks in corporations. Researchers Anne Donnellon and Nan Langowitz found that women's networks are unique spheres of influence that enable members to connect with others (survive), develop personally and professionally (thrive), and grow their business (drive).[64] The more evolved the network, the more it can contribute to venture growth and social change.

- *Survive*: This stage of network maturation focuses on connectedness and sharing common identities and experience. Women get advice from other women about how to navigate a male-dominated business environment and on how to develop their competencies and their business venture.
- *Thrive*: This point in development is focused more on professional development, business growth, or both, as women share information about opportunities, receive assistance and advice in accessing resources and solving problems, and identify role models from whom they gain advice and inspiration.
- *Drive*: At this advanced stage of development, women come together to affect change. They are motivated to enable and promote the advancement of women in a broader context. They understand the role of entrepreneurship in driving social change as well as policy in affecting programs for the betterment of women's economic prosperity.

REFLECTIONS

Are you an active member of a formal or informal women's network? If so, what benefits do you realize from these networks? How evolved is your network in terms of the three stages just described: survive, thrive, or drive? Does it help you to grow your business and drive social change? Could it contribute more to the advancement of women? How can your network(s) be leveraged to realize more value?

Final Thoughts

In this chapter, we looked at the importance of building social capital, relationships that translate into improved entrepreneurial outcomes. We deconstructed the components of social capital and highlighted the potential influences of being female on network configurations. We devoted this chapter to social capital because many women perceive they are disadvantaged with respect to accessing networks and social brokers.[65] Fortunately, there are strategies to manage contacts, networks, and other relationships, since not all relationships are of equal value—value you can bank on.

Increasingly, women entrepreneurs are harnessing the power of social media to reach out to potential business partners and customers. This is not surprising, given that feminine capital assets are advantageous in this new arena. Skills such as building trust, collaboration, open communication, and mutual empowerment are ideally suited to the Internet's dynamic environment. Social media is an ideal channel to leverage. Simply put, women are well equipped to thrive in the digital age. This is evidenced in several ways. In the United States, for example, a 2014 survey found that, compared to men, a greater percentage of women use top social media sites: Facebook, Tumblr, Pinterest, Instagram, and Twitter.[66] Women are also leading the trend toward accessing social media via their mobile devices such as cell phones and tablets. Ironically, the only social network that boasts more men than women is the *professional* networking site LinkedIn. This final point underscores the importance of consciously managing your social capital, in a strategic way; and this chapter has presented evidence-based insights and tips to help you do so.

Money Matters

6

Most of us enjoy hearing stories about rags-to-riches entrepreneurs, self-made women who start with nothing and build global enterprises from their apartments or garages. Like the women profiled in this book, such accomplishments inspire others. Successful startup and growth, however, require more than just dreams—they require financial capital. Money matters. Capital is needed to bridge the costs of production until eventual payment. Capital helps in weathering periods of tight cash flow. Capital is needed to finance the growth of the firm's productive assets. Undercapitalized firms forego growth opportunities. Yet there is evidence that suggests that many female entrepreneurs undercapitalize their ventures.[1]

This chapter presents a snapshot of the sources of capital available to aspiring entrepreneurs and how being female is associated with preferences for potential sources of capital and with success at obtaining financing. For example, we speak often with women who believe that banks discriminate against female business owners, but is this perception true? Information about sources of capital is presented in this chapter by considering four popular myths about money matters. The chapter also presents information that will help you to match your entrepreneurial intentions with the appropriate types of financial capital and that will help you to estimate your fiscal literacy.

There are numerous small-business finance books and online resources on this topic. Given regional differences in capital market structure and tax legislation, we encourage you to read several of these primers after digesting this chapter. Decisions about how to finance your venture are best left to you, your small-business advisor, your mentor, and, ideally, your accountant. We also suggest reading *A Rising Tide: Financing Strategies for Women-Owned Firms* by Susan Coleman and Alicia Robb.[2] Coleman and Robb's book provides more in-depth information about financing that is beyond the scope of this one chapter.

We begin this chapter by addressing one very popular belief about business financing: that venture creation is the best way to make money.

Myth 1: Venture Creation Is the Best Way to Make Money

Venture creation is not the only way that one can create wealth. Goals of work-family balance, professional autonomy, and opportunity to commercialize ideas are all attractive reasons to consider venture creation. But the financial implications of these motives cannot be taken lightly. Almost all entrepreneurs begin venture creation with optimism and an unshaken belief in the success of their ideas. Objective assessment, however, can be burdened by enthusiasm. The harsh reality is that half of all new small businesses face discontinuance in the first five years. This can be for fortunate reasons (for example, a merger or sold the firm) or for unfortunate reasons (such as bankruptcy or lack of revenue). Understanding the viability of a startup idea is best considered before hanging out the proverbial shingle.

While the decision to enter into venture creation often depends on a degree of choice, some are pushed into self-employment and business ownership. Researchers refer to these enterprising women as *necessity entrepreneurs*.[3] Studies of women who enter venture creation nonvoluntarily indicate that many do so as a result of

- Limited availability of once unionized or secure employment
- Corporate downsizing and outsourcing to offshore workers
- Glass ceiling, glass walls, and discrimination
- Work-family demands, including elder and child care.[4]

Necessity entrepreneurship is particularly evident in industries and regions undergoing economic restructuring.[5] Necessity entrepreneurs typically are older and have limited education. Immigrants are overrepresented. The firm that results is often that of an unincorporated, home-based service enterprise with no employees. Almost half of necessity entrepreneurs report that they experience financial difficulties and would be willing to exit venture creation for employment. Among all the reasons for having to enter venture creation, work-family demands were most often associated with relatively low earnings. What scholar Karen Hughes points out is that, for some business owners, venture creation is not an attractive substitute for paid employment, particularly for those who leave employment for work-family reasons.

Among businesses, particular sectors are especially risky, with histories of high frequencies of loan defaults. Certain service enterprises fall into a relatively higher risk category, as do firms characterized as having low complexity and technological innovation. These include young firms operating in the food, accommodation, beverage, retail, and wholesale sectors. Service enterprises in which the business owner retains little supplier autonomy and those engaged in repetitive or routine tasks that face inexpensive foreign competitors are also vulnerable to failure.[6] So too are firms operating in niches characterized as intensely competitive, with low barriers to entry and few or no industry standards, certifications, or accreditations.[7] Such firms are considered to be high risk and therefore are not particularly attractive to lending institutions. Unfortunately, these also tend to be among the sectors in which female-owned firms have historically been concentrated. Fortunately, this is changing quickly as women recognize economic opportunities in more lucrative markets.

Cross-country comparisons illustrate other patterns in entrepreneurial intention. Among male and female entrepreneurs, the incidence rate of entrepreneurial intention reflects an inverted U-Shape, with the highest levels associated with those in intermediate levels of per capita daily income.[8] The lowest prevalence rate is among those living in countries with the highest levels of daily income.[9]

Globalization has also had an impact on whether small businesses succeed or fail. Reduced customs barriers and tariffs, shortened product lifespans, and the presence of offshore services dampen the financial viability of many businesses. Lenders and professional investors are aware of these risk factors, risks that influence their investment decisions. Even established entrepreneurs who fall into one or more of the following categories face relatively more difficulty in financing a startup:[10]

- *Self-employed*: Many self-employed workers have higher credit scores and net worth than paid employees; however, lenders often prefer salaried earnings in the decision to grant credit. Self-employed workers typically lower their taxable income by maximizing business expenses and other deductions. While tax arbitrage reduces personal taxable earnings, low net income can erode lender confidence. Following the 2008 financial crisis, new lending regulations introduced to protect borrowers also make it even more difficult to secure debt (and mortgages) given discounted (taxable) earnings.
- *Young firms operating in certain fields*: Wholesale, retail, and knowledge-intensive sectors (that is, technologically advanced goods and services) are more likely to be turned down for debt capital than manufacturing, resource exploitation, and professional services firms.
- *Firms that operate in certain regions*: Firms in rural or remote communities are less likely to receive loans.
- *Owners with little industry experience*: Owners with little experience and those who do not have a history of conducting their personal banking with the prospective lender are also more likely to face loan turndowns.

In consideration of these factors, the narrowing gender gap in wages and salaries in most countries makes paid employment more attractive for many women who are contemplating venture creation.[11] From a financial perspective, the decision to invest in a startup should be compared to other investment opportunities. For example, given the high discontinuance rate of new ventures, it is sometimes more prudent to invest savings and other startup capital in safer investments.

There are useful benchmarks from which to compare the anticipated return on investment in a new venture. For example, long-term rates of return on diversified portfolios of exchange-listed stocks provide returns that are higher than inflation. Investments in relatively diversified high-risk stock-market-listed securities can yield around 7 to 9 percent over the long term. Of course, these investments may be volatile on a short-term basis. These benchmarks do not even consider foregone employment earnings, benefits, and advancement opportunities. These observations suggest that it is wise to be conservative about the prospect of securing startup commercial funding from a bank or other lending institution, even with an established client relationship, self-employment earnings profile, industry experience, or all of the above. As a result, for many startups, credit (debt) is structured as personal loans guaranteed by personal collateral.

Sources of Capital

Once the decision to start a venture has been made, how do most entrepreneurs finance their enterprises? To determine which sources and amounts of capital are appropriate, nascent entrepreneurs must first determine the firm's ownership structure—preferably early in the venture creation process—and the balance among the CDEs of finance (cash flow, debt, and equity).

- *Cash flow* is the amount and flow of funds from operations of the firm over a designated period of time. Cash flow differs from net income posted on an income statement, as net income reflects non-cash items and expenses such as depreciation. Cash flow is much more than keeping up with creditors. Cash flow projections signal potential investors
  - If and when you will make enough money for personal needs and for the business and still earn profit
  - Whether or not the enterprise is viable; for example, if, when, and how you can afford to grow by hiring staff and expanding into new markets and products.
- *Debt* is a financial obligation to a lender. It reflects a contractual agreement specifying the amount of capital borrowed and terms of debt, including interest payable.
- *Equity* is capital investment that results in a portion of firm ownership. For a small minority of firms with strong growth prospects, *external equity* comes in the form of investments from new partners, business angels and angel syndicates, venture capital pools, and possibly initial public offerings once the firm has matured.[12]

The CDEs of venture creation imply that the owner must make difficult trade-offs early in the venture creation process. Television shows such as *Dragon's Den* in Britain and Canada and *Shark Tank* in the United States are entertaining and revealing about the negotiations between entrepreneurs and investors. But dragons and sharks rarely discuss all the alternative types of financing. Certain characters also personify "bully investment," when the primary focus is the investors rather than the investment relationship and entrepreneurs are ridiculed.[13]

In reality, founders must decide if the enterprise is to be incorporated, a partnership, or sole proprietorship, and if incorporated, what the stock allocations will be for external and internal investors. Stock is a vehicle that enables owners, or principals, to share investment opportunities and wealth creation. The decision to offer equity infers a willingness to accept external investment and, often, dilute ownership and control. Bank credit assumes other financial obligations. Figure 6.1 presents a visual overview of the sources of capital, broken down by stage of firm development.

On the left-hand side of the continuum are new ventures. Nascent entrepreneurs typically rely on personal savings; investment by family and friends, or what is commonly referred to as "love money"; credit cards; and bank loans for startup capital. As owners and firms mature and gain market legitimacy, a minority of growth-oriented firms attract external investment from angels, venture capitalists, or the public through initial public offerings (or IPOs).

Investment by Family and Friends (Love Money)

Like all capital, love money has advantages and disadvantages. From an owner's perspective, love money tends to be patient; repayment and interest obligations are often less onerous than for other sources of capital. Generosity enables some women the opportunity to move up the learning curve, to establish credit scores, and to refine their startup ideas. This is particularly important for those who bring limited industry experience and credit history to venture creation. This source of capital also brings well-intentioned advice and expertise. The caveat is that the quality of advice is rarely equivalent to that of arm's length professional investors and others who remain independent parties to the investment. For example, external equity from angel investors is often coupled with other benefits: various forms of nonfinancial value-added assets including advisory networks, business mentoring, technological support, and industry visibility. Defaulting on love money can also infuse long-term strife in close and important relationships. In many cases, the risks of love money may not outweigh the rewards. This brings us to our second myth.

Figure 6.1: Framework of financial capital

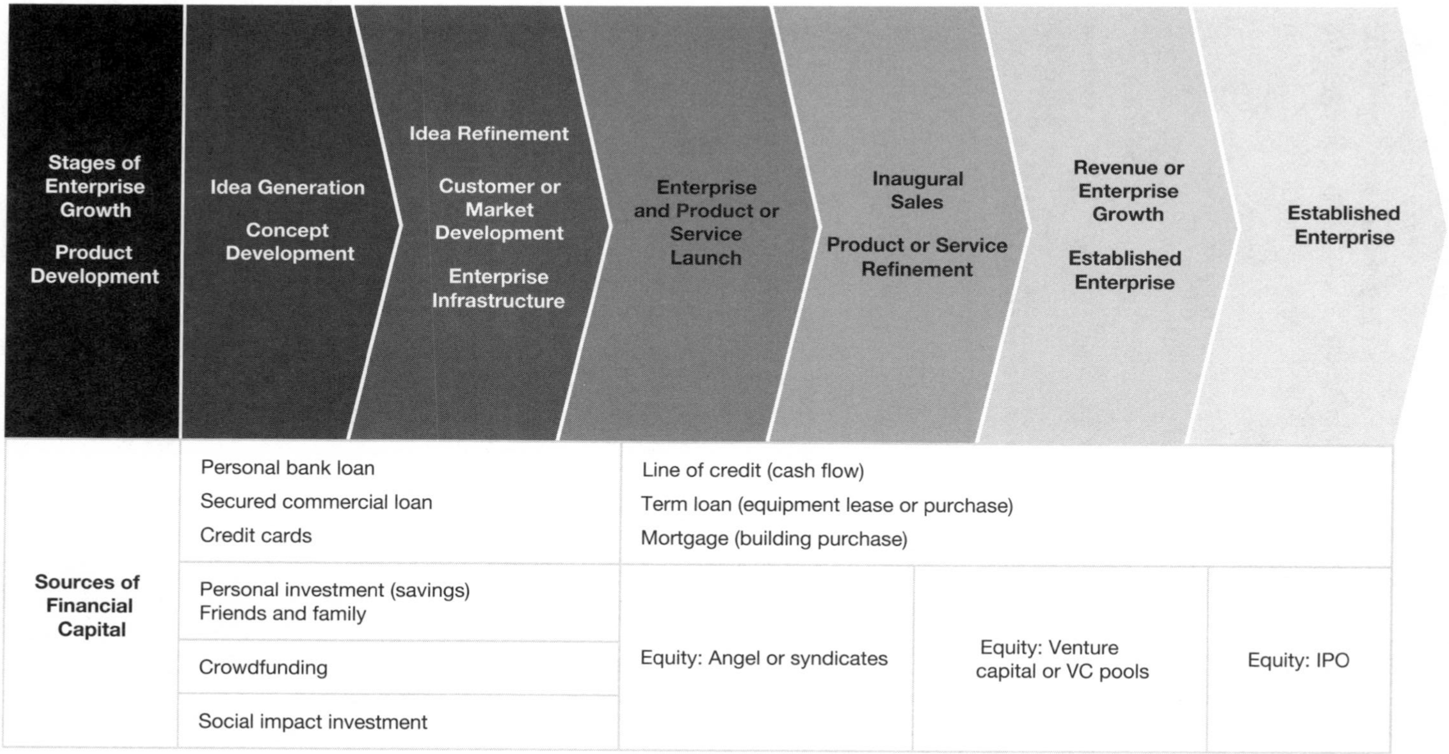

Stages of Enterprise Growth

- Product Development
- Idea Refinement
- Idea Generation / Concept Development
- Customer or Market Development / Enterprise Infrastructure
- Enterprise and Product or Service Launch
- Inaugural Sales / Product or Service Refinement
- Revenue or Enterprise Growth / Established Enterprise
- Established Enterprise

Sources of Financial Capital

- Personal bank loan
- Secured commercial loan
- Credit cards
- Personal investment (savings) / Friends and family
- Crowdfunding
- Social impact investment
- Line of credit (cash flow)
- Term loan (equipment lease or purchase)
- Mortgage (building purchase)
- Equity: Angel or syndicates
- Equity: Venture capital or VC pools
- Equity: IPO

Myth 2: Investing in Family and Friends Pays Off

Investment in any business is risky, but investment in enterprises owned by family and friends is particularly vulnerable to financial loss. From the investor's perspective, value is rarely realized. Our studies of small enterprises that have compared the rates of return on investment between firms that are arm's length from relatives and firms that are not arm's length found that most of the time investments by family and friends simply did not pay off.[14] On average, arm's length investors make more money! Among family and friends, the odds of making money are not impressive. Six in ten investors who invest capital in a venture owned by family or friends lose money. Only one in ten realizes gains of more than a 50 percent return on investment. Among those who invested in arm's length ventures, the odds of earning a reasonable return increased significantly. This may be due to the fact that many angel investors—who tend to invest at arm's length—have investment expertise, experience, and strong financial motives.

Given the likelihood of loss, love money in many cases amounts to a gift. Like reality television, any request for capital should be based on the merits of the owner, including her demonstrated skills and competencies, anticipated revenue potential predicted on evidence of lead customers, inaugural sales, ability to service debt repayment obligations, and an appreciation of investor risk. Anticipated returns should also be benchmarked against alternative investment vehicles. It is the responsibility of the business owner to spell out on paper comparative returns on the investment and expected terms of lending. It is also reasonable and professional to articulate how the money will be used, when it will be paid back, the amount of interest charged (if any), and what will happen in the case of default. Given that financial loss is a likely outcome, another alternative is to advance capital with no strings attached, wish your friends or family member well, and move on.

There are more lessons which can be learned about love money that are important to remember. First, there is an assumption that female entrepreneurs prefer to finance firms through investment by family and friends, versus other financial vehicles. Economic psychologists have explained this tendency by describing female entrepreneurs as being more risk averse compared to male entrepreneurs.[15] Women business owners are seen to be "more cautious, less confident, less aggressive, easier to persuade and have inferior leadership and problem solving abilities when making decisions under risk compared to men, reinforcing stereotypical views that women are less able managers."[16]

Recent studies find that such gender stereotyping is outdated. For example, on average, female business owners across Canada are just as likely as males to seek debt capital for financing their firms.[17] Across most developed economies, there are numerous sources of microcredit and startup funding available to nascent entre-preneurs. A source of information about microcredit is Women Advancing Micro-credit, an example of collective feminine capital in action.[18] Many federal and state governments support loan guarantee schemes.[19] Administered by financial institu-tions on behalf of government, loan guarantees help offset the risk and administra-tion cost of small business loans.[20] Before asking family and friends to kick in, we encourage you to work with a small-business advisor and your bank. If multiple requests for capital are turned down by lending agencies and your financial institu-tion (professional managers who are backed by well-honed credit scoring systems), ask yourself why it is reasonable to request that family and friends invest in a ven-ture viewed by experts as too risky.

Bank Lending

Among small-firm clients, bank credit is typically advanced in the form of personal loans, credit cards, term loans, or operating loans. Term loans are used to acquire fixed assets such as equipment or to supplement the permanent component of working capital. Repayment schedules are predetermined and typically reflect both principal and interest amounts. Operating loans are commonly referred to as *lines of credit*, when capital is drawn down on an as-needed basis. Interest rates generally are based on prime plus a rate of interest that reflects the financial risk associated with the owner and her firm. Loan application and administration fees are charged for managing the relationship. Term and operating loans are among the lowest-cost sources of capital, especially given that interest is tax-deductible and borrowing dilutes neither ownership nor autonomy.[21]

Assessment Criteria

From a lender or banker's perspective, financing small enterprises is a risky, high-volume, low-margin, labor-intensive business.[22] Lenders have fiduciary obligations to depositors and shareholders. Given the financial risks described throughout this chapter, early-stage lending decisions are often predicated on the principal's credit-worthiness and almost always are adjudicated using credit scoring techniques that use client profile data obtained from a credit bureau together with personal data and information on the loan application. Centralized and automated credit scoring has removed much of the subjectivity that historically has affected lending deci-sions, subjectivity that had fueled suspicions of gender discrimination. Credit is also typically extended on the basis of the firm's real or projected

- Cash flow, and ability to service debt obligations
- Level of current assets relative to debts.

Banks further mitigate their risk by imposing conditions in the lending relationship. Such conditions can create tension between those who seek capital and lenders, tensions captured in Table 6.1.

Depending upon their situation, business owners must calibrate the availability, cost, terms, and obligations of bank credit. For example, collateral is often pledged as security to offset risk. Consider the situation described in Scenario 1. From the owner's perspective, reliance on debt (lending, referred to as financial leverage) can increase the firm's vulnerability to economic conditions. In addition, reliance on debt, even along with retained earnings and cash flow, is often not enough to finance rapid growth.

Scenario 1: No Surprises Please

Asha Sing was perplexed. Her company had been doing well. International sales had been increasing rapidly, and a profitable year end was almost a shoo-in. Payroll was due in two days, and the firm could demonstrate lots of accounts receivable. Why then had the bank refused yesterday's request to provide an operating line of credit? The refusal placed Asha in a terrible position. She was sure the cash shortfall was temporary.

This scenario plays out all too frequently. Growing firms can face cash flow problems due to the increased investment required in inventory and receivables

Table 6.1: Tensions in lending relationships

Key Determinants of Lending Decisions	Owner Perspectives on Lenders	Lender Perspectives on Owners
Firm age and size	They provide insufficient startup funding, advice, and counsel.	Their lack of experience is associated with risk.
Ability to service debt (such as cash flow)	They charge excessive interest, particularly on charge cards.	They do not realistically appraise firm value or capital needs.
Strength of guarantee or security; value of collateral	They require excessive collateral.	They don't understand lender requirements and risk tolerance.
Ratio of debt to equity	They are unwilling to lend on character.	They invest too little personal equity in the firm.
Level and credibility of working capital	Their local account managers often lack authority to make decisions or do not understand business.	They assume banks are the only source of capital (other sources are personal equity, external equity, family, friends).
Client risk; strength, depth, and experience of client	They do not explain turndowns or other sources of capital.	They communicate poorly, ask in untimely manner (during crisis).

Source: Adapted from A. Riding and B. Orser, *Beyond the Banks: Creative Financing for Canadian Entrepreneurs* (Toronto: John Wiley & Sons, 1997): 52–61; copyright © 1997 by Allan L. Riding and Barbara J. Orser.

that tie up cash. However, cash flow shortfalls should not be a surprise. They are often predictable. What is also predictable is that the bankers and other investors will give the cold shoulder to management if they are taken by surprise by this type of cash flow problem. Barring major catastrophes (which can occasionally happen), management should be able to make good predictions of cash flow deficits. Poor cash flow forecasts speak volumes to lenders and investors about the founder's ability to be a good steward of loans and capital investments. The worst time to approach a bank for a loan is on the eve of a crisis. It is far better to sort things out with the loan account manager in advance, according to reasonable estimates based on a well-considered financial plan.

Table 6.1 provides criteria that can prepare for a lending discussion. For example, Asha should be equipped with documentation such as a recent value appraisal of her firm, summary of financial contributions by the firm to the bank over time, a list of current account receivables, and a backup plan in the event that funding is not forthcoming (such as personal investment). She should also proactively address potential lender concerns, such as those listed on the right-hand column.

Myth 3: Banks Discriminate Against Women

Most loan officers prospect clients who manage stable, profitable enterprises, regardless of gender. The evidence, at least in North America, is mixed with respect to the gender influences in accessing debt capital. Our large-scale studies indicate that, after accounting for owner experience, firm size, and sector (assessment criteria commonly associated with credit risk), females are just as likely as male business owners to receive external financing in the form of debt, leases, and supplier credit, with one exception: external equity capital.[23] Despite the perception of many women that they suffer discrimination from financial institutions, there was no evidence of gender discrimination with respect to bank loan approval and turndown rates, and the costs of capital.[24] However, among young firms (startups that have been in operation for less than five years), those with joint ownership (50-50 male-female ownership distribution) were significantly more likely to be loan applicants compared to either majority male-owned or majority female-owned firms. Majority male- and female-owned young firms did not differ appreciably in terms of the likelihood of being loan applicants. Among established firms (more than five years in operation) this was not the case. Majority female-owned firms were significantly less likely to be loan applicants than either majority male-owned or jointly owned (50-50 female-male) enterprises.[25]

What appears to be gender discrimination is more likely an artifact of, as mentioned previously, a congregation of female-owned firms in relatively high-risk sectors.[26] Firm size and sector account for what might seem like gender effects in the terms of credit advanced in commercial loans, leases, and supplier financing.[27] One conclusion is that, when these factors are accounted for, the terms of lending are nearly identical across gender of firm owners. Another is that North American lending institutions increasingly understand that women mean business and women understand that money matters.

It may be that gender-based differences in lending are driven by demand rather than supply.[28] Some business owners forgo applying for debt capital, even if they need financing and often even if they might be otherwise eligible for bank loans. "Fear of denial" is one explanation for this behavior.[29] Our research discovered another important insight. When thousands of female business owners were asked why they did not seek financing, the vast majority cited "financing was not needed." Less than 4 percent of respondents classified themselves as "discouraged borrowers," business owners who do not apply for a bank loan because they feel that they would have been rejected.[30] In other words, fear of denial is not the only reason why women business owners are less likely to seek debt capital. Many believe that capital is not needed.

So why does this myth persist? We suspect several dynamics are at play. Historical practices of gender discrimination fuel this misperception. Country-level lending practices differ. It is unreasonable to assume that criteria and adjudication processes of North American lenders mirror firms operating in many other nations. Traditionally, banking studies did not consider female business owners who were informally discouraged from completing loan applications. Some banking studies about the borrowing experiences of female entrepreneurs are based on owners' perceptions rather than actual lending outcomes. Without disaggregated gender data, such studies do not actually test if females were disadvantaged. Even today, few banking studies control for systemic differences in firm and owner attributes (such as, are identical male- and female-owned firms equally likely to get financing?). Fewer studies consider the frequencies with which men and women apply for financing. The media are also found to attribute bank turndowns or requirement of spousal or partner co-signatures and collateral to being female rather than to creditworthiness and the risk profile of the applicant.

Approval decisions in large lending institutions are typically supported through centralized credit scoring. This is not the case for startup equity investment. Gender differences attributed to banks may be, in part, the product of judgment, such as angel and venture capital in which gender influences are more likely to be reported. Finally, perceptions of gender bias may reflect owner preferences. For example, one large-scale American study found significant gender differences in financing of new technology-based firms: female founders were found to invest about half the amount of male founders. Furthermore, almost half of male founders secured outside equity investment compared to less than 5 percent of female founders. Conversely, female founders were twice as likely as males to employ personal debt.[31] "[W]omen went on to raise significantly lower amounts of incremental debt and equity in years two and three even controlling for a variety of firm and owner characteristics including the level of initial start-up capital and firm sales."[32] In contrast, our large-scale Canadian study found no gender differences in the use of debt financing among new knowledge-intensive firms.[33]

The absence of large-scale, comparative studies and use of anecdotal storytelling serve to reinforce misperceptions about gender biases in debt lending.

Equity Capital

For the minority of firms with strong growth prospects, external equity financing comes in the form of investments from business angels and angel syndicates, venture capital pools, and initial public offerings (IPOs). *Business angels* are wealthy individuals who invest their own money directly in the firm. Angels are hard to find and even harder to secure. While angels may be obscure, researchers speculate that the pool of angel investment exceeds by a wide margin the entire venture capital market.[34] Angels typically reject upward of 97 percent of proposals, three out of four at first sight. On average, they expect an annualized 25 to 40 percent rate of return on their investments.[35] In other words, one dollar invested by an angel investor is expected to return approximately seven dollars in six to seven years.[36] Decisions are also predicated on personal relationships: trust, integrity, and confidence outweigh innovation or technological viability. In studies that have examined decision protocols of business angels, scholar Allan Riding describes the "Toledo factor." The term arises from an angel investor who cited this as *the* criterion for investment viability. When asked to explain, the term referred to his willingness to spend a weekend together with the prospective entrepreneur in Toledo (with apology to readers in Toledo). That is, the prospective investee had better be very impressive.

Venture capitalists are professional investors, merchant banks, corporate subsidiaries of institutions such as insurance companies, public sector funds, and, increasingly, small-business lenders. The National Venture Capital Association estimates that in the United States there is approximately $26 billion dollars in total venture capital (VC) investment annually.[37] Such investors tend to specialize by investment size, sector, or other guidelines. Many have a preference for technology- and knowledge-based firms. Most invest in the expansion phase of development and, increasingly, in early stage activities. Several rounds of VC financing are to be expected.

An *initial public offering* (or IPO) refers to a transaction in which a private firm sells equity through investment dealers to the public by offering shares for sale. The IPO is a means by which small growing firms raise considerable amounts of capital.

IPOs also present an exit ramp for a small percentage of owners and their initial investors. It is at the IPO where many successful entrepreneurs cash in.

Equity capital enables entrepreneurs to diversify their dependence on the leading source of capital (debt) and to ease tensions with financing institutions such as their bank. Equity also provides a means to overcome bank conservatism such as the preference for mature, goods-producing firms with long-standing commercial borrowing relationships. For example, Table 6.2 illustrates the financial implications of debt and equity capital. What the table shows is that leverage is very helpful in periods of economic prosperity (boom) but can be a disaster for borrowers in difficult economic times (bust).

Attracting Equity Capital

Financial value is typically created through growth—in relational or social capital, revenues, market expansion, new product or service introductions, and retained earnings. Growth requires new financing. Often, equity investors seek some level of control over the firm and its founders. This may imply compromise and loss, particularly losses in terms of the decision autonomy for founders. Such a decision can challenge the founder's values and direction. For example, founders who weigh success in nonfinancial terms (such as autonomy, sense of achievement, or industry recognition) may choose to eschew growth. The decision to grow is therefore often a departure point between self-sustaining enterprises and ventures that are attractive to equity investors. For entrepreneurs who prefer a steady state, self-investment, supplier, and bank credit are likely sources of capital. Among equity investors, capital flows to the most promising of ventures, of which "promising" is defined as having the ability to service fiscal obligations and generate return on an investment. Investors may be interested in the social mandate of the organization, but their primary focus traditionally is on the ability of the founder(s) and the startup team to generate financial value and wealth.

So what creates financial value? The classic view of capital growth is summed up in the concept and estimation of net present value of future cash flows. Growth-oriented entrepreneurs invest cash and effort in order to create enterprise capacity in the form of new products, market expansion, and talent acquisition. Firms then generate incrementally more cash from the new assets financed by the investment, ideally creating value that exceeds the initial investment. Owners and investors work to determine what assets and liabilities are required to create future cash flow.

Firms employ various practices that influence cash flows. For example, one firm might have generous collection policies (such as net ninety days). Another might adhere to "collect on delivery." The more generous the repayment practices or industry norms, the more the firm ties up cash in the exchange process. Year after

Table 6.2: Leverage: Debt and equity investment

To illustrate how leverage works, suppose that your firm has assets of $100,000 and makes an operating* return of 10 percent on assets during booms, but only 3 percent during downturns. Now, suppose that you financed the firm only from shareholders who collectively hold 1,000,000 shares. The following table computes earnings per share for both booms and busts.

Scenario A: A Firm with No Debt Obligations		
	Boom	Bust
Operating income*	$100,000	$30,000
Less interest payments	None	None
Equals taxable income	100,000	30,000
Less taxes (@30%)**	30,000	9,000
Equals net income	70,000	21,000
Earnings per share***	$0.07	$0.02

Now, suppose your firm had instead financed assets by borrowing $500,000 at 8 percent interest and from the sale of 500,000 shares. Earnings per share would now look like this.

Scenario B: A Firm with Debt Obligations		
	Boom	Bust
Operating income*	$100,000	$30,000
Less interest payments	40,000	40,000
Equals taxable income	60,000	−10,000
Less taxes (@30%)**	18,000	−3,000
Equals net income	42,000	−7,000
Earnings per share***	$0.08	$(0.014)

Note: In this second scenario, the firm is more highly leveraged because it faces fixed interest costs. Earnings per share are better during prosperous times than for the original unleveraged firm. However, downturns particularly threaten the earnings and cash flow of leveraged firms.

*Operating income is revenue less direct operating expenses (for example, cost of goods sold, direct labor, materials).

**In the interest of keeping the example simple, taxation and accounting are simplified.

***Earnings per share = Net income/Shares outstanding

Source: Adapted from A. Riding and B. Orser, Beyond the Banks: Creative Financing for Canadian Entrepreneurs (Toronto: John Wiley & Sons, 1997): 9; copyright © 1997 by Allan L. Riding and Barbara J. Orser.

year, new sources and uses of cash produce a net cash flow. Owners keep a share of earnings associated with the cash flow after payment to others, including lenders, investors, and so on. Entrepreneurs trade off cash flow and enterprise growth. They do so by managing financial inputs and expected outcomes. The take-away is that business owners must weigh personal and commercial values when considering how to finance their firm.

Benefits and Risks of External Capital

The high discontinuance rate of new ventures implies that there are hurdles in creating financial value or wealth. To offset the liabilities of newness and to bolster inaugural capacity,[38] many entrepreneurs seek strategic alliances, including collaboration with investors.[39] External investment can bring an industry or financial expert onto the team. Learning Aid 6.1 presents the benefits and risks of external sources of capital, provided by intermediaries that fund new and growing ventures. These risks and benefits are drawn from studies that have examined the behavior and financial performance of firms that have obtained angel and venture capital.[40] While only a small percentage of enterprises attract substantial equity investment, the risks and benefits are relevant to most entrepreneurs. This includes founders who seek less traditional sources of capital, such as equity investment from crowd-funding, suppliers, and clients.

Use this tool to brainstorm about strategies that leverage the benefits and offset the risks of acquiring external capital. For example, Maria Guidi is weighing the decision to seek debt (bank) versus equity capital. In making the decision, she has developed a list of questions for her banker and the business angel. She is aware that, compared to her banker, the local angel brings considerable social capital, including introductions to prospective clients in the construction sector. She is concerned, however, that due diligence may make her firm competitively vulnerable given that disclosure of proprietary information with an industry insider. After reviewing the listed criteria, she is better prepared to mitigate her concerns about sharing proprietary information and has proposed several ways to avert potential investor defection.

Myth 4: Accessing Equity Is a Level Playing Field

As we described earlier, in North America, female business owners obtain equity capital less frequently than males.[41] For example, in the United States, less than 5 percent of venture capital is placed in majority female-owned enterprises.[42] In 1999, a team of leading entrepreneurship researchers (The Diana Project) teamed up with Springboard Enterprises to understand the aspirations of American female

Learning Aid 6.1: Benefits and risks of external capital

Potential Benefits	Potential Risks
☐ Return on investment: Cost of capital is offset by financial gains.	☐ Equity: Anticipated return on investment does not reflect deal valuation or information asymmetry: it is difficult to estimate the financial value of investor knowledge at the outset of the investment. Size and terms of capital investment may not accurately reflect the associated costs (such as expenses associated with due diligence, collateral obligations, terms of repayment, or potential loss of control or ownership). Debt: Fixed interest obligations do not reflect market conditions.
☐ Social capital: Investors provide referrals and matchmaking services, and signal prospective clients and suppliers that the founder or startup team is reputable. This reduces search costs and time otherwise spent on prospecting for quality clients and suppliers.	☐ Distraction: High up-front search costs to locate and secure investment can detract founder efforts to bring new services or products to market.
☐ Technical capital: Investors can augment founder or team technical competencies with sector or specific technological skills and knowledge.	☐ Complacency: External advice can create complacency about developing in-house technical skills.
☐ Strategy: Investors often advise founders about vision and assist in objectively assessing founder or firm capabilities.	☐ Leverage: Limited resources (leverage) and negotiating skills make it difficult to assess the quality and value of advice.
☐ Surveillance: External capital is associated with productivity and enterprise growth through expert (experienced) insights. Investors typically alert founders about emergent threats and opportunities (for example, new technologies, market rumors, where to find top talent and capital).	☐ Broadcasting "asks" can alert competitors about strategic direction, patents, and intellectual property. Disclosure can dilute patent effectiveness and increase the risk of leaking confidential and proprietary information (such as market intelligence, R&D, innovative technology).
☐ Performance: Investors negotiate milestones and performance benchmarks (such as anticipated return on investment, time to market). This leads to improved structure, governance, and oversight of the enterprise.	☐ Expropriation or investor defection: Threat of investor expropriation of the firm, or firm's intellectual property. Investor focus on short-term returns on investment can dilute long-term investment in R&D, growth, and so on.
☐ Other:	☐ Other:

entrepreneurs who sought venture capital and the expectations of those who supply venture capital financing.[43] One finding of this project is that entrepreneurs need knowledge to make appropriate decisions about the capital structure of their firm and strategies to maintain a healthy cash flow. A second is that equity investment is not gender blind.

In a similar U.K.-based study to explain why few female-owned enterprises raise early stage (angel) and later stage (venture) capital, Colin Mason and Richard Harrison (editors of *Venture Capital*, an international journal of entrepreneurial finance), attribute the low number of deals in part to an absence of female angels and venture capitalists.[44] It is estimated that less than 5 percent of all business angels are female.[45] There are even fewer female venture capitalists.[46] That is, women have much less social capital in this sphere. Furthermore, social capital is produced and reinforced through investment interactions, both on the demand side (female entrepreneurs) and supply side (angels, venture capital) of an interaction, so they have less opportunity to produce additional social capital through these relationships. Dated assumptions and gender stereotypes remain. For example,

- The Diana team found that among some VC investors, the perception remains that women prefer to start firms in sectors that are unattractive to investment. The researchers reported that networks in the venture capital market are closed to women and deals typically are made through established male-to-male relationships. Women are also noticeably absent in the executive suites of venture-funded capital pools.[47] However, when female venture capitalists were at the table, they tended to attract female-led ventures.

- Gender bias is also evidenced from studies that examined perceptions of the value of IPOs. In an experiment to simulate the potential influence of gender in the assessed value of male- and female-led IPOs, American researchers found that despite identical CEO qualifications and firm financial performance, MBA students consistently discounted female-led firms in comparison to male-led firms.[48] Gender bias was also evidenced in performance expectations. Female founders and CEOs were seen to be "less capable" than their male counterparts. The conclusion: female-led IPOs were less attractive investments. A word of caution is required. While there are a limited number of studies about gender and equity investment, study findings lean toward stereotyping in the mind-set of venture capitalists and students. What is particularly concerning is that students represent future leaders, and potentially another generation of potentially sexist investors.

The Diana Project offers strategies to increase women's access to venture capital. These are summarized in Learning Aid 6.2. After reviewing the table, consider what steps you or your organization can take to facilitate these changes.

Crowdfunding: An Emerging Source of Startup Capital

MIT Tech Review ranks crowdfunding among the top ten milestones that will have the greatest impact on shaping innovation in years to come.[49] This emerging source of capital provides startup investment through relatively small contributions from the general public in order to attain a certain goal.[50] For example, in 2013 crowdfunding generated approximately $5 billion in investment capital. Exchange is

Learning Aid 6.2: Strategies to increase women entrepreneurs' access to capital

To encourage and facilitate equity investment in female-led entrepreneurial ventures, the following strategies have been advanced by a team of leading entrepreneurship scholars.

1. **Encourage and educate women to participate in the investment process** (angels, corporate venture funds, and venture capital firms). The objective is not to encourage all women business owners to seek equity capital but to encourage women to develop an understanding of the growth process, and the role and fit that equity might play in that process. It is through this understanding that informed choices about business ownership and growth would best be made.

2. **Encourage investors to seek out and consider investment in women-led ventures** by expanding their networks beyond their traditional contacts.

3. **Fund programs to educate and prepare women to lead fast growth businesses** whether high-tech or not. Programs to foster development of relevant educational and experiential programs would broaden the participation base for these opportunities.

4. **Sponsor forums and events** to link women with potential investors. Increased visibility of strong deals generates awareness and investment interest.

5. **Sponsor and disseminate the results of research about women's entrepreneurship** and comparative research on financing and growth of women-owned and men-owned ventures. Myths are best overturned by solid data.

6. **Track investments and performance of investments by gender** in all venture-funded companies. A complete understanding of the participants and the process of equity investment is hindered by incomplete information.

Source: C. Brush, N. Carter, P. Greene, and M. Hart, *Gatekeepers of Venture Growth: A Diana Project Report on the Role and Participation of Women in the Venture Capital Industry* (Kansas City, MO: Kauffman Center for Entrepreneurial Leadership, 2004).

predicated on online communication; viewers connect with a pitcher's vision and project. Following are some examples:

- First-to-market platforms such as Indiegogo and Kickstarter in the United States, and UInvest in the Ukraine, match funds in exchange for product or rewards.[51]

- Investment entrants include crowdfunding platforms such as Angel-List, MyMajorCompany, MicroVentures, and SeedInvest for tech start-ups; MissionMarkets, Bolstr in the United States and Seedsup Canada or Fundco.ca in Canada for social enterprises and small businesses; and CircleUp for consumer-product companies.

- Women-targeted platforms, such as Bad Girl Ventures, promise access to capital, education, and mentorship to growth-oriented women business owners.

A growing inventory of sites offer would-be financiers the opportunity to back startups through a diversity of investment models: *donation-based*, used primarily but not exclusively by nonprofit and charitable enterprises; *pre-purchase* with a promise of product receipt; peer-to-peer *lending* (for example, Prosper); *equity investment* that provides backers an ownership stake in the business or share of profits (such as Kickstarter); and *club model*, in which participants are deemed as being members of a club (for example, BeerBankroll, MyFootballClub).[52] Payout options vary, as follows:

- *Nothing*—a philanthropic or charitable model
- *Nonfinancial compensation*, including tokens of appreciation (for example, sponsorship-based incentives such as a T-shirt, name recognition, and so on)
- *All or nothing*, when funding goals must be met within a time limit established by the project creator and if reached, backers' credit cards are charged and funds to the project created (such as Kickstarter)
- *All or more model*, in which creators keep the capital raised even if the funding goal is not achieved (for example, RocketHub, Indiegogo).[53]

Investor engagement can be *active*, reflecting the ability to have an impact on the creators' project, or *passive*, having no influence over the endeavor.

For entrepreneurs, early studies are helping to identify factors associated with successful outcomes. Obtaining funds is associated with

- A clear signal of the underlying project, product, or service quality
- The strength of the founders' online social networks
- The amount requested, when reasonable
- Rapid market launch of the product
- The opportunity for active engagement by backers.[54]

Equity-based models appear to raise more funds than other reward or donation-based opportunities. Firm age has little influence on the amount of funds raised or, ultimately, project success. These observations suggest that there is little value in delaying a campaign on the basis of date of firm establishment.[55]

Myth 5: Crowdfunding Will Resolve Gender Biases in Access to Capital

Richard Harrison, editor of *Venture Capital*, describes the dynamics of crowdfunding as a disintermediation of the finance market, as online platforms play an increasing role in the equity market.[56] Indiegogo founder and market catalyst Danae Ringelmann sees crowdfunding as the democratization of investment. Forty-seven percent of Indiegogo campaigns fund women-led firms: "We're literally changing the industry by showing it without having to talk about it. It's just happening. . . . I left finance because it was biased and created these buddy systems. We're building a system where everyone has access to equal opportunity."[57] Shereen Shermak, CEO of the venture capital firm Launch Angels, agrees. She compares this level of funding to the meager 4 to 7 percent of venture capital that is directed to female-led firms, pointing out the huge leap forward that online platforms provide for women.[58]

To inform investment decisions, Julie Weeks, founding president and CEO of Womenable, suggests that female investors who seek to support women-led firms form peer circles to gather information, seek opinions, and check references. *Forbeswomen*[59] offers more tips for would-be investors and entrepreneurs:

- *Diversify, place small bets across different industries.* Crowdfunding is a high-risk investment with potential for high returns. It is best to start investing with a secure, diversified portfolio (lower-risk, blue chip stocks).
- *Check the leadership.* There are an increasing number of nascent crowdfunding websites. Until regulatory norms are established, investors should assess the background and demonstrated expertise of the firm's founder(s) and management team.
- *Evaluate the platforms.* Peggy Wallace, managing director of Golden Seeds, cautions, "There's a stampede of companies launching crowdfunding platforms. You want to make sure that you're using a reputable one. The crowdfunding platform plays a critical role in screening companies. Review and compare the platforms' criteria before choosing the one you'll use. To ensure that platforms adhere to the highest standard, the industry has developed an accreditation program. Using an accredited crowdfunding platform reduces the chances of fraudulent businesses using crowdfunding to bilk would-be investors".[60]
- *Look to the millennials for role models.* "Younger women are really in front of this trend," says Amy Millman of Springboard Enterprises. "Millennial women may not be able to participate in equity and debt crowdfunding yet, but they are contributing or donating to projects on platforms such as Kickstarter and Indiegogo. They get how to use social media for crowdfunding purposes and will be at the forefront of developing best practices."[61]

For many advocates, crowdfunding facilitates equitable market engagement and provides a means to circumvent poor or nonexistent credit ratings and closed investment networks. While such assertions are encouraging, particularly for women entrepreneurs with limited startup experience, it is still a myth that this source of capital will resolve gender biases in capital markets. The reality is that later-stage investors (angel investors, venture capitalists) bring key assets to venture creation, including concept validation, technical know-how, and social capital (such as industry insights, network access, prestige). While crowdfunded investment in female-owned enterprises is "just happening," it will take time for investment practices of later-stage capital pools to catch up with this rapidly growing entry in the capital marketplace.

Making Financial Literacy Part of Feminine Capital

This chapter has focused on sources of entrepreneurial capital. We discussed five myths that shape decisions about entrepreneurial capital. It is important to understand capital markets, given that the ability to attract investment is a proxy for founders' managerial acumen. Yet too often investment decisions are anchored in dated assumptions about women entrepreneurs, such as their risk-taking behavior.[62] The more knowledge that entrepreneurs and investors retain about the viability of the firm, the better able they are to make sound decisions that are free of gender bias.[63]

One solution to increasing women entrepreneurs' access to capital is female-focused equity funds such as Karmijn Kapitaal in the Netherlands,[64] Astia[65] and Golden Seeds[66] in the United States, or social enterprises such as Springboard Enterprises and The Pipeline Fellowship.[67] Another strategy is gender-sensitive financial training for suppliers, educators, and users of capital.

Financial literacy affects the status of women around the globe, including their economic health and empowerment. For instance, The Organization for Economic Co-operation and Development (OECD) has reported on the need to increase women's financial literacy, citing gender differences in financial management experience and knowledge as early as the "teen" years.[68] Financial literacy affects the ability to develop and interpret financial statements, identify performance benchmarks (industry norm, points of reference), set goals, and present financial data to investors and taxation authorities. The impact of not managing financial information is significant; fiscal management is linked to enterprise growth and survival.

Yet the construction of financial literacy is more complex, influenced by a myriad of factors such as age, type of knowledge, and country. It is a myth that men are more financially literate than women. For instance, the U.S. National Council on Economic Education examined teens' knowledge associated with five financial domains: economics and the consumer; factors pertaining to production; money, interest rates, and inflation; government and trade in economics; and personal finance. In this study, the overall performance of young males was higher than females.[69] Conversely, in another international survey, gender differences in financial acumen were found in particular knowledge domains: for example, in New Zealand, men and women demonstrated similar understandings of "interest concepts" while in the United Kingdom, women outperformed men at "keeping track of finances."[70] The results of a Canadian survey indicated that women marginally outperformed men on "making ends meet" and "keeping track of finances."[71]

An Australian study has reported that women's "composite financial scores" on numeracy, attitudes, and behaviors were significantly lower than men's: "Whilst women's control of day-to-day financial matters is equal to that of men, this does not spill over to the full spectrum of knowledge, skills, attitudes and behaviors associated with wealth accumulation, i.e. understanding of compounding, planning and engaging with the financial marketplace. Worryingly, women appear to be less likely to stay abreast of new developments, making them more vulnerable to being left behind in the face of financial innovation."[72] Despite the mixed evidence about gender differences in financial literacy, improving women's financial literacy bolsters their feminine capital, both at the individual and the collective level.

We close this chapter with two challenges, one targeted at entrepreneurs and the other at small-business educators.[73]

- *Challenge 1, for entrepreneurs.* Assess your entrepreneurial financial literacy. Were you aware of the different types of debt and equity that we touched on in this chapter? To what degree are you able to create and evaluate a balance sheet, an income statement, and a cash flow statement? Financial literacy can help you avoid undercapitalizing and underestimating the value of female-owned ventures.[74] If you are not familiar with sources of capital and basic planning tools, enroll in a small-business training program. Many are available online or through adult learning centers, colleges, and financial institutions.
- *Challenge 2, for educators.* Check curricula and teaching practices for gender biases. This includes understanding the expectations, confidence, learning preferences, and styles of male and female program participants.[75] If you are not familiar with gender influences in teaching and learning, contact a women's enterprise center. Many have developed gender-sensitive small-business accounting and finance training programs.[76]

"If I only knew *then* what I know *now*. . . ." is a refrain voiced by many. Understanding money matters, including the ABCs of small-business finance, can shorten the timeline between then and now.

Power in Policy

7

Forbeswomen labels women's entrepreneurship as the new women's movement.[1] Mechanisms to accelerate the movement are politics, policies, and training programs. Politics is the process of influencing others. Policies are the means by which governments carry out business and distribute services and goods through the implementation of acts, regulations, and program guidelines.[2] Policies can also enact limitations. Training programs, delivered through the private and public sectors, are vehicles through which policy can be operationalized. In this chapter we focus on institutional-level support for female entrepreneurs. We do so by describing the collective power of women entrepreneurs and the impact of intermediary advocacy groups. We also explore the rationales for engaging in advocacy and policy reform to increase women's economic empowerment.[3]

Economic empowerment facilitates access to and control of resources and the ability to challenge and change existing power relations.[4] To strengthen women entrepreneur's presence in policy debates, this chapter opens with five reasons why business owners should care about public policy. Examples that illustrate the practicalities of gender bias in entrepreneurship policy are then presented. Diagnostics and assessment criteria that can be used to examine and challenge entrepreneurship policies follow. These lead to a discussion about market interventions, including the relative merits of mainstream versus female-focused small-business programs. The chapter closes with more strategies to support women in business.

Why Should You Care About Public Policy?

The value of engaging more women business owners in policymaking is captured in reports[5] and taskforces.[6] A unifying theme across all is the call for formalized and systemic interventions that create increased access to economic opportunities for women. Without advocacy, the media, bureaucrats, and politicians are prone to ignore the contributions of female entrepreneurs. The underperformance hypothesis is also a comfortable platform from which to dismiss economic discrimination and, therefore, the need for female-focused market interventions.[7] The need for policy reform stems from criticisms that many public policies favor male-dominated sectors,[8] bias that comes with economic and social consequences.

To answer the question, "Why should business owners care about public policy?" we reached out to five "women-in-enterprise champions." Each is engaged in global advocacy, education, and design of entrepreneurship programs. All are playing leadership roles in improving the ecosystem of support for women entrepreneurs. Their stories and profiles inspired us and may encourage you to visit their websites to learn more about how these leaders are accelerating women's entrepreneurship through advocacy, consultation, and collaboration.

Get into Politics or Go Out of Business

Virginia Littlejohn, co-founder and CEO of Quantum Leaps, uses the acronym GIPOGOOB (get into politics or get out of business) to explain why women entrepreneurs should care about policy.[9] As she points out, "While governments have introduced numerous regulations intended to facilitate business startup and growth, many are counterproductive to doing business. Many policymakers do not understand what business owners need to succeed. Women entrepreneurs need to advocate on the issues, policies, and programs that they deem necessary to succeed. Change only happens when women demand it."

Virginia Littlejohn also believes firmly in the power of fact-finding. She encourages business owners to equip themselves with evidence and to thoroughly investigate the issue when advocating for change. During our interviews, she referenced a number of indices that report on the status of women entrepreneurs.

Table 7.1 captures some of the indices that support the contention that economic growth does not always reflect equitable outcomes or the interests of women.[10] Advocacy groups and government agencies tasked with the advancement of women use these international benchmarks to establish goals, monitor progress, and compare the impacts of country-specific interventions. For example, the Global Entrepreneurship Development Index presents a composite profile of entrepreneurial processes, predicated on entrepreneurial attitudes, entrepreneurial abilities, and entrepreneurial aspirations. A contribution of this index is multicountry evidence that gender equality does not correlate with economic development by entrepreneurs.[11] Policymakers cannot assume that legislation and other progress translates into economic benefits for female entrepreneurs.

The World Bank Group's *Doing Business* report monitors regulations and measures their effects on small to medium-sized enterprises. In 2007, The World Bank Group began to document legal and regulatory barriers that women entrepreneurs

Table 7.1: Global indices associated with women's entrepreneurship

Index	Description
Ease of Doing Business	The World Bank's *The Ease of Doing Business* captures time, cost, and procedures for starting a small business.
Women, Business and the Law	The World Bank's *Women, Business and the Law* report captures gender gaps in country-level legislation.
Gender Inequity Index	The United Nation's index measures inequality across three dimensions: reproductive health status, women's economic empowerment, and labor market participation.
Gender Global Entrepreneurship Development Index	The Gender GEDI measures the development of high-potential female entrepreneurship, defined as "innovative, market expanding, and export oriented." The index captures percentage of female startups and gross measure of equality of economic participation.
Global Entrepreneurship Monitor	The GEM index is an assessment of the entrepreneurial activity, aspirations, and attitudes of individuals across countries. Reports measure differences in the level of entrepreneurial activity between countries, including factors leading to entrepreneurial activity and policies that enhance the national level of entrepreneurial activity.
Gender Empowerment Measure	The Gender Empowerment Measure estimates representation in economic and political power, and considers gender gaps in earnings, political representation, and women's advancement in professional and managerial positions.
Social Institutions and Gender Index	This OECD index measures drivers and determinants of gender discrimination in over one hundred countries. Metrics quantify early marriage, discriminatory inheritance practices, violence, son bias, access to public space, and other resources.
Women's Entrepreneurial Venture Scope	WEVenture Scope ranks Latin American countries and the Caribbean on the basis of the degree to which they provide enabling environments for women entrepreneurs.
Women's Economic Opportunity Index	Published by the Economist Intelligence Unit, this report monitors twenty-six indicators of regulatory practice and social customs that affect female workers and entrepreneurs.

confront. An associated report, *Women, Business and the Law*, reported that 90 of the 143 economies surveyed had at least one legal difference restricting women's economic opportunities.[12] Differences have an impact on credit histories, access to capital, marital assets, and land ownership, and therefore bargaining power and ability to conduct business affairs. Not surprisingly, in countries that "rank high for their ease of doing business, women's unemployment is low and there are numerous women entrepreneurs. In countries that rank low, the opposite is true."[13] The very act of data collection has also become a means to stimulate policy discussion about women's entrepreneurship.[14]

The Women's Economic Opportunity Index gauges female entrepreneurs' access to finance programs. Indicators include three types of programs: initiatives to provide financial accounts to women (for example, current accounts, savings accounts, and deposit accounts); outreach efforts aimed at improving women entrepreneurs' access to credit, loans, lines of credit, and so on; and provision of financial literacy and risk-management programs to women.

Use the list of indices and assessment criteria presented in Table 7.1 to explore the changing status of women's entrepreneurship in your region or country. The indices can also be used to estimate the cost of doing business, including how easy or difficult it is to close or sell a business.[15]

Policy Can Create a Level Playing Field

"Policy turns into funding and funding turns into resources that affect business growth. Resources, such as small business training, help women to grow their firms. As a leader, my role is to create results that vindicate policy decisions. This is how change happens." These are the words of Sandra Altner, president of the Canadian Council for Small Business[16] and chief executive officer of the Women's Enterprise Centre of Manitoba (Canada).[17] Sandra heads one of an expanding network of female-focused small-business centers around the world. The Women's Enterprise Centre administers a multimillion dollar loan fund for business owners who wish to start, expand, or purchase businesses.[18] Other services include advisory services such as assistance with business planning and one-on-one counselling. Training and skills development are delivered through seminars and workshops covering topics such as marketing, startup planning, and financial management.

As Altner says, "A rationale for women's enterprise centers is that innovative programming can lead to a revolution in the way women do business. Many are 'seed programs' that address issues that impede the growth of women-owned businesses. But such initiatives are rarely self-sustaining. Most cannot exist without supportive policy directives and funders that recognize the societal importance of the program outcomes."

The establishment of women's enterprise centers is one response to gender-blind small-business initiatives that make few or sometimes no arrangements for the unique needs of female entrepreneurs.[19] For example, in the European Union, Central Europe, and Eastern Europe over 70 percent of small-business member organizations make no provision for women entrepreneurs.[20] Consequently, women in business centers and networks operate in parallel with mainstream small-business organizations, vying for the attention of clients, politicians, and policymakers.

If you are a member of a small-business or industry association, ask whether female-focused policies and programming are part of the organization's mandate:

if not, why not? Remember that membership and contributions should represent all members' interests.

Policy Leads to Business Opportunities

Founded in 2001, Women Impacting Public Policy (WIPP) is influencing entrepreneurship policy across the United States and increasingly around the world. Barbara Kasoff, the founding president of WIPP, tells us, "For more than a decade, WIPP has worked to make the Women-Owned Small Business (WOSB) Procurement Program an effective means to achieve and exceed the U.S. federal government's 5 percent contracting goal for women-owned small businesses. When the program was launched in 2011, WIPP began spreading the news to the women's business community. Through a partnership with American Express OPEN, we developed the 'Give Me 5 Program' to educate women who were new to contracting on the fundamentals of contracting. More recently, WIPP expanded this partnership to include the Small Business Administration and launched the 'ChallengeHER Campaign.' We are taking the outreach message nationwide.[21] But WIPP has gone beyond education, using our broad coalition of women entrepreneurs to advocate in Washington for improvements to the program. More work remains. WIPP is now focused on bringing sole-source authority, an important contracting tool, into the program. Right now, the women's procurement program is the only small-business procurement program without this option. As the program continues to evolve, we will continue to advocate and educate to ensure contracting opportunities and success are attainable for women business owners."

Barbara Kasoff understands how policies lead to business opportunity. "When one woman succeeds, others succeed as well. The trickle-down effect is evidenced when a woman business owner lands a contract. Women business owners hire other women, making the community stronger economically." The WIPP *Economic Blueprint, Women Business Owners' Platform for Growth* can be viewed at www.wipp.org. "This document serves to focus WIPP member activities. The report can also serve as a discussion tool for other advocacy groups on how to build a strategy to increase women's business opportunities."

Business Owners Must Deal with Cascading Policies

An academic by profession, Patricia Greene is the academic director of Goldman Sachs Foundation's 10,000 Small Businesses Initiative and a professor at Babson College in the United States.[22] She is also a founding member of the Diana Project, the world's largest and most comprehensive research initiative focusing on women's entrepreneurship. The Goldman Sachs (U.S.) project reflects a $500 million investment to help entrepreneurs create jobs and economic opportunity by providing access to education, financial capital, and business support services. Patricia Greene's work focuses on program design "to create scale and efficiencies for more high-impact training to support growth-oriented business owners." She is also an advisor to Goldman Sachs' 10,000 Women Project.[23]

Patricia Greene believes that "few policymakers understand the gestalt of how policy impacts women's lives and that policy impacts women in broader ways than men. We need to encourage more women to know what the policies are and to think about ways to become active in policy discussions. Public policy is about who gets educated and who can participate in different markets. Policy dictates the availability of child care. Even in countries that support generous social and family benefits, such as the Nordic nations, women who own small businesses cannot access such benefits. The challenge is to streamline the policy ecosystem, given a cascading of policies that impact small business owners."

Patricia offers practical advice to business owners. "A first step is to pay attention to legislation that is going to directly impact your business. Think about getting involved in subfederal [local] policy because there are few watching how country- and state-level policies align with federal legislation."

Advocacy Can Build and Strengthen Community

Marsha Firestone, president and founder of the Women Presidents' Organization (WPO)[24] has learned that policies "can make or break a business. Policies can bolster enterprise growth or can aggravate inequalities and reverse women's social and economic gains. Change is not a linear process. Policy affects all facets of our personal and business lives. Women business owners must recognize that just about everything they do is affected by policy. At the same time, the economic impact that women business owners make is still overlooked. For example, women are still perceived as starting and running very small businesses. Not enough credit is given to women in the ways that they help economies in the countries in which they operate. Engagement in policy strengthens the women's business community."

Founded in 1997, the WPO operates 115 chapters on six continents. Marsha Firestone's key message is that women's entrepreneurship is big business. "WPO membership generates aggregate revenues of $19 billion. To be eligible for membership, women business owners must generate minimum revenues of $1,000,000 if service-based and $2,000,000 if product-based. Members employ over 142,000 workers and generate an average of $13 million in sales. Currently, the top policy issues for WPO members in the United States include health care, credit policy [monetary policies and initiatives that control the money supply, credit policy of lenders], taxation, and dealing with unions."

What Are the Impacts of Gender Bias in Policy?

We have heard from our women-in-enterprise champions about why we should care about public policy. So what are the implications? What does gender bias look like in terms of policy? In this section, we introduce four examples, remedial solutions, and commonly used analytic techniques to address gender bias that have been drawn from our experiences as policy advisors.

Economic gender bias occurs when a person of one sex does not meet program application or usage criteria and the reason is a lack of qualifications associated with the person's gender.[25] Empowerment is a process of awareness and capacity building leading to greater participation, to greater decision-making power and control, and to transformative action.[26] In your experience, can you think of any examples of gender bias in policy or programming?

Entrepreneurship Capabilities

Across North America and Europe, females constitute the majority of university students. Yet the bulk of research and infrastructure funding is targeted at faculties engaged in technology, engineering, and material sciences. Male students disproportionately populate these faculties. In management schools, business case competitions are an important vehicle for training elite entrepreneurship students. Female students are significantly underrepresented among award beneficiaries. Female faculty are underrepresented in university incubation and technology transfer centers.[27] Few funding agencies hold universities and colleges accountable for the participation of females in awarding of grants, research assistantships, and other types of financial and training support.[28]

What remedial strategies can be undertaken to rectify this imbalance? One solution is funding guidelines that explicitly acknowledge the value of women's knowledge and mandate equitable participation and awarding of funds. This implies proactive outreach to female students and targeted funding to female-dominated faculties or disciplines, such as communications, nursing, and natural sciences. National and regional business case competitions and other student-focused extracurricular experiences should also include equitable participation criteria across participating universities and colleges.

Funding R&D and Technology

Many governments support tax schemes that are intended to stimulate private investment in research, development, and the commercialization of advanced technologies. Funding support has multiplier benefits and gender biases. Males are more likely to start firms that benefit from such schemes. Males are more likely to be hired into occupational roles that are supported by such schemes. Males are more likely to acquire experience that they can subsequently leverage in an enterprise startup. Males lead most lobby organizations that advocate for such schemes.

Remedial strategies include the introduction of tax schemes that explicitly target female-dominated sectors or occupational roles such as tax relief to support marketing and public relations activities, functional roles that are more likely to be populated by females.

Self-Employment Training

Another remedial strategy employed by many governments is small-business training initiatives targeted at disadvantaged populations. Program guidelines typically include compensation for unemployed workers while participating in self-employment training. Program funding and program evaluation criteria typically are based on the number of new or incremental jobs created. Gender-based analysis of Canada's largest self-employment training initiative found that evaluation criteria, predicated on the number of jobs created, resulted in staff favoring the selection of growth-oriented male applicants.[29] Paradoxically, cherry-picking candidates countered the program mandate to support disadvantaged groups, including women.

Response strategies include tying funding to inclusive representation of unemployed workers, conducting gender-sensitivity training of staff responsible for recruitment, recognizing potential conflicts between job creation and equitable access to such programs, and expanding program performance criteria to include material, perceptual, and relational change.

Availability of Female-Focused Policies

Few small-business policies consider the gender profile of participants or program impacts on men and women. The cataloguing of small-business policies and programs provides evidence of the need for advocacy. Learning Aid 7.1 is a short exercise for learning about the construction of entrepreneurship policies, including the state of women's entrepreneurship programming across different nations. Complete the exercise by working through the three steps.

The next section presents three analytical tools and the criteria used to assess potential biases in entrepreneurship policy and programming.

Identifying Gender Biases in Entrepreneurship Policies

There are a variety of approaches used by advocates, academics, and policymakers to assess how entrepreneurship policy can affect women and men differently. Two questions underlying most analyses are

- Does the policy support equitable participation of women and men?
- Does the policy discriminate in process, inputs, or outcomes?[30]

Learning Aid 7.1: Women-focused entrepreneurship policy

Step 1: The International Centre for Entrepreneurship Policy is an international forum for sharing information about entrepreneurship policy and programming. The Centre's website enables visitors to search online for case studies about entrepreneurship policies and programs.

Visit the site http://www.inter-cep.com and then locate the search function and enter the word *growth*.

Conduct a second search using the word *technology*.

Conduct a third search using the terms *women* and *gender*. What are your observations? In the first two searches, multiple policies and programs are referenced. Recall that gender is a key marker of enterprise growth. How many female-focused policies can you identity?

Step 2: Using an online search engine, input the words *women* and *entrepreneurs*. What are your observations? One lesson is that there is an emerging global infrastructure of "by women, for women" business associations and networks. Women entrepreneurs are meeting to share experiences. Many of these organizations are engaged in influencing policy.

Step 3: Visit the website for Women Impacting Public Policy (http://www.wipp.org). This nonprofit, bipartisan U.S.-based organization is a leading change agent for entrepreneurship policy. Having reviewed sample pages on the website, what are your observations? One conclusion is the demonstrated need for policy reform. The links that connect economic discrimination, empowerment, and enterprise growth are not always evident. To determine policy and program priorities to address economic discrimination, advocates and bureaucrats rely on several well-established sex- and gender-based analytical techniques.

The answers to these questions are rarely straightforward. Entrepreneurship policies differ markedly across different countries, as do the ideologies that fuel advocacy.[31] For example, governments such as Spain and Italy prefer a non-interventionist approach. Sweden, Finland, and Norway are pro-egalitarian and pro-entrepreneurship, and lead the world in training programs to support women entrepreneurs.[32] According to Virginia Littlejohn, "India, South Korea, the Philippines, and China are actively building women's entrepreneurship programs and policies. The China Association of Women Entrepreneurs and Women's Chamber of Commerce are aggressively leading initiatives focused on poverty alleviation. South Africa has introduced federal procurement policy. Malaysia has introduced women and export trade programming by coupling initiatives with corporate sector partners, such as IBM. Japan retains an intense need for program and policy work, given its infancy with regards to women's economic empowerment."

The United States and Canada present contrasts in policy emphasis, within close geographic proximity. In the United States, federal supplier diversity is the most advanced in the world. The U.S. government has challenged private sector contractors to meet the federal 5 percent set-aside goals. By comparison, Canada supports no federal procurement set-asides explicitly for female-owned firms.[33] Paradoxically, Canada was a world leader in stipulating the obligation to report on equity provisions among private firms who sought to do business with the government. While the Canadian government nominally mandates suppliers to report on equity, today it makes no such provision on federal purchasing. Canadian legislation does, however, mandate parental leaves, including benefits for self-employed workers. Among developed economies, the United States is distinct in the scarcity of parental benefits, including those for the self-employed.

Once gender inequities are recognized, remedial response strategies are also rarely straightforward. The rough waters of public opinion—and divergent agendas of small-business interest groups—must be navigated. For example, attempts to redress inequities in trade and small business export promotion (such as eligibility criteria that have been seen to favor firms in male-dominated sectors) have led to female-only trade missions, export training, and networks such as the Organization of Women in Trade. Public responses include claims of reverse discrimination and policy that favors political correctness. The presence of female-focused export promotion programs has also led to legislative challenges that position such initiatives as actionable subsidies under bilateral trade agreements.[34]

Given such complexities, you may be wondering, "What can I do? How can I break through the bureaucratic machinery of government?" As Virginia Littlejohn advises, acquiring evidence is critical. To do so requires engaging others in the process of data gathering and using established approaches to identify potential gender biases within entrepreneurship policies. Three such approaches are

- Sex- and gender-based analysis
- Value chain analysis
- Diversity management.

Sex- and Gender-Based Analysis

Stemming from equal opportunity legislation introduced in the United States during the 1970s, sex- and gender-based analysis (SGBA) seeks to capture material, perceptual, and relational changes that result from the introduction of policies and programs.[35] Material changes reflect economic security and access and control of other resources such as health, child care, nutrition, and housing. Perceptual changes imply self-confidence, vision, and understanding one's individuality and capabilities. Relational changes capture the role of women in the household, local and national communities, and the ability to act independently (that is, reduce one's independence on intermediation by others).

Gender responsive budgeting (GRB) is then used to determine how governments should allocate resources in a more equitable manner. Gender responsive budgeting considers how the criteria above are reflected in funding and the degree to which ministries of finance incorporate gender equality into the budgetary process.[36] GRB entails tracking the allocation of spending in terms of equality outcomes, awareness, and capacity building. Accountability implies a long-term commitment to equality objectives. Ultimately, this also implies changes to government budgeting and policies.

Value Chain Analysis

Value chain analysis extends sex- and gender-based investigation into the sequences of activities that bring products and services to markets. Value chain analysis is most often operationalized through two types of interventions: supplier diversity and trade impact analysis.

Supplier diversity reflects procurement initiatives that link sellers and buyers. The availability of such programs is increasing rapidly within both the private and public sectors, particularly among American and European firms. *Trade impact analysis* is used primarily by governments and NGOs to examine the impacts of trade agreements, international development, and foreign aid on women. Each is described in the following text.

Supplier Diversity Programs

The objective of supplier diversity programming is to integrate products and services offered by economically disadvantaged groups, including majority female-owned firms, into regional and global supply chains.[37] Advocates argue that supplier diversity is a means to stimulate economic growth and address challenges that confront small-firm suppliers. Benefits are reflected in increased managerial capacity, revenue growth, skills development, and transfer among sellers.[38] Governments are often the target of advocacy, given that they are among the largest customers in the world.[39] Key concerns among business owners include lack of transparency, complicated bidding, jargon, expectation creep, and specifications that are not commensurate with requested products or services. Such challenges increase paper burden and, therefore, demands from time-strapped business owners.[40]

If you are not yet familiar with supplier diversity programming for women-owned firms, here are two easy tasks: visit the website of WEConnect International (http://weconnectinternational.org) and then read about the global impact of this initiative in *Buying for Impact: How to Buy from Women and Change Our World* by Elizabeth Vazquez and Andrew Sherman.[41]

Trade Impact Assessment

In 2004, the United Nations Conference on Trade and Development called for gender-based analysis during the negotiations phase of new free trade agreements. The objective was to understand the impact of policy on inputs such as prices, sexual division of labor, working conditions, consumption, and the availability of social services.[42] In a number of countries, legislation mandates that international trade and investment agreements undergo sex- and gender-based analysis.[43] This requirement stems from decades of research that reports that trade agreements and economic legislation differ in gender outcomes. Assessment criteria consider the impacts within the

- Texts of the trade agreement
- Implementation and enforcement mechanisms
- Norms that influence gender roles and women's opportunities.[44]

Analysis also considers, by country, legislation relevant to the economic and social status of women, including

- Treaty commitments to women
- Constitutional guarantees of nondiscrimination and equality
- Affirmative action and other laws providing special treatment, such as small-business assistance and procurement preferences (for example, laws pertaining to fair wages, food labeling, health, and safety)
- Biases in application or enforcement of laws that benefit women and other vulnerable groups (such as labor laws and maternity benefits)
- Religious, traditional, or customary laws and practices, especially relating to rights to land and other assets.[45]

When gender biases are identified, remedial strategies emphasize skills development and training, improving production capacities and upgrading the product quality of female-owned enterprises.[46] The following excerpt from a study on free trade agreements[47] illustrates the findings of a gender-based trade assessment in Latin America.

Textile and garment exports in Colombia have experienced sustained growth over the past few years. In 2007, sector exports grew 50 percent over the previous year, in 2009 they rose by 42 percent, and in 2010 by 15 percent.[48] In 2010, the sector supported 8,905 firms. These firms generate a significant number of permanent and contractual jobs, 60 percent of which are held by women. Supported by the 2004 Domestic Agenda for Productivity and Competitiveness, the Columbian government promotes the manufacture of cottons, fibres, textiles, and garments.[49] The trade promotion policy seeks to strengthen distribution channels, access new markets, and further integrate global value chains.

A key concern from a gender perspective is that outsourcing is common. Small and informal satellite businesses that depend on contracts from medium- and large-sized enterprises have proliferated. These employ a predominately informal female labor force, illustrating typical gender inequalities in the sector labor profile.[50] Another issue is the effect that trade has had on SMEs, in which women are disproportionately employed.

Liberalization in the country began in 1991, and by the mid-1990s, 55 percent of Columbian SMEs had disappeared. Trade liberalization instigated an increase in imports, which dampened growth.[51] This has impacted women in a number of ways: as workers, they were most affected by falls in wages, economic insecurity, and job precariousness; as small business owners, women were adversely affected by the increased international competition;[52] as consumers, however, women benefited from lower prices and a larger variety of products.

Diversity Management

Diversity management is a third approach to assessing potential gender biases within SME policies. Predicated on the principles of meritocracy, the objective is to encourage "all people to maximize their potential contribution."[53] Also referred to as "gender-based analysis plus," diversity management acknowledges the heterogeneity of women entrepreneurs by considering their broader psycho-demographic identities.[54] In this context, identity is defined inclusively as gender, mother tongue, physical and mental abilities, education, cultural or ethnic background, sexual orientation, and so on. Analysis seeks "to find a way to address the specificity of experiences of gender, while at the same time attending to broader commonalities and configurations that have social and political significance."[55] Emphasis is placed on individual competencies.

Critics refer to diversity management as the rebranding of mainstream analysis, a process that negates evidence of women's subordination, power, and structural disadvantages[56] and a view that removes gender from the policy discussion and minimizes the impact by including it with all other marginalized groups.[57]

A summary of the three approaches and associated policy levers is presented in Table 7.2. The table can be used to identify the principles, common criticisms, and areas of policy reform. Refer back to this table as you continue to work through the following discussion about strategies to support women's entrepreneurship.

Strategies to Support Women Entrepreneurs

Having worked with your team of advocates and advisors to assemble evidence of gender bias in policies and programming, in this section we summarize two options that can be used to facilitate women's enterprise growth and social change: mainstream versus female-focused small-business programs. Sample programs are presented to illustrate the strengths of each option. Conflicting ideologies among industry advocates, politicians, and bureaucrats can undermine efforts to support women entrepreneurs. Common tactics used to dismiss taskforce recommendations are then presented.

Table 7.2: Approaches to assessing economic gender discrimination

	Sex- and Gender-Based Analysis*	Value Chain Analysis**	Diversity Management*
Principles	Social justice and fairness, labor rights, and ways of learning Impetus: Legislation, rights-based, compliance	Market inputs and outputs such as prices, cost of labor, sexual division of labor, earnings, access and control over resources, household time burdens, consumption, and social services Impetus: Inclusion and economic opportunity	Meritocracy and individualism; pragmatic intervention strategies Impetus: Inclusion and economic opportunity
Opportunity	Eradication of resource and power inequities; examination of enabling environments and policies from a "gender perspective"	Captures the globalization of trade and labor rather than focusing solely on domestic legislative affairs (hence, international cross-agency collaboration)	Recognizes the heterogeneity of women (for example, double or triple marginalization in the context of other identities such as disability or minority ethnicity); provokes less hostility and resistance than affirmative action
Criticism	Little evidence that it is used to design rather than audit public policy (that is, little more than rhetoric); analysis is based on weak anti-discrimination legislation, with little questioning of underlying power relations and interests; few repercussions	Rarely has an impact on actual trade processes; in many economies, exports are concentrated in a few, capital-intensive sectors such as extraction, natural resources, and manufactured goods which are populated by large firms; women entrepreneurs are not typically involved in these sectors	So inclusive that it is meaningless, and distracts from salient differences such as gender; analysis negates power and structural disadvantages, and is more about image building than progress in equality goals
Policy Levers	Positive (affirmative) actions, explicit program performance guidelines (participation, outcomes) among underrepresented groups	International treaties, bi- and multilateral trade agreements	Individual entrepreneurial self-efficacy, skills, and competencies; policy emphasizes program selection based on multiple demographic criteria, in addition to being female

Sources: *G. Kirton and A-M. Greene, "What Does Diversity Management Mean for the Gender Equality Project in the United Kingdom? Views and Experiences of Organizational Actors, *Canadian Journal of Administrative Sciences* 27, no. 3 (2010): 249–262.

**E. McGill, "Poverty and Social Analysis of Trade Agreements: A More Coherent Approach?" Boston College *International & Comparative Law Review, Student Publications* 27, no. 2 (2004): 429–452.

Mainstream Entrepreneurship Policies

There is an array of mainstream policy levers that can be used to create social, economic, and regulatory environments that are conducive to business startup and growth, including regulations and legislation; research, development, and technology; entrepreneurial capabilities; culture; access to finance; and market conditions.[58] This approach assumes that firm growth is hindered by unfavorable economies of scale (for example, small firms are less efficient than large firms)[59] and that gender-related barriers to startup and growth can be addressed through conventional entrepreneurship policies. Each lever comprises a suite of policy options that collectively create environments conducive to business startup, growth, and survival.

Proponents of mainstream programming argue that entrepreneurs benefit equally from such policies, and that well-structured entrepreneurship policies

- Improve the quality and number of firms
- Enhance the skills and decision-making ability of nascent entrepreneurs
- Provide value-added advice and role models to support and encourage entrepreneurial intentions
- Increase the social legitimacy of business ownership
- Create forums for entrepreneurs to exchange information.

From a political perspective, the anticipated outcomes of most entrepreneurship policies are job creation, economic recovery, and the commercialization of innovation.[60] Different governments enact different mainstream policies on the basis of their dominant ideology about factors that lead or constrain growth and the country's economic structure and circumstances.[61] Learning Aid 7.2 captures the concerns voiced by women business owners. It provides a menu of policy levers to bolster women's entrepreneurship. Use the tool to create a policy framework. Build expert knowledge teams. Then, appoint spokespersons for each of the policy domains.

Integration of Women's Issues in Mainstream Policy and Programming

Monitoring agencies report that integration of women's issues within mainstream policy is weak. Female-focused initiatives remain selective (that is, token, one-off, and pilot projects). Women's economic empowerment remains a tertiary policy consideration. Budgetary emphasis is placed on analysis rather than on the long-term commitment to material, perceptual, and relational change for women. "While more than 120 countries have a national action plan for the advancement of women . . . many of them remain 'wish lists' without an adequate budget for implementation."[62] Women in business taskforces also report that political and program support is limited.

Learning Aid 7.2: Entrepreneurship policy levers

Instructions: Use the learning aid to stimulate discussion about potential policy and program reform. How might some of the challenges affect your business or intentions? Indicate those challenges that you have experienced or are currently experiencing.

Regulation

☐ **Administrative burden (time):** Onerous bureaucracy and administrative fees dissuade women from venture creation. In countries with high levels of corruption, women face gender-intensified constraints including negotiating complex and costly procedures.

☐ **Social and health security:** Women are more likely to operate home-based firms and undertake low value, piece-rate work (such as data inputting). Personal health and security, low earnings, and workplace safety have a disproportionate impact on women.

R&D and Technology

☐ **R&D investment:** Disproportionate R&D and technology funding target sectors in which women business owners are underrepresented.

☐ **University-industry interface:** Male faculty and students are overrepresented in patent registration and sharing and other aspects of the commercialization of innovation.

☐ **Technology diffusion:** Male faculty and students are more likely to access and benefit from technology transfer services within postsecondary institutions. Male faculty and students are more likely to hold patents and commercialize their intellectual property.

☐ **Entrepreneurship education:** Females are less likely to enroll in entrepreneurship courses. Having completed entrepreneurship course work, males are more likely to aspire to venture creation. Governments play a key role in mandating gender-sensitive curricula, availability and diffusion of information about women's entrepreneurial opportunities, and promotion of female role models.

☐ **Entrepreneurial infrastructure:** Female students and faculty are less likely to utilize small-business infrastructure supports (for example, startup or incubation centers).

☐ **Immigration:** Women are less likely to qualify for "business immigration programs" that seek to attract immigrants who possess commercial acumen and pre-immigration intentions of starting firms in the host countries.

Culture

☐ **Risk attitude:** Culture influences the degree to which risk taking is valued and failure is stigmatized. Women are perceived as risk averse. Contributions are undervalued. Government can play a role in creating positive images of female entrepreneurs, and celebrating entrepreneurial success with awards.

☐ **Attitudes:** Attitudes toward entrepreneurs continue to be "think entrepreneur = think male"; "think women entrepreneurs = think micro-enterprise." Women compose half the North American labor force and one-third of small-business owners.

Access to Finance

☐ **Debt:** Some governments provide targeted funding instruments for female-owned firms. Funding should move beyond microcredit to working capital instruments and equity. There should be support for financial literacy, including understanding of preconditions for financial success.

☐ **Equity** (angel investment): Women business owners are less likely to be linked to equity investment networks. There should be assistance for business owners to meet informal investors.

☐ **Venture Capital:** Government can play a role in capacity building and information sharing, given that women garner less than 5 percent of funds invested by venture capitalists. VC funding is based on referrals in closed, male-dominated networks.

☐ **IPO**, other sources of capital: There is a lack of female-led IPOs in all countries. Simulation studies suggest that despite identical qualifications, female CEOs are perceived as less capable.

Market Conditions

☐ **Access to markets:** Women business owners are more likely to operate low-value-added micro-enterprises, with intensive competition. Lack of sector experience limits access to commercial sector information and inputs. There are smaller profit margins to invest in marketing.

☐ **Procurement:** Gender-based procurement policies seek to integrate products and services by women-owned firms into government supply chains.

What might account for widespread, lethargic responses by governments to the concerns of women entrepreneurs? Responses are, in part, a product of compartmentalizing women's economic empowerment within government agencies tasked with addressing social development. This approach fails to recognize that women are not a homogenous "group." Women's directorates are not in the business of growing firms. Expertise within such agencies or departments is limited, relative to that of departments or ministries explicitly tasked with economic development, innovation, and trade. Within women's directorates, competitive bidding for limited funds pits women's economic empowerment against social well-being (for example, violence and abuse prevention). Solidarity is weakened as women in business advocates become competitors to other women's interests groups. We have observed simple, practical business development discussions become entangled in complex debates about women's subordination.[63]

Here are more tactics used to stifle the efforts of women in business advocates and other interest groups.[64] Do you recognize any?

- *Denial*: Stating that gender equity is not a concern for the country, or that a particular policy or program does not discriminate.
- *Speaking on behalf of women*: Generalizing one or two experiences into a broad statement about all women or presuming that one's own experience justifies a statement about 'what women want' or need (generally ignoring the fact that women are not a homogenous group).
- *Token action*: Acknowledging that something should be done, but selecting an action that can only have limited impact (a small add-on project or project component) or focusing on women's use of a project activity, rather than the project's impact on gender equality.
- *Lip service*: Acknowledging the issues at the level of rhetoric but failing to take meaningful action.
- *Commissioning a study*: Delaying decisions by setting up a study to provide more information (often in the hope that the need to address the issue will disappear with the delay).
- *Appointing a token woman*: Resolving the need to act by appointing a woman to a committee or a decision-making process."

Despite criticism of mainstream entrepreneurship policy, our research found examples of interventions that appear to address the needs of women. Following is the profile of one such program, the Goldman Sachs 10,000 Small Businesses Initiative.

In the words of Dr. Patricia Greene, "The Goldman Sachs program is predicated on a collaborative design and delivery model, taking the best of content and culture from private and public sector partners, including consultancies, nonprofit agencies, and academic experts from Babson College. Programs are delivered through community colleges throughout the U.S. Continuous improvement entails ongoing assessment and modification of content and program delivery. An annual review is conducted to consider major program changes.

"The program is tactical, timely, and personal, with a 99 percent program retention rate. Case-based learning embraces a broad definition of entrepreneurship and is predicated on what participants want to accomplish. All content is hands-on, applied knowledge. The delivery model is peer-to-peer learning with a direct focus on the participant's business. Eligibility criteria include business ownership for at least two years, revenues between $150,000 and $4,000,000, and owners with the intention to grow their firm. The objective is to create jobs and grow revenue: entrepreneurship meets economic development.

"Cohort composition reflects a diversity of participants. Particular attention is paid to recruiting women. Half are female, a participation rate that exceeds most growth-focused small-business training programs. Recruitment is undertaken through national and local partnerships. Training is based on entrepreneurial mind-sets and skills, focusing on identifying opportunities, organizing resources, and providing leadership. Attention is also paid to participants' aspirations. This reflects clarification and metrics that capture personal and business goals, goals that are based on a clear sense of what he or she hopes to create that has value for themselves and their family, communities, and society."

Female-Focused Entrepreneurship Policies

Several explanations justify female-focused entrepreneurship policy and programming. One school of thought views female-focused policies as a means to alleviate poverty, by increasing women's per-capita income. A second considers investment in female-focused programs as a means to stimulate overall economic growth, while a third centers on women's lived experiences rather than third-party interests and agendas. All three rationales assume that gender inequalities are the product of durable social norms that disadvantage women, and that women are economically and socially disadvantaged often due to caregiver responsibilities. All three schools of thought seek to

- Promote entrepreneurship to women and increase women's participation in business ownership
- Build awareness about the availability of capital and support
- Offer role models and assist women in developing skills, credit histories, and contacts

- Promote economic equity between men and women
- Communicate strategies to address barriers to startup and growth.

Each is now defined. Further explanations and critiques of female-focused entrepreneurship policies are presented in Table 7.3.

Poverty Alleviation

The premise of such policies is self-sufficiency. Clients are typically nascent business owners or the self-employed. Programming focuses on ensuring access to training and startup capital. Training emphasizes confidence building, financial competencies, networking, and knowledge sharing. Career services encourage women to enter nontraditional fields and sectors.[65] Impact is typically measured in terms of self-sufficiency, increased female participation in business ownership, and awareness of entrepreneurship as a career option.[66]

Economic Growth

This perspective implies that women-owned enterprises constitute an underutilized or underperforming resource, one to be supported for employment creation and economic growth. In other words, female-focused programs are another means of generating employment. Curriculum is intended to address gender-related barriers to firm growth such as accessing business contacts and contracts, growth-capital, and networking that lends explicitly to business development. Sample programs include female-only trade missions, venture capital funds, and industry associations.

Entrepreneurial Feminism

Building on the earlier discussion about entrepreneurial feminism, this market-led rationale suggests that economic growth, without gender-focused policies and program interventions, reinforces women's subordination. Women entrepreneurs are seen as key agents in creating and sharing knowledge and skills. Entrepreneurship is a mechanism for women to gain power and therefore negotiate wider change to redress economic inequality and discrimination. The anticipated outcomes of policy and program intervention are holistic and focus on women's empowerment as the end goal.[67] Training focuses on personal development and self-efficacy.[68] More rationales for female-focused entrepreneurship follow.

As with mainstream policies and programs, there is little evidence to objectively compare the effectiveness of female-focused initiatives.[69] To better understand why women business owners value female-focused services, we asked over two hundred clients of the Mount Saint Vincent University Women's Enterprise

Table 7.3: Rationales for female-focused entrepreneurship policies

	Poverty Alleviation	Economic Growth	Entrepreneurial Feminism
Principles	Advocacy is associated with ensuring access to education, capital, provision of quality child care, and other policies that support the "care economy" and social protection.	Policy objectives include economic recovery and growth, retraining, and helping women make the transition to higher value-added enterprises.	Economic growth without female-focused policy interventions reinforces women's subordination.
Focus	Policy emphasizes the marginalization of historically disadvantaged workers. Self-employment and access to capital (such as microlending) are associated with women's economic self-sufficiency and social independence.	Focus is on enhanced economic productivity and efficiencies through technology adoption. Investment in girls and women is viewed as a means to stabilize economies (for example, economies characterized by military conflict such as the Middle East).	Women act in accordance with internal wisdom (for example, conflict resolution and intra-group support). Women learn from women. Egalitarian, partnership-based decisions are reflected in commercial transactions, webs of socioeconomic relationships, cooperation, empathy, and mutual trust.
Implementation	Training emphasizes self-employment and small-scale or niche production.	Policy and programs encourage women to "think big" (for example, enterprise growth), and to enter nontraditional fields or sectors.	Advocacy focuses on coalition building, collaboration, hubs for sharing best practices, and removal of gender stereotyping from educational curriculum.
Policy Levers	These include subsidized earnings during self-employment training and social insurance schemes, including maternity and parental leave for self-employed workers.	Procurement and spending are directed at female business owners. Communities of experts assemble to share best practices about leveraging private and public supplier diversity opportunities.	There are explicit guidelines for women's inclusion in all economic development policies, training, and rigorous gender-based analysis of policy inputs, processes, and outcomes.
Criticisms	The need remains to "fix" mainstream policy, embedding women's issues into training for the benefit of all. Programs are redundant and do not adequately prepare women to compete in the market. Self-employment is confined to gender-segregated sectors and traditional occupational roles.	Programs reinforce rather than eliminate stereotypes. Macro-level economic gender issues remain. Such programs assume "female deficiencies," as described earlier under the "underperformance hypothesis" of female-owned firms.	Feminist-focused programs promote over-adherence to being "disadvantaged" versus focusing on female capital (advantage).

Centre (Canada) to explain their motives for accessing the small-business center. Following are some of our findings.[70]

Center clients describe three primary reasons for using the service. Two are similar to those associated with mainstream small-business programming; the third is not. These women sought access to

- Managerial capital
- Enhanced social capital
- Services that are explicitly female-focused (to enhance feminine capital).

Most respondents stressed that the female-only focus was a strong drawing card: they were attracted to the center as a place where they could connect with and learn from "women like me." The center clients sought advisors who understood their personal and commercial needs, as women. Some women identified with other female clients. Program users described outcomes such as feeling empowered, comforted, and supported and emphasized sharing and like-mindedness.

When asked to compare female-focused programs to other support agencies, the majority of women felt that the center had unique attributes. One dominant theme was "women learn from women." Program users described the value of learning and sharing information with other women using descriptors such as warm and safe, comfortable, friendly, less intimidating, and supportive. The atmosphere was inviting and "risk-free." Their experiences reflect those of women who have used other female-focused centers.

Learning Aid 7.3 summarizes the clients' motives and other studies that report on female-focused small-business services.[71] You can use this tool to reflect on your preferred training needs. When meeting with counsellors, for example, walk through each of these motives, discussing the relevance of each. Trainers can use this tool to draft clients' learning objectives and to inform assessment criteria (for example, examine the relevance or importance of each and the extent to which the learning objectives are attained).

Advancing Women's Entrepreneurship

As this chapter explains, entrepreneurial success is not solely the consequence of intention. Policy ecosystems play a role. To close this chapter, we share more parting insights from the women-in-enterprise champions about the power in policy. A common theme is that creating environments that support women entrepreneurs takes organization and leadership.

- "Having political and policy influence implies having a large and strong community of support."

Learning Aid 7.3: Motives for using female-focused entrepreneurship programs

Instructions: Review the list of program motives and outcomes. Indicate which reflect your learning needs. Then draw on the learning aid to work with an advisor or trainer to create a learning environment and curriculum that is right for you.

- ☐ **Networking:** I need to build my business networks.
- ☐ **Women like me:** I need to connect with other women experiencing similar challenges.
- ☐ **Guidance:** I seek a safe place to learn how to run my business.
- ☐ **Women-focused:** I prefer to work with others who understand my needs as a woman.
- ☐ **Learn more about my target market:** My target clients are women. I seek business-to-business opportunities.
- ☐ **Trust:** I value the feeling of being on the same page as the person with whom I am speaking.
- ☐ **Approachable:** I seek a learning environment in which people are approachable.
- ☐ **Being taken seriously:** I prefer a community where my business ideas will be taken seriously.
- ☐ **Self-reflection:** I need to clarify attitudes and feelings about myself in relation to other work and personal roles.
- ☐ **Learning from women like me:** I expect to learn about issues women face in managing their firms.
- ☐ **Imposter syndrome:** I tend to dismiss the success that I have attained.
- ☐ **Leadership:** I need to learn about leadership styles that work for me.
- ☐ **Understanding power:** I need to understand concepts of power and the application of power in my business practices.
- ☐ **Safe learning environment:** I like to test my ideas against the experiences of other women.
- ☐ **Collective:** I need to participate and share in a collective women's experience.
- ☐ **Feminist knowledge:** I wish to integrate feminist principles into my business practices.
- ☐ **Relevant curriculum:** Given personal demands, I need to learn more about time management.
- ☐ **Financial literacy:** I have little confidence in my financial literacy.
- ☐ **Relational approach:** I wish to work with others who know that learning is relational.
- ☐ **Role incongruity:** I sometimes feel conflicted between my caregiving and occupational roles.
- ☐ **Respect:** I feel more respected in my work and accomplishments.
- ☐ **Language:** I need to work with trainers who don't use jargon.
- ☐ **Peer-to-peer:** I learn best from my colleagues and peers.
- ☐ **Family demands:** I need day care support while in training.
- ☐ **Counseling:** I would benefit from counseling about continued learning and job acquisition.
- ☐ **Moral support:** I need support, as I am dealing with difficult personal issues at this time.
- ☐ **Business culture:** I wish to learn more about business culture from successful women.

- "There remains a need to continue to build communities of women business owners who share like-minded interests."

A second message relates to creating a clearly identified constituency.

A third message is that "Economically empowered women make for a strong economy. Fairness is always back of everyone's mind, but focusing on economic impact is a political agenda that all parties can get behind. In creating a constituency, establish clear business goals at the outset to motivate engagement. For example, the initial purpose of the U.S. Association of Women Business Owners was to gain access to capital and federal contracts. This brought growth-oriented women entrepreneurs to the table. American success followed government recognition that 'women business owners' is a defined sector."

The fourth message pertains to catalyzing change.

- "Call for hearings on women entrepreneurship and hold conferences and economic summits to create national and local visibility. Track and report on the number of women-owned firms. Publish directories of women-owned businesses and annual reports about the needs of women entrepreneurs.
- Acknowledge wins. Celebration is a strategy to maintain momentum. It also helps to build a vision of what the business environment should be for women entrepreneurs."

A final take-away focuses on the importance of engaging both the private and public sectors in the design and execution of female-focused small-business training. Figure 7.1 showcases illustrative public, private, and collaborative programs that are helping to build the ecosystem of support for all entrepreneurs. We encourage you to visit the websites of these organizations to learn more about what's out there, in terms of available policies and programs.

Table 7.4 then summarizes the recommendations of the women-in-enterprise champions for making policy change happen. The lessons learned focus on building community, framing policy, and creating operational tactics to increase women's economic self-sufficiency through entrepreneurship policy and programming. Use these insights in planning discussions with like-minded entrepreneurs and market intermediaries to prepare briefs for elected and senior government officials. An early step in the planning process is first to build community. Outreach to political connections of all parties enhances credibility and helps to ensure that your efforts are not viewed as partisan. This likely includes drafting a list of women with political connections that can inform your action plan. This task can help the team

Figure 7.1: Landscape of women's entrepreneurship and small-business programs

	Mainstream ◄————————————————————————► Female-Focused

	Mainstream	Female-Focused
Public	Most entrepreneurship policies and programs (investment in R&D schemes, training, loan guarantees, industry or university interfaces, self-employment initiatives) are predicated on a mainstream strategy.	Training: Women's Business Centers Microcredit: Grameen Bank, BRAC Research centers: Cranfield International Centre for Women Leaders, Anita Borg Institute for Women and Technology Websites: wbl.worldbank.org; Constitutions.unwomen.org
Private / Public	Training consortia: Goldman Sachs Foundation 10,000 Small Businesses Taskforces for women's enterprise growth Department and ministry SME advisory boards	
Private	Chambers of commerce, boards of trade Small-business (private) mentoring circles Industry and trade associations Incubation centers, startup garages Training: SME development banks Crowdfunding: Kickstarter, Indiegogo, AngelList, SeedInvest, MissionMarkets, Bolstr, Fundco.ca, CircleUp	Networks: Women Presidents' Association, Prowess 2.0 Women in Business Network (U.K.) Associations: Organization for Women in Trade (OWIT), The International Alliance of Women (TIAW), Canadian Women in Communications and Technology Supplier diversity: WIPP/American Express "Give Me 5%" Initiative, WEConnect International Equity funds: Astia, Golden Seeds, The Pipeline Fellowship, Karmijn Kapitaal (Netherlands), Global Women's Equity Fund Training: Springboard Enterprises, FemTechNet, Women 2.0

Table 7.4: Strategies to make policy change happen

Build Community	**Be guided by women with political connections.** Recruit politically savvy leaders to help construct strategies to educate others about the nature of women's entrepreneurship (for example, policymakers, academics). Link messages to political issues (globalization of trade, innovation, sustainability).
	Build capacity. Advocates are only as successful as the people behind them. This implies educating coalition members to ensure that they too are advocates (for example, Women Influencing Public Policy employs a full-time government relations team, but WIPP professionals are only as good as the leadership of its coalition members). Successful advocacy takes leadership by many.
	Align advisory and government agencies. Consider execution through an Interagency Committee on Women's Business Enterprise, one that includes key government agencies. This requires commitment to comply with existing legislation (where available) and to undertake analysis of policies and programs (such as SGBA, value chain analysis, diversity management). Reporting can track progress.
	Structure a coalition. Coalition building recognizes that the missions of members are diverse (economic, social, charitable, or all) and that not all participants have the same needs or issues. Determine common interests; agree upon a set of issues that you can work on together.
Create a Policy Framework	**Focus on an economic agenda.** Women-in-business representatives must have a clear understanding about what needs to be accomplished, and then how to draft a consistent message.
	Issues cannot be politically driven. Discussion should be driven by policy and legislation (for example, when WIPP personnel speak to bureaucrats or politicians, staff approach their roles from an "educational perspective," focusing on the facts and not what the media pundits report).
	Quantify the issues. Research, backed by brand-name firms, builds legitimacy. Campaign for more studies about women's entrepreneurship, working with the private sector to fund research.
	Not only "women's issues" need to be on the agenda. Virginia Littlejohn, CEO of Quantum Leaps, reflected on how a small group of women were able to help pass twenty-six of twenty-seven policies at the White House Conference. "Many of the policies did not focus on women entrepreneurs. We found specialists in pension reform, on insurance. . . . The process of engaging female specialists led to the training of over two hundred high-profile women business owners who were elected as representatives to the White House Conference. All issues were adopted through block voting among the team of delegates."
Tactics	**Educate.** Form educational alliances with government, not-for-profit, and industry groups. Then train partners about small-business policymakers and women's issues.
	Create national and local visibility. Simultaneously launch advocacy chapters in more than one city. Track and report on the number of women-owned firms. Call for hearings on women entrepreneurship. Hold conferences and economic summits. Publish directories of women-owned firms and annual reports about the contributions and needs of women entrepreneurs.
	Advocacy takes time and energy. A challenge is to work with women who have time to contribute to sustained advocacy. Barbara Kasoff, founding president of WIPP, cautions that women who are in a startup, or who manage micro-enterprises (revenue of less than $200,000 U.S.), are likely too engaged in dealing with day-to-day demands of the firm to engage fully in advocacy.
	Celebrate "wins." Celebration recognizes the strategic importance and history of women effecting social and economic change. For example, in 1988 the U.S.-based National Association of Women Business Owners (NABO) organized congressional hearings that led to the passing of the Women's Business Ownership Act. Today, NABO is planning a high-profile celebration on Capital Hill to recognize the thirty-year anniversary of the legislation. A fifty-year celebration (FastForward! 2038) is also being planned.
	"Velvet, silk and pearls, guerrilla infiltration tactics." Reflecting on her early years of advocacy, Virginia Littlejohn used this phrase to capture how teams of women worked to populate boards and agencies. They caucused on issues before and after meetings in order to move the women's economic agenda forward. Such discussions remained out of the purview of larger committee memberships. Most board members were not aware of a collective action by female members. The relevance of this strategy is dependent on the maturation of the country, sector, and so on in engaging women in all aspects of decision making.
	Build trust. Effecting change requires building trust and credibility among policymakers and all political parties. For example, WIPP members constantly brief political and policy stakeholders, an educational role that demands investment in time and that builds trust.

Source: Interviews with five "women-in-enterprise champions." Augmented with V. Littlejohn, *A Brief Overview of the Women's Entrepreneurial Movement in the United States*, OECD Conference on Women Entrepreneurs in Small and Medium Enterprises: A Major Force in Innovation and Job Creation, Paris, May 16–18, 1997.

conserve time and energy by ensuring that efforts are focused on decision makers. Seasoned political connections can also advise on the wording of briefs, in a language that resonates with political agendas and spending priorities.

To further set the stage, you will find a brief history of the development of the U.S. women's entrepreneurship policy framework posted on the book website. We posted this information to illustrate the impact of collective action by a relatively small group of dedicated people and to present a context to better understand why the United States has one of the most advanced entrepreneurship policy ecosystems in the world. Around the world, similar communities of women-in-business advocates are leading policy and program reform on behalf of others. If you aren't already, we encourage you to do the same. Your efforts can make a difference!

Never Underestimate
the Underestimated Woman

8

Feminine capital is changing the architecture of power around the world.[1] "Between 2002 and 2007, women's income (globally) increased by nearly $4 trillion to $9.8 trillion. By 2017, women's income will jump by almost $6 trillion to $15.6 trillion."[2] By 2028, it is expected that women will control close to 75 percent of discretionary spending worldwide.[3] Women's increasing wealth is helping to reduce poverty and improve health standards.[4] As the global economic bar moves upward, so does the educational attainment of girls and women.[5] The multiplier effects of entrepreneurship become evident. Women hire women, including other entrepreneurs.[6] And compared to men, women spend a greater percentage of their wealth on food, housing, and education for their children, raising their family's economic prospects.[7]

Connecting the Dots

What do these statistics mean for you? It is time to return to the questions posed in the introduction of this book. How does gender affect the way you do business? How has your perspective changed?

For many, being female is an inherent component of entrepreneurial identity: an asset for many, a liability for some. There are still many female business owners who perceive that they are not taken seriously. We believe that it is those who understand the nature and contributions of female entrepreneurs who will gain competitive advantage in the changing marketplace. To inform your decision making, throughout this book we offered new insights and showcased peer-reviewed studies about gender influences in venture creation processes. We dispelled misperceptions about resource acquisition and advanced practical tips to better manage all types of capital.

To illustrate how gender is infused in entrepreneurial endeavors, we advanced a gendered matrix of venture creation. Gender was depicted along a continuum of entrepreneurial processes and enterprise outcomes. The matrix positioned traditional indicators of enterprise performance, such as growth in revenue and profit, within a broader array of criteria that reflect holistic enterprise outcomes. Social and community welfare are not separate or distinct from economic vitality. A subset of entrepreneurs identified in the matrix we labeled feminist entrepreneurs: for women, by women business owners. Feminist entrepreneurs employ venture creation as a means to generate economic wealth and improve the quality of life and well-being of others, particularly girls and women.

Like the heroines described throughout this book, the nature of feminine capital varies. For many female business owners, relationships are based on trust, sense of community, and reciprocity. Results are achieved by inspiring and empowering others. Participative leadership reflects an ethic of care. Another lesson learned is that there is no best way to resource or grow an enterprise. As the case studies demonstrate, paths and outcomes of venture creation are rarely predictable.

Entrepreneurial Heroines

Today, Susan Ross generates a modest living as a self-employed professional, earning significantly less than her former corporate colleagues. Susan sees the decision as enabling her to better balance work and personal demands.

During her fifth year in business, a multinational rival filed a lawsuit for brand infringement against Asha Sing's enterprise. Prior to a legal decision being made, expenses led to the bankruptcy of her firm. Asha is not alone. Court harassment is an unscrupulous practice used by larger firms to deplete the resources of smaller competitors without the means to defend themselves in court. She is considering new opportunities.

Recall that Maria Guidi, the proprietor of a small construction firm, registered her firm with WEConnect International. The investment has paid off. Their online network provides Maria with access to corporations and business owners operating in over seventy countries. She looks forward to attending an affiliated annual conference, along with over three thousand women business owners and corporate representatives.[8]

Dr. Elaine Jolly's vision to build a women-centered health care facility met initially with little support from senior hospital administration. Through perseverance and visionary leadership, she managed to mobilize public support for the center. The Shirley E. Greenberg Women's Health Centre now provides exemplary, patient-focused services. A linchpin in ensuring that the project was successful was the establishment of an advisory council comprising influential patients and other women leaders. A large lead donation was critical in signaling the legitimacy of her vision.[9] Upon securing the resources needed to fund the facility and related infrastructure, operations were turned back to the central hospital administration. This was disappointing for many council members. The main concern was a lack of ongoing input by the women's community.

Professor Cynthia Goh continues to mentor academic entrepreneurs. She also leads a popular entrepreneurship course, having developed a suite of programs for budding entrepreneurs in the advanced technology sectors.[10] Within her workshops, Cynthia emphasizes that what is really required is an ability to work with a diverse team of experts. Technical credentials, such as an engineering, chemistry, or computer science degree, are not prerequisites to business ownership. "In some cases, entrepreneurs with management experience hire scientists and technicians to help create their firms' intellectual property. In other cases, engineers and scientists hire professional managers to lead their firms. Success rests on evidence of both technical and management skills."[11]

On the day of our last interview with Debra Moore, co-founder of Just Us! Coffee Roasters, she had just returned from the bargaining table. Recently, a group of workers in one of the coffee houses had petitioned for a union. The petition had generated considerable media attention. Debra viewed this development as an opportunity, one that would bring Just Us! values into union negotiations. "I am excited about being at the table. It is the chance to take the values of Just Us! into a new arena. The details may not be fun, but wow, this is what Just Us! set out to do. We are challenging the unions, as they have little experience with a worker co-op, but in many ways we are all on the same side of workers' rights. It has its challenges, as we are learning, but the process is strengthening Just Us! as well as the union."

When we last reached Janet Longmore, president of Digital Opportunities Trust, her email arrived from Uganda, where she was traveling enroute from Cairo, Lebanon, and Kenya. Her message moved us. "It is so rewarding to see the leadership of so many young women in the technology and entrepreneurship field across a variety of cultures and environments. As always, I am so impressed by the depth of their commitment to positive change, even in the complexities and challenges of environments like the communities of the Bekaa Valley who are so affected by the Syrian crisis. They are truly trailblazers." This response is another reminder of the power of entrepreneurship.

Julie Weeks, CEO of Womenable, continues to consult with governments, corporations, and multilateral agencies such as the International Trade Center (Geneva) and Inter-American Development Bank (Ecuador). "In conversation with colleagues, I hear a change in focus. Supporting women's enterprise growth is a priority. I am working with governments, developing strategies to assist women in internationalizing their firms, tapping supply chains, and selling services to multinationals." Womenable is also under contract with several South American banks. "We are reviewing lending data to understand gender differences in access to and utilization of capital. This is a departure from first-wave policies that sought to stimulate startups and legitimize entrepreneurship as a career option for women. Where policy was once seen as a means to promote social equality, many see the economic value of doing business with women. There are other catalysts. Governments and corporations are asking why there remains a gender gap, reflected in firm size. More and more women also want to move up the growth continuum. Many have been in business for some time."

Closing the Gap Between Entrepreneurship and Feminism

In our interviews with community advocates and thousands of women business owners, we also learned that not everyone thinks women's economic self-sufficiency is worthy of celebration. The potential for misunderstanding is high. Rather than viewing wealth as a means to effect change and enable others, for some financial success is viewed with suspicion. We heard reservation in refrains from others, such as

- "Successful women pull up the ladder on the way to the top."
- "Queen bees don't help others."
- "Small-business owners seek to suppress wage rates."
- "These women just want to make money."

It is important to probe such suspicions. Advocates and entrepreneurs should not be estranged. These change agents have much in common. Two women-in-enterprise champions explain why. In the words of Professor Patricia Greene, Babson professor and academic director of Goldman Sachs Foundation's 10,000 Small Businesses Initiative, "Entrepreneurship focuses on breaking down issues and looking at equality of opportunities and equality in accessing resources. Entrepreneurship tells us that there are different ways to solve problems. Every feminist asks, 'What value am I trying to create, what is the change?'" Marsha Firestone, founding president of Women Presidents' Organization, also believes that entrepreneurship is the great equalizer for women. "Business ownership is a place where women can have more power and more influence. Women can control their time working when they want and need to. Women entrepreneurs have more control. What feminism can learn is that there are many ways to achieve goals and there are many approaches. There are many different doors that provide women with access to economic opportunities. Those doors can be opened using a variety of approaches." The challenge is to find common ground and then to leverage women's entrepreneurial competencies in social, financial, and political spheres.

Table 8.1 presents a summary of strategies to support women's entrepreneurship.

Table 8.1: Strategies to support women's entrepreneurship

Training	☑	Business readiness: create opportunities for women to objectively assess their startup ideas, including increased provision of pre- and post-startup support.
	☑	Female-focused entrepreneurship curriculum, including female role models and confidence building to enhance entrepreneurial self-efficacy. Women also need increased access to technical, entrepreneurial, and managerial courses.
	☑	Peer-to-peer learning: Construct and facilitate group-learning environments that enable women to learn from other women.
Culture	☑	Promote entrepreneurship as a viable career option for women.
	☑	Increase media visibility and positive messaging about women entrepreneurs. Focus should be more than "mompreneurs" (for example, showcase women in export, born global enterprises, innovative financing).
	☑	Host regional and national recognition and awards programs.
	☑	Ensure that women are included in business hall of fame awards.
Information	☑	Disseminate information about successful women business owners at conferences and conventions. Support web-based information, virtual networks, webinars, TED-talks, and so on.
	☑	Establish women in enterprise research centers that inform evidence-based policies and practices.
	☑	Increase the quality and availability of gender-disaggregated data. Mandate reporting about the users (recipients) of publicly funded small-business training programs, business development grants, innovation investment funds, loan-guarantee schemes, and so on.
Capital	☑	Increase access to microloans (debt), equity, leases, and supplier credit.
	☑	Promote female-targeted equity investment funds.
	☑	Set clear terms of lending such as the cost of loan applications, interest, and other repayment expenses.
	☑	Construct and report on nonsexist loan application scoring criteria.
	☑	Financial literacy: Gender-sensitive training should include self-assessment of entrepreneurial self-efficacy. Other topics could include understanding the language of finance and the importance of female role models, coaches, and mentors.
Public Support	☑	Similar to the United States, governments should legislate opportunities for women business owners to advise on national economic policies and activities. Financial support is needed to establish and sustain women in enterprise centers, and to support women business-owner associations, sector associations, and networks.
	☑	Set targets to ensure the engagement of women within all economic development services (for example, boards of institutions such as banks, agencies, and related programs). Conduct proactive recruitment for female entrepreneurs on the women's committees within boards of trade and chambers of commerce).
Access to Markets	☑	Mandate public supplier diversity or procurement initiatives, particularly targeted at the service sectors.
	☑	Offer gender-sensitive market (export) development training (for example, women's trade missions, support of the Organization of Women in Trade).
Family	☑	Provide affordable day care.
	☑	Provide family (maternity, paternity) benefits for self-employed workers.

Feminism has come full circle. As calls for the advancement of women in corporations go unheeded, ambitious and talented women will deploy their wisdom and skills through entrepreneurial ventures. Some bring feminist ideals on their journey. Women entrepreneurs are teaching feminist scholars and advocates about how to get things done. In the words of Virginia Littlejohn, founder and CEO of Quantum Leaps, "New definitions and perspectives are needed to describe the global change that entrepreneurship brings to feminism." Feminine capital is one such definition.

Strategies to Propel Women's Entrepreneurship

Successful women business owners are not entrepreneurial at birth. More support is needed. International and national communities are working hard to increase access to resources by influencing policymakers. Taskforce reports and "roadmaps" document the momentum and need for change.[12] The underlying message is that investment in women's enterprise bolsters prosperity. Female-owned businesses constitute an underutilized resource, one to be supported for employment creation and economic growth.

Only when governments, at all levels, recognize the need to integrate the needs of women within mainstream entrepreneurship policy will their full contributions be realized. We are not there. It is perplexing that in many developed economies, politicians are more likely to support sex- and gender-based analysis via international development agencies than within domestic economic policy. To test this assertion, compare the messages, photos, and program links posted on the websites of your own country's international development agency to those displayed by domestic industry or economic agencies (for example, USAID; U.K. Department for International Development; Foreign Affairs, Trade and Development Canada). Chances are high that girls and women will be far more prominent on the international development agency home page. Photos of technology will likely dominate the latter. More female-focused policies and programs are also needed.

This book scratches the surface of feminine capital. It is our hope that you leave this book with a sense of what it is; and how powerful it can be for female-led firms, and for economies the world over. We encourage you to revisit your written reflections from the introductory chapter to assess how gender influences your business practices and the venture creation process. It is left to you, the reader, to challenge our ideas, to define feminine capital, and then put your thoughts into action.

Notes

Introduction

1. Global Entrepreneurship Research Association, *Global Entrepreneurship Monitor 2012 Women's Report*, accessed at http://www.gemconsortium.org; P. Reynolds, "Entrepreneurship in Development Economies: The Bottom Billions and Business Creation," *Foundations and Trends in Entrepreneurship* 893 (2012): 141–277.

2. M. L. Chang, *Shortchanged: Why Women Have Less Wealth and What Can Be Done About It* (New York: Oxford University Press, 2010), 2.

3. Centre for Women's Business Research, "The Economic Impact of Women-Owned Businesses in the United States," accessed at http://www.nwbc.gov/sites/default/files/economic impactstu.pdf.

4. Information about the "Women of Wolfville" theater group can be accessed at http://www.womenofwolfville.ca.

5. H. Ahl, "Why Research on Women Needs New Directions," *Entrepreneurship Theory and Practice* 30, no. 5 (September 2006): 595–621.

6. L. Warren, "Negotiating Entrepreneurial Identity: Communities of Practice and Changing Discourses," *International Journal of Entrepreneurship and Innovation* 5, no. 1 (2004): 25–35.

7. H. Florén, "Collaborative Approaches to Management Learning in Small Firms," *Journal of Workplace Learning* 15, no. 5 (2003): 203–216.

Chapter 1

1. C. G. Brush and others, "The Diana Project: Women Business Owners & Equity Capital—The Myths Dispelled," *Venture Capital Review* Summer, no. 10 (2002): 30–40; N. F. Krueger and A. L. Carsrud, "Entrepreneurial Intentions: Applying the Theory of Planned Behaviour," *Entrepreneurship & Regional Development* 5, no. 4 (1993): 315–330.

2. V. Gupta and others, "The Role of Gender Stereotypes in Perceptions of Entrepreneurs and Intentions to Become an Entrepreneur," *Entrepreneurship Theory and Practice* 33, no. 20 (2009): 397–417.

3. A. Smith, *An Inquiry into the Nature and Causes of the Wealth of Nations* (London: Methuen, 1904).

4. J. S. Mill, "On the Definition of Political Economy, and On the Method of Investigation Proper to It," in *Essays on Some Unsettled Questions of Political Economy*, 2nd ed., Essay V (London: Longmans, Green, Reader & Dyer, 1874); R. Buchholz and S. Rosenthal,

"Toward a Contemporary Conceptual Framework for Stakeholder Theory," *Journal of Business Ethics* 58 (2005): 137–148; L. Dunham, "From Rational to Wise Action: Recasting Our Theories of Entrepreneurship," *Journal of Business Ethics* 92 (2010): 513–530.

5. Buchholz and Rosenthal, "Toward a Contemporary Conceptual Framework for Stakeholder Theory"; Dunham, "From Rational to Wise Action"; Mill, "On the Definition of Political Economy."

6. J. A. Schumpeter, *The Theory of Economic Development: An Inquiry into Profits, Capital, Credit, Interest, and the Business Cycle* (New York: Oxford University Press, 1961).

7. Ibid.

8. R. H. Brockhaus, "Risk Taking Propensity of Entrepreneurs," *Academy of Management Journal* 23, no. 3 (1980): 509–520.

9. G. T. Lumpkin and Gregory G. Dess, "Clarifying the Entrepreneurial Orientation Construct and Linking It to Performance," *Academy of Management Review* 21, no. 1 (1996): 135–172.

10. S. Nadin, "Entrepreneurial Identity in the Care Sector: Navigating the Contradictions," *Women in Management Review* 22, no. 6 (2007): 456–467.

11. M. P. Follett, *Creative Experience*, reprint 1951 ed. (New York: Peter Smith, 1924); M. P. Follett, *Dynamic Administration*, reprint 1942 ed. (New York: Harper & Brothers, 1927).

12. B. Friedan, *The Feminine Mystique* (New York: W. W. Norton, 1963).

13. E. Chell and S. Baines, "Does Gender Affect Business 'Performance'? A Study of Microbusinesses in Business Services in the UK," *Entrepreneurship and Regional Development* 10, no. 2 (1998): 117–135.

14. Mill, "On the Definition of Political Economy"; M. Belenky and others, *Women's Ways of Knowing: The Development of Self, Voice, and Mind* (New York: Basic Books, 1986).

15. C. G. Brush, "Research on Women Business Owners: Past Trends, a New Perspective and Future Directions," *Entrepreneurship, Theory and Practice* 16, no. 4 (1992): 5–30.

16. S. L. Bem, "The Measurement of Psychological Androgyny," *Journal of Consulting and Clinical Psychology* 42, no. 2 (1974): 155–162. The purpose of the Bem Sex Role Inventory was to investigate socially "desirable behavior for men and women." As Bem noted, "The BSRI was founded on a conception of the sex-typed person as someone who has internalized society's sex-typed standards of desirable behaviour for men and women; these characteristics were selected as masculine or feminine on the basis of sex-typed social desirability and not on the basis of differential endorsement by males and females as most other inventories have done" (p. 155).

17. V. E. Schein, "The Relationship Between Sex Role Stereotypes and Requisite Management Characteristics," *Journal of Applied Psychology* 57, no. 2 (1973): 95–100; V. E. Schein, "Relationships Between Sex Role Stereotypes and Requisite Management Characteristics Among Female Managers," *Journal of Applied Psychology* 60, no. 3 (1975): 340–344.

18. V. Gupta and C. Fernandez, "Cross-Cultural Similarities and Differences in Characteristics Attributed to Entrepreneurs," *Journal of Leadership & Organizational Studies* 15, no. 3 (2009): 304–318. Also see V. Gupta, D. Turban, S. A. Wasti, and A. Sikdar, "The Role of Gender Stereotypes in Perceptions of Entrepreneurs and Intentions to Become an Entrepreneur," *Entrepreneurship Theory and Practice* 33, no. 20 (2009): 397–417.

19. A. Du Rietz and M. Henrekson, "Testing the Female Underperformance Hypothesis," *Small Business Economics* 14, no. 1 (2000): 1–10. Also see P. Rosa, S. Carter, and D. Ham-

ilton, "Gender as a Determinant of Small Business Performance: Insights from a British Study," *Small Business Economics* 8, no. 6 (1996): 463–478.

20. S. M. Yohn, "Crippled Capitalists: The Inscription of Economic Dependence and the Challenge of Female Entrepreneurship in Nineteenth-Century America," *Feminist Economics* 12, no. 1–2 (2006): 85–109.

21. E. Bardasi, S. Sabarwal, and K. Terrell, "How Do Female Entrepreneurs Perform? Evidence from Three Developing Regions," *Small Business Economics* 37, no. 4 (2011): 417–441.

22. Du Rietz and Henrekson, "Testing the Female Underperformance Hypothesis."

23. L. Stevenson, "Some Methodological Problems Associated with Researching Women Entrepreneurs," *Journal of Business Ethics* 9, no. 4–5 (1990): 439–446.

24. R. Reuber and E. Fischer, "Reconceptualizing Entrepreneurs' Experience," presentation to the Academy of Management, Vancouver, May 1995. Also see E. Fischer, R. Reuber, and L. Dyke, "A Theoretical Overview and Extension of Research on Sex, Gender, and Entrepreneurship," *Journal of Business Venturing* 8, no. 2 (1993): 151–168.

25. K. Mirchandani, "Feminist Insight on Gendered Work: New Directions in Research on Women and Entrepreneurship," *Gender, Work and Organization* 6, no. 4 (1999): 224–235.

26. Fischer, Reuber, and Dyke, "A Theoretical Overview." An important contribution of feminist scholars, such as Fischer, Reuber and Dyke, to entrepreneurial research is the challenge to be ever mindful of research techniques (such as gathering information, data interpretation) and researcher bias, including which topics pass as being of scientific merit or legitimacy. This includes preconceptions about the value of comparing female against male experiences.

27. H. Ahl, *The Scientific Reproduction of Gender Inequality* (Copenhagen: CBS Press, 2004).

28. Ibid.

29. M. Wollstonecraft, *A Vindication of the Rights of Women* (Boston: Peter Edes for Thomas and Andrews, 1792); J. S. Mill, *The Subjection of Women* (New York: A. Keley, [1829] 1967).

30. A. L. Kalleberg and K. T. Leicht, "Gender and Organizational Performance: Determinants of Small Business Survival and Success," *Academy of Management Journal* 34, no. 1 (1991): 136–161; J. Watson, "Comparing the Performance of Male- and Female-Controlled Businesses: Relating Outputs to Inputs," *Entrepreneurship Theory and Practice* 26, no. 3 (Spring 2002): 91–100; J. Watson and S. Robinson, "Adjusting for Risk in Comparing the Performances of Male- and Female-Controlled SMEs," *Journal of Business Venturing* 18, no. 6 (2003): 773–778.

31. Fischer, Reuber, and Dyke, "A Theoretical Overview."

32. A. Ellis, D. Kirkwood, and D. Malhotra, *Economic Opportunities for Women in the East Asia and Pacific Region* (Washington, DC: World Bank, 2010).

33. D. Kelley and others, *Global Entrepreneurship Monitor Report: Women Entrepreneurs Worldwide. Executive Report* (Babson Park, MA: Babson College, 2010).

Chapter 2

1. For foundational works about the antecedents of intention, see I. Ajzen and M. Fishbein, "Understanding Attitudes and Predicting Social Behaviour," *Journal of Experimental Social Psychology* 5 (1990): 400–416; N. F. Krueger and A. L. Carsrud, "Entrepreneurial In-

tentions: Applying the Theory of Planned Behaviour," *Entrepreneurship & Regional Development* 5, no. 4 (1993): 315–330.

2. K. Deaux and B. Major, "Putting Gender into Context: An Interactive Model of Gender-Related Behavior," *Psychological Review* 94, no. 3 (1987): 369–389.

3. B. J. Orser and L. Dyke, "The Influence of Gender and Occupational-Role on Entrepreneurs' and Corporate Managers' Success Criteria," *Journal of Small Business and Entrepreneurship* 22, no. 3 (2009): 275–301.

4. S. Down and L. Warren, "Constructing Narratives of Enterprise: Clichés and Entrepreneurial Identity," *International Journal of Entrepreneurial Behaviour and Research* 14, no. 1 (2008): 4–23.

5. Down and Warren, "Constructing Narratives of Enterprise"; M. Cardon and others, "The Nature and Experience of Entrepreneurial Passion," *Academy of Management Review* 34, no. 3 (2009): 511–532.

6. K. Mirchandani, "Feminist Insight on Gendered Work: New Directions in Research on Women and Entrepreneurship," *Gender, Work and Organization* 6, no. 4 (1999): 224–235.

7. I. Verheul, L. Uhlaner, and R. Thurik, "Business Accomplishments, Gender and Entrepreneurial Self-Image," *Journal of Business Venturing* 20 (2005): 483–518.

8. B. J. Orser and S. Hogarth-Scott, "Opting for Growth: Gender Dimensions of Choosing Enterprise Development," *Canadian Journal of Administrative Sciences* 19, no. 3 (2002): 284–300; M. Morris and others, "The Dilemma of Growth: Understanding Venture Size Choices of Women Entrepreneurs," *Journal of Small Business Management* 44, no. 2 (2006): 221–244.

9. G. A. Akerlof and R. E. Kranton, "Economics and Identity," *The Quarterly Journal of Economics* 115, no. 3 (2000): 715–753.

10. Orser and Dyke, "The Influence of Gender and Occupational-Role"; R. Jones, J. Latham, and M. Betta, "Narrative Construction of the Social Entrepreneurial Identity," *International Journal of Entrepreneurial Behaviour & Research* 14, no. 5 (2008): 330–345.

11. B. J. Orser, C. Elliott, and S. Findlay-Thompson, "Women-Focused Small Business Programming: Client Motives and Perspectives," *International Journal of Gender and Entrepreneurship* 4, no. 3 (2012): 236–265; B. J. Orser, C. Elliott, and J.D. Leck, "Feminist Attributes and Entrepreneurial Identity," *Gender in Management* 26, no. 8 (2011): 561–589; A. Werner, "The Influence of Christian Identity of SME Owner-Managers' Conceptualisations of Business Practice," *Journal of Business Ethics* 82 (2008): 449–462; B. J. Orser, A. L. Riding, and J. Stanley, "Women in Advanced Technology: Examining the Influence of Role Orientation and Firm Structure on Perceived Gender Challenges," *Entrepreneurship & Regional Development* 24, no. 1 (2011): 1–22.

12. Orser, Elliott, and Leck, "Feminist Attributes and Entrepreneurial Identity."

13. S. L. Bem, "The Measurement of Psychological Androgyny," *Journal of Consulting and Clinical Psychology* 42, no. 2 (1974): 155–162. Also see V. E. Schein, "Relationships Between Sex Role Stereotypes and Requisite Management Characteristics Among Female Managers," *Journal of Applied Psychology* 60, no. 3 (1975): 340–344; V. E. Schein, "The Relationship Between Sex Role Stereotypes and Requisite Management Characteristics," *Journal of Applied Psychology* 57, no. 2 (1973): 95–100.

14. Down and Warren, "Constructing Narratives of Enterprise"; C. Essers and Y. Benschop, "Muslim Businesswomen Doing Boundary Work: The Negotiation of Islam, Gender and Ethnicity Within Entrepreneurial Contexts," *Human Relations* 62 (2009): 403–423.

15. S. Nadin, "Entrepreneurial Identity in the Care Sector: Navigating the Contradictions," *Women in Management Review* 22, no. 6 (2007): 456–467.

16. A. Xia and B. H. Kleiner, "Discrimination in the Computer Industry," *Equal Opportunities International* 20, no. 5/6/7 (2001): 117–120.

17. V. Gupta and C. Fernandez, "Cross-Cultural Similarities and Differences in Characteristics Attributed to Entrepreneurs," *Journal of Leadership & Organizational Studies* 15, no. 3 (2009): 304–318. Also see V. Gupta and others, "The Role of Gender Stereotypes in Perceptions of Entrepreneurs and Intentions to Become an Entrepreneur," *Entrepreneurship Theory and Practice* 33, no. 20 (2009): 397–417. It is notable that both studies employ dated diagnostics that were constructed in the 1970s and 1980s.

18. Verheul, Uhlaner, and Thurik, "Business Accomplishments, Gender and Entrepreneurial Self-Image"; E. Fagenson and E. Marcus, "Perceptions of the Sex-Role Stereotypic Characteristics of Entrepreneurs: Women's Evaluations," *Entrepreneurship, Theory & Practice* 15, no. 4 (1991): 33–47; Orser, Riding, and Stanley, "Women in Advanced Technology"; C. Simard and others, *Climbing the Technical Ladder: Obstacles and Solutions for Mid-Level Women in Technology* (Boulder: National Center for Women and Information Technology, University of Colorado, 2008).

19. Prowess, *Under the Microscope: Female Entrepreneurs in SECT: Science, Engineering, Construction and Technology*, (2008). See www.prowess.org.uk.

20. H. Ahl, *The Scientific Reproduction of Gender Inequality* (Copenhagen: CBS Press, 2004); Essers and Benschop, "Muslim Businesswomen Doing Boundary Work."

21. A. Bruni, S. Gherardi, and B. Poggio, "Entrepreneur-Mentality, Gender and the Study of Women Entrepreneurs," *Journal of Organizational Change Management* 17, no. 3 (2004): 256–268.

22. Down and Warren, "Constructing Narratives of Enterprise."

23. The three entrepreneurial identity categories of "founder," "inventor," and "developer" are drawn from M. S. Cardon, J. Wincent, J. Singhe, and M. Drnovsek, "The Nature and Experience of Entrepreneurial Passion," *Academy of Management Review* 34, no. 3 (2009): 511–532 and M. Cardon and others, "A Tale of Passion: New Insights into Entrepreneurship from a Parenthood Metaphor," *Journal of Business Venturing* 20, no. 1 (2005).

24. Down and Warren, "Constructing Narratives of Enterprise."

25. M. Cardon and others, "A Tale of Passion"; Essers and Benschop, "Muslim Businesswomen Doing Boundary Work."

26. T. Fenwick and S. Hutton, "Women Crafting New Work: The Learning of Women Entrepreneurs," paper presented at the Annual Adult Education and Research Conference, University of British Columbia, Vancouver, June 2000; C. Ridgeway, "Linking Social Structure and Interpersonal Behavior: A Theoretical Perspective on Cultural Schemas and Social Relations," *Social Psychological Quarterly* 69, no. 1 (2006): 5–16; Bruni, Gherardi, and Poggio, "Entrepreneur-Mentality, Gender and the Study of Women Entrepreneurs."

27. D. McClelland, *The Achieving Society* (Princeton, NJ: D. Van Nostrand, 1961).

28. Down and Warren, "Constructing Narratives of Enterprise."

29. P. Kyro, "Women Entrepreneurs Question Men's Criteria for Success: Proceedings of the 2001 Entrepreneurship Research Conference and *Frontiers of Entrepreneurship Research 2001 Edition*" (Babson Park, MA: Babson College, 2001); M. d'Arleux, "Success as a Psychological and Social Construct: The Influence of the Entrepreneur's Nature on His/Her

Conceptions of Success, Babson College," *Frontiers of Entrepreneurship Research 1998 Edition* (Babson Park, MA: Babson College, 1998); B. Parker and L. Chusmir, "A Comparison of Men and Women Managers' and Nonmanagers' Perceptions of Success," *Human Resource Development Quarterly* 3, no. 1 (Spring 1992): 73–84; D. M. Ray and D. V. Trupin, "Crossnational Comparison of Entrepreneurs' Perceptions of Success," *Entrepreneurship & Regional Development* 1, no. 1 (1989): 113–127; M. Ruderman and others, "How Managers View Success," *Leadership in Action* 18, no. 6 (Spring 1999): 6–10.

30. R. Chaganti, "Management in Women-Owned Enterprises," *Journal of Small Business Management* 24, no. 4 (1986): 18–29; H. E. Buttner, "Examining Female Entrepreneurs' Management Style: An Application of a Relational Frame," *Journal of Business Ethics* 29 (2001): 253–269; S. Helgeson, *The Female Advantage: Women's Ways of Leading* (New York: Doubleday, 1990).

31. S. M. Yohn, "Crippled Capitalists: The Inscription of Economic Dependence and the Challenge of Female Entrepreneurship in Nineteenth-Century America," *Feminist Economics* 12, no. 1–2 (2006): 85–109.

32. Mirchandani, "Feminist Insight on Gendered Work."

33. S. Sandberg, *Lean In: Women, Work, and the Will to Lead* (New York: Alfred A. Knopf, 2013).

34. B. J. Orser, C. Elliott, and J. Leck, "Entrepreneurial Feminists: Perspectives About Opportunity Recognition and Governance," *Journal of Business Ethics* 109, no. 3 (2012).

35. A. L. Kalleberg and K. T. Leicht, "Gender and Organizational Performance: Determinants of Small Business Survival and Success," *Academy of Management Journal* 34, no. 1 (1991): 136–161; S. E. Abraham and others, "Managerial Competencies and the Managerial Performance Appraisal Process," *Journal of Management Development* 20, no. 10 (2001): 842–852.

36. Ray and Trupin, "Crossnational Comparison of Entrepreneurs' Perceptions of Success"; J. Sturges, "What It Means to Succeed: Personal Conceptions of Career Success Held by Male and Female Managers at Different Ages," *British Journal of Management* 10, no. 3 (1999): 239–252; E. Fagenson, "Personal Value Systems of Men and Women Entrepreneurs Versus Managers," *Journal of Business Venturing* 8 (1993): 409–430; L. W. Fernald and G. T. Solomon, "Value Profiles of Male and Female Entrepreneurs," *Journal of Creative Behaviour* 21, no. 3 (1987): 234–247.

37. Orser and Hogarth-Scott, "Opting for Growth."

38. B. J. Orser, "Understanding the Influence of Intention, Managerial Capacity and Gender on Small Firm Growth," PhD. diss., Bradford University School of Management, 1997.

39. G. N. Powell and K. A. Eddleston, "The Paradox of the Contented Female Business Owner," *Journal of Vocational Behavior* 73, no. 1 (2008): 24–36.

40. P. Lovett-Reid and D. Green, *Surprise! You're Wealthy: A Woman's Guide to Protecting Her Wealth* (Toronto: Key Porter, 2002); H. Lee-Gosselin and J. Grise, "Are Women Owner-Managers Challenging Our Entrepreneurship?" *Journal of Business Ethics* 9 (1990): 423–433; Kyro, "Women Entrepreneurs Question Men's Criteria for Success."

41. Powell and Eddleston, "The Paradox of the Contented Female Business Owner"; J. Acker, "The Gender Regime of Swedish Banks," *Scandinavian Journal of Management* 10 (1994): 117–130.

42. Orser and Dyke, "The Influence of Gender and Occupational-Role."

43. Orser, "Understanding the Influence of Intention."

44. S. G. Walter, K. P. Parboteeah, and A. Walter, "University Departments and Self-Employment Intentions of Business Students: A Cross-Level Analysis," *Entrepreneurship Theory and Practice* 37, no. 2 (2013): 175–200.

Chapter 3

1. P. Drucker, *Innovation and Entrepreneurship: Practice and Principles* (New York: Harper Row, 1985).

2. C. Henry and K. Johnston, "Introduction," in *Female Entrepreneurship: Implications for Education, Training and Policy: Routledge Advances in Management and Business Studies*, ed. N. M. Carter, C. Henry, B. O. Cinnéide and K. Johnston (London: Routledge, Taylor & Francis Group, 2006), 1–7.

3. D. A. Shepherd and D. R. DeTienne, "Prior Knowledge, Potential Financial Reward and Opportunity Identification," *Entrepreneurship Theory and Practice* 29, no. 1 (2005): 91–112.

4. F. Warner, *Power of the Purse: How Smart Businesses Are Adapting to the World's Most Important Consumers* (New Jersey: Prentice-Hall, 2006).

5. S. Alvarez, J. Barney, and S. Young, "Debates in Entrepreneurship: Opportunity Formation and Implications for the Field of Entrepreneurship," in *Handbook of Entrepreneurship Research, International Handbook Series on Entrepreneurship*, ed. Z. J. Acs and D. B. Audretsch (New York: Springer Science + Business Media (2010): p. 25.

6. L. Mosek, M. Gillin, and L. Katzenstein, "Evaluating the Tension Within a Not-for-Profit Organization, When Developing a Business Model for the Maintenance of a Sustainable Profitable Business Venture," *2008 Regional Frontiers of Entrepreneurship Research*, Australian Graduate School of Entrepreneurship, Swinburne University of Technology, Melbourne, Australia, February 5–8, 2008, 501–516.

7. B. Løwendahl, *Strategic Management of Professional Service Firms*, 3rd ed. (Copenhagen: Copenhagen Business School Press, 2005).

8. H. Westlund and R. Bolton, "Local Social Capital and Entrepreneurship," *Small Business Economics* 21, no. 2 (2003): 77–112.

9. E. Fischer and R. Reuber, "The Good, the Bad, and the Unfamiliar: The Challenges of Reputation Formation Facing New Firms," *Entrepreneurship Theory and Practice* 31, no. 1 (2007): 53–75.

10. R. D. Putnam, *Bowling Alone: The Collapse and Revival of American Community* (New York: Simon & Schuster, 2000).

11. To locate sample "business plan" templates, search the U.S. Small Business Administration, U.K. Department of Industry and Trade, or Industry Canada websites.

12. B. J. Orser, C. Elliott, and J. Leck, "Entrepreneurial Feminists: Perspectives About Opportunity Recognition and Governance," *Journal of Business Ethics* 109, no. 3 (2012).

13. B. J. Orser, M. Cedzynski, and R. Thomas, "Modelling Owner Experience: Linking Theory and Practice," *Journal of Small Business and Entrepreneurship* 20, no. 4 (2007).

14. B. Aliouat, C. Camion, and Y. Gasse, "Managerial Practices and Core Competencies of Entrepreneurs: A Contingency Framework of Performance," *Frontiers of Entrepreneurship*, (Babson Park, MA: Babson College, 1999); Watson Wyatt, *The Human Capital Index: Linking Human Capital and Shareholder Value: Summary Report* (New York: Watson Wyatt World-

wide, 2000); R. Cressy, *Staying with It: Some Fundamental Determinants of Business Startup Longevity*, Working Paper no. 17 (Warwick, England: Warwick Business School, Small and Medium Enterprise Centre, 1994).

15. A. Bandura, *Social Foundations of Thought and Action: A Social Cognitive Theory* (Englewood Cliffs, NJ: Prentice-Hall, 1986).

16. A. L. Anna, G. N. Chandler, E. Jansen, and N. P. Mero, "Women Business Owners in Traditional and Non-Traditional Industries," *Journal of Business Venturing* 15, no. 3 (2000): 279–303.

17. J. E. Jennings and C. G. Brush, "Research on Women Entrepreneurs: Challenges to (and from) the Broader Entrepreneurship Literature?" *The Academy of Management Annals* 7, no. 1 (2013): 663–715.

18. W. Cukier, *Attracting, Retaining and Promoting Women: Best Practices in the Canadian Tech Sector* (Ottawa: Canadian Advanced Technology Alliance, 2009). Also see W. Cukier, *Developing Tomorrow's Workforce Today*, paper prepared on behalf of the Information and Communications Technology Council (2007), Accessed at http://www.ryerson.ca/tedrogersschool/diversityinstitute/news/Diversity-The-Competitive-Edge.pdf; B. J. Orser, A. L. Riding, and J. Stanley, "Women in Advanced Technology: Examining the Influence of Role Orientation and Firm Structure on Perceived Gender Challenges," *Entrepreneurship & Regional Development* 24, no. 1 (2011): 1–22.

19. S. G. Peitchinis, *Women at Work: Discrimination and Response* (Toronto: McClelland & Stewart, 1989); B. R. Bergmann, *The Economic Emergence of Women* (New York: Basic Books, 1986); B. J. Orser, "Growth Strategies of Women Entrepreneurs in Technology-Based Firms," in *Female Entrepreneurship and the New Venture Creation: An International Overview*, ed. D. Kariv (London: Routledge, 2013), 504–518.

20. A. de Koning and D. F. Muzyka, *Conceptualizing Opportunity Recognition as a Socio-Cognitive Process* (Stockholm: Centre for Advanced Leadership, 1999). Also see A. de Koning, "Strategy & Entrepreneurship Dissertation: Opportunity Development as a Socio-Cognitive Process: The Case of Serial Entrepreneurs," Ph.D. diss., INSEAD, June 1999.

21. S. Sarasvathy, "Causation and Effectuation: Towards a Theoretical Shift from Economic Inevitability to Entrepreneurial Contingency," *Academy of Management Review* 26, no. 2 (2001): 243–263.

22. Ibid. In describing the work of Saras Sarasvathy, Alvarez and others (2010, p. 28) write that the effectuation process is rooted in a *constructionist perspective* of entrepreneurship, in which opportunities emerge from induction, interactions, and interpretations of people, and in which "knowledge may be constructed by individuals but it is validated through social cross-validation."

23. J. T. Perry, G. N. Chandler, and G. Markova, "Entrepreneurial Effectuation: A Review and Suggestions for Future Research," *Entrepreneurship Theory and Practice* 36, no. 4 (2012): 837–861.

24. To learn more about the effectuation process, visit Society for Effectual Action at http://effectuation.org.

25. Sarasvathy, "Causation and Effectuation."

26. J. Florin and E. Schmidt, "Creating Shared Value in the Hybrid Venture Arena: A Business Model Innovation Perspective," *Journal of Social Entrepreneurship* 2, no. 2 (2011): 165–197.

27. L. Dunham, "From Rational to Wise Action: Recasting Our Theories of Entrepreneurship," *Journal of Business Ethics* 92, (2010): 513–530.

28. R. Buchholz and S. Rosenthal, "Toward a Contemporary Conceptual Framework for Stakeholder Theory," *Journal of Business Ethics* 58, (2005): 137–148.

29. G. Surie and A. Ashley, "Integrating Pragmatism and Ethics in Entrepreneurial Leadership for Sustainable Value Creation," *Journal of Business Ethics* 81, (2008): 235–246.

30. Florin and Schmidt, "Creating Shared Value."

31. S. Read, M. Song, and W. Smit, "A Meta-Analytic Review of Effectuation and Venture Performance," *Journal of Business Venturing* 24, no. 6 (2009): 573–587.

32. Ibid.

33. S. L. Koen, "Feminist Workplaces: Alternative Models for the Organization of Work," Ph.D. diss., The Union for Experimenting Colleges and Universities, 1985.

34. Learning Aid 3.3 draws on the work of Malte Brettel, René Mauer, Andreas Engelen, and Daniel Küpper, who present a multifactor measurement model of effectuation and causation. See M. Brettel, R. Mauer, A. Engelen, and D. Küpper, "Corporate Effectuation: Entrepreneurial Action and Its Impact on R&D Project Performance," *Journal of Business Venturing* 27, no. 2 (2012): 167–184.

35. H. E. Aldrich and J. E. Cliff, "The Pervasive Effects of Family on Entrepreneurship: Toward a Family Embeddedness Perspective," *Journal of Business Venturing: The Evolving Family / Entrepreneurship Business Relationship* 18, no. 5 (2003): 573–596.

36. C. G. Brush, "Research on Women Business Owners: Past Trends, a New Perspective and Future Directions," *Entrepreneurship, Theory and Practice* 16, no. 4 (1992): 5–30.

37. D. Cetindamar, V. K. Gupta, E. E. Karadeniz, and N. Egrican, "What the Numbers Tell: The Impact of Human, Family and Financial Capital on Women and Men's Entry into Entrepreneurship in Turkey," *Entrepreneurship & Regional Development* 24, no. 1–2 (January 2012): 36.

38. G. N. Powell and K. A. Eddleston, "Linking Family-to-Business Enrichment and Support to Entrepreneurial Success: Do Female and Male Entrepreneurs Experience Different Outcomes?" *Journal of Business Venturing* 28, no. 2 (2013): 261–280.

39. P. McGowan, C. L. Redeker, S. Y. Cooper, and K. Greenan, "Female Entrepreneurship and the Management of Business and Domestic Roles: Motivations, Expectations and Realities," *Entrepreneurship & Regional Development* 24, no. 1–2 (2012): 53–72.

40. B. J. Orser and S. Hogarth-Scott, "Opting for Growth: Gender Dimensions of Choosing Enterprise Development," *Canadian Journal of Administrative Sciences* 19, no. 3 (September 2002): 284–300.

41. Aldrich and Cliff, "The Pervasive Effects of Family on Entrepreneurship."

42. J. E. Jennings, K. Hughes, and P. D. Jennings, "The Work-Family Interface Strategies of Male and Female Entrepreneurs: Are There Any Differences?" in *Women Entrepreneurs and the Global Environment for Growth*, ed. C. G. Brush, A. de Bruin, E. J. Gatewood and C. Henry(Cheltenham, UK: Edward Elgar, 2010), 163–186.

43. T. Fenwick and S. Hutton, "Women Crafting New Work: The Learning of Women Entrepreneurs," paper presented at the Annual Adult Education and Research Conference, University of British Columbia, Vancouver, June 2000).

44. McGowan, Redeker, Cooper, and Greenan, "Female Entrepreneurship."

45. Adapted from McGowan, Redeker, Cooper, and Greenan, "Female Entrepreneurship." Illustrative quotations are from pages 64–67.

46. Cetindamar, Gupta, Karadeniz, and Egrican, "What the Numbers Tell," 29–51.

47. Ibid.

48. England and McCreary cited in Orser and Hogarth-Scott, "Opting for Growth," p. 143.

49. S. Sandberg, *Lean In: Women, Work, and the Will to Lead* (New York: Alfred A. Knopf, 2013).

50. B. Bird and C. Brush, "A Gendered Perspective on Organizational Creation," *Entrepreneurship Theory and Practice* 26, no. 3 (2002): 41–65.

51. Ibid.

52. S. M. Yohn, "Crippled Capitalists: The Inscription of Economic Dependence and the Challenge of Female Entrepreneurship in Nineteenth-Century America," *Feminist Economics* 12, no. 1–2 (2006): 85–109; H. Ahl, "Why Research on Women Needs New Directions," *Entrepreneurship Theory and Practice* 30, no. 5 (September 2006): 595–621.

53. B. J. Orser and J. Leck, "Physician as Feminist Entrepreneur: The Gendered Nature of Venture Creation and the Shirley E. Greenberg Women's Health Centre," in *Women Entrepreneurs and the Global Environment for Growth*, ed. C. G. Brush, A. De Bruin, E. J. Gatewood, and C. Henry (Cheltenham, UK: Edward Elgar, 2010).

54. T. K. Forsythe, "CECNB Takes Leadership Role in Social Enterprise Sector," *The Atlantic Co-Operator* (May-June 2013): 16; C. Seelosa and J. Mairb, "Social Entrepreneurship: Creating New Business Models to Serve the Poor," *Business Horizons* 48, (2005): 241; S. Venkataraman, "The Distinctive Domain of Entrepreneurship Research," in *Advances in Entrepreneurship, Firm Emergence and Growth*, ed. J. Katz, vol. 3 (Greenwich, CT: JAI Press), 119–138; S. Dorado, "Social Entrepreneurial Ventures: Different Values So Different Process of Creation, No?" *Journal of Development Entrepreneurship* 11, no. 4 (2006): 319–343.

55. H. Ahl, *The Scientific Reproduction of Gender Inequality* (Copenhagen: CBS Press, 2004), 58; J. S. Coleman, "Free Riders and Zealots: The Role of Social Networks," *Sociological Theory* 6, no. 1 (1988): 52–57; Putnam, *Bowling Alone*.

56. See http://www.thefundingportal.com.

57. To learn more about The Funding Portal from CEO Teri Kirk, search Youtube for "NOXTROM D.M. / XEAYZ.COM Yvonne Pilon interviews Teri Kirk."

58. See http://www.ottawahospital.on.ca.

59. Orser and Leck, "Physician as Feminist Entrepreneur."

60. See http://springboardenterprises.org.

61. For more information about Springboard Enterprise and the firms the organization has helped to launch, search Youtube for "Impact investing-women fuel 21st century economy: Kay Koplovitz at TEDxBayArea."

62. Orser, Elliott, and Leck, "Entrepreneurial Feminists."

63. B. J. Orser and S. Hogarth-Scott, "Case Analysis of Canadian Self-Employment Assistance Programming," *Entrepreneurship & Regional Development* 10, no. 1 (1998): 51–69.

Chapter 4

1. OECD, *Small Businesses, Job Creation and Growth: Facts, Obstacles and Best Practices.* Accessed July 22, 2013 at http://www.oecd.org/industry/smes/2090740.pdf.

2. B. J. Orser and S. Hogarth-Scott, "Opting for Growth: Gender Dimensions of Choosing

Enterprise Development," *Canadian Journal of Administrative Sciences* 19, no. 3 (September 2002): 284–300.

3. B. J. Orser, A. L. Riding, and O. Jung, "Gender of Ownership and the Growth of Young Enterprises," paper read at the Babson Conference Research Conference, Lyon, France, June 8–11, 2013.

4. Ibid., 165–197.

5. G. Hamel, *Leading the Revolution* (Boston: Harvard Business School Press, 2000), 59, as referenced in B. W. Wirtz, *Business Model Management: Design-Instruments-Success Factors* (Wiesbaden: Gabler, 2011), 52.

6. J. Magretta, "Why Business Models Matter," *Harvard Business Review* 80, no. 5 (May 2002): 86–92, as referenced in Wirtz, *Business Model Management,* 52.

7. D. C. Hambrick and J. W. Fredrickson, "Are You Sure You Have a Strategy?" *The Academy of Management Executive* 19, no. 4 (2005): 51–62.

8. J. Florin and E. Schmidt, "Creating Shared Value in the Hybrid Venture Arena: A Business Model Innovation Perspective," *Journal of Social Entrepreneurship* 2, no. 2 (2011): 168.

9. E. T. Penrose, *The Theory of the Growth of the Firm* (London: Basil Blackwell, 1959).

10. P. Preisendorfer and T. Voss, "Organizational Mortality of Small Firms: The Effects of Entrepreneurial Age and Human Capital," *Organization Studies* 11, no. 1 (1990): 107–129; D. J. Storey, *Understanding the Small Business Sector* (London: Routledge, 1994).

11. J. Baldwin, *Strategies for Success: A Profile of Growing Small and Medium-Sized Enterprises (GSMEs) in Canada* (Ottawa: Firm Strategy and Adjustment Project, Statistics Canada, 1994).

12. L. Foss, L., K. Woll, and M. Moilanen, "Creativity and Implementations of New Ideas: Do Organizational Structure, Work Environment and Gender Matter?" *International Journal of Gender and Entrepreneurship* 5, no. 3 (2013): 298–322.

13. Ernst & Young, *Global Job Creation: A Survey of the World's Most Dynamic Entrepreneurs,* 2013, EYG no. CY0422.

14. Baldwin, *Strategies for Success.*

15. In this study, small was defined as less than five hundred employees. See Z. J. Acs and D. B. Audretsh, *Innovation and Small Firms* (Cambridge, Mass: MIT Press, 1990).

16. OECD, *Small Businesses, Job Creation and Growth.*

17. Ibid.

18. Ibid., p. 28.

19. J. Barsh, M. M. Capozzi, and J. Davidson, "Leadership and Innovation," *McKinsey Quarterly* (2008), accessed at http://www.mckinsey.com/insights/innovation/leadership _and_innovation.

20. J. A. Schumpeter, *The Theory of Economic Development: An Inquiry into Profits, Capital, Credit, Interest, and the Business Cycle* (Cambridge, MA: Harvard University Press, 1934), as cited by G. A. Alsos, E. Ljunggren, and U. Hytti, "Gender and Innovation: State of the Art and a Research Agenda," *International Journal of Gender and Entrepreneurship* 5, no. 3 (2013): 236–256.

21. Alsos, Ljunggren, and Hytti, "Gender and Innovation."

22. K. Pettersson and M. Lindberg, "Paradoxical Spaces of Feminist Resistance: Mapping the Margin to the Masculinist Innovation Discourse," *International Journal of Gender and Entrepreneurship* 5, no. 3 (2013): 323–341.

23. M. Lindberg, "A Striking Pattern: Co-Construction of Innovation, Men and Masculinity in Sweden's Innovation Policy" in *Promoting Innovation-Policies, Practices and Procedures*, ed. S. Andersson, K. Berglund, J. Thorslund, E. Gunnarsson, and E. Sundin, (Stockholm: Vinnova, 2012), 47–67.

24. D. Doloreux and S. Parto, "Regional Innovation Systems: Current Discourse and Unresolved Issues," *Technology in Society* 27, no. 2 (2005): 133–153, as cited by Alsos, Ljunggren, and Hytti, "Gender and Innovation."

25. L. E. Duxbury, L. S. Dyke, and N. Lam, *Managing High Technology Employees* (Scarborough, ON: Carswell, 2000).

26. B. J. Orser, A. L. Riding, and J. Stanley, "Perceived Career Challenges and Response Strategies of Women in the Advanced Technology Sector," *Entrepreneurship & Regional Development* 24, no. 1–2 (2012): 73–93.

27. P. Westhead, "Survival and Employment Growth Contrasts Between Types of Owner Management High-Tech Firms," the 18th National Institute for Small Business Affairs Conference proceedings, Paisley, Scotland, November 15–17, 1995, 605–636. This explanation has also been referred to as population ecology and institutional theory. We use the heading "reputation and legitimacy" as these are the practical outcomes associated with each theoretical perspective.

28. E. Fischer and R. Reuber, "The Good, the Bad, and the Unfamiliar: The Challenges of Reputation Formation Facing New Firms," *Entrepreneurship Theory and Practice* 31, no. 1 (2007): 53–75.

29. A. Eagly, W. Wood, and A. Diekman, "Social Role Theory of Sex Differences and Similaries: A Current Appraisal," in *The Developmental Social Psychology of Gender*, ed. T. Eckes and H. M. Trauter (Mahwah, NJ: Lawrence Erlbaum Associates, 2000): 123–174.

30. Fischer and Reuber, "The Good, the Bad, and the Unfamiliar".

31. Ibid.

32. Ibid.

33. Bem defines gender schemas as "cognitive structures of organized prior knowledge regarding the role expectations of individuals based on biological sex." See M. A. Lemons and M. Parzinger, "Gender Schemas: A Cognitive Explanation of Discrimination of Women in Technology," *Journal of Business and Psychology* 22, no. 1 (2007): 91.

34. Prowess, *Under the Microscope: Female Entrepreneurs in SECT: Science, Engineering, Construction and Technology* (2008), accessed at www.prowess.org.uk.

35. Orser, Riding, and Stanley, "Perceived Career Challenges and Response Strategies of Women"; W. Cukier, *Attracting, Retaining and Promoting Women: Best Practices in the Canadian Tech Sector* (Ottawa: Canadian Advanced Technology Alliance, 2009); H. Mayer, "Economic Trends and Location Patterns of Women High-Tech Entrepreneurs," in *Frontiers in Entrepreneurship*, ed. A. Zacharakis (Babson Park, MA: Babson College, 2006), 298–312.

36. C. Aislabie, "The Implications for Survival in Small Firm Failure Studies," paper presented at the Fifth National Small Business Conference Proceedings, University College of Southern Queensland, Toowoomba, 1992; T. Bates, "An Analysis of Small Business Size and Rate of Discontinuance," *Journal of Small Business Management* 27, no. 4 (1989): 1–7; S. Cromie, "The Problems Experienced by Young Firms," *International Small Business Journal* 9, no. 3 (1990): 44–60; B. J. Orser, S. Hogarth-Scott, and A. L. Riding, "Performance, Firm Size and Management Problem Solving," *Journal of Small Business Management* 38, no. 4 (2000): 42–58.

37. Statistic cited in M. Schnack, "Accessing International Markets," in *The Roadmap to 2020—Fueling the Growth of Women's Enterprise Development*, ed. V. Littlejohn (Washington, DC: Quantum Leaps, 2010), 47, accessed at http://nawbo.org/imageuploads/Roadmap to2020.Pdf.

38. International Monetary Fund, *World Economic Outlook Database* (2012).

39. F. Neville, B. J. Orser, A. Riding, and O. Jung, "Do Young Firms Owned by Recent Immigrants Outperform Other Young Firms?" *Journal of Business Venturing* 29, no. 1 (2014): 55–71; Orser, Riding, and Spence, *Canadian SME Exporters.*

40. B. J. Orser, A. L. Riding, and M. Spence, *Canadian SME Exporters—SME Research and Statistics (Archived)* (2010), accessed at http://www.ic.gc.ca/eic/site/061.nsf/eng/h_02 115.html.

41. Neville, Orser, Riding, and Jung, "Do Young Firms Owned by Recent Immigrants Outperform Other Young Firms?"

42. Orser, Riding, and Spence, *Canadian SME Exporters.*

43. B. J. Orser, R. Riding, and J. Townsend, "Exporting as a Means of Growth for Women-Owned Canadian SMEs," *Journal of Small Business and Entrepreneurship* 17, no. 3 (July 2004): 153–174; B. J. Orser, M. Spence, A. L. Riding, and Christine A. Carrington, "Gender and Export Propensity," *Entrepreneurship: Theory & Practice* 34, no. 5 (2010): 933–957.

44. Orser, Riding, and Townsend, "Exporting as a Means of Growth for Women-Owned Canadian SMEs."

45. M. A. Reavley, T. Lituchy, and E. McClelland, "Exporting Success: A Two Country Comparison of Women Entrepreneurs in International Trade," *International Journal of Entrepreneurship and Small Business* 2, no. 1 (2005): 57–78.

46. For many enterprises, international trade introduces challenges. Onerous bureaucratic procedures and regulations, and foreign exchange risks stymie international trade. Business owners also report challenges such as lack of market intelligence, finding suitable foreign partners, the adaptation of products and services to meet foreign demand, and sourcing export capital. In the case of Digital Opportunities Trust, founder Janet Longmore also overcame challenges of trade within emerging economies, including limited infrastructure and supply chains and few customers with disposable income.

47. J. E. Cliff [now Jennings], "Does One Size Fit All? Exploring the Relationship Between Attitudes Towards Growth, Gender, and Business Size," *Journal of Business Venturing* 13, no. 6 (1998): 523–542.

48. B. Philips and B. Kirchhoff, "An Analysis of New Firm Survival and Growth," *Frontiers in Entrepreneurship Research* (1988): 266–267; S. Scheinberg and I. MacMillan, "An 11 Country Study of Motivations to Start a Business," *Frontiers in Entrepreneurship Research* (1988): 669–687.

49. P. Reynolds, D. J. Storey, and P. Westhead, "Cross-National Comparisons of the Variation in New Firm Formation Rates," *Regional Studies* 28, no. 4 (1994): 443–456.

50. OECD, *Small Businesses, Job Creation and Growth.*

51. E. Bardasi, S. Sabarwal, and K. Terrell, "How Do Female Entrepreneurs Perform? Evidence from Three Developing Regions," *Small Business Economics* 37, no. 4 (2011): 417–441.

52. For example, see European Commission Enterprise Directorate General, *Good Practices in the Promotion of Female Entrepreneurship: Examples for Europe and other OECD Countries* (Vienna: Austrian Institute for Small Business Research, December 2002); OECD,

Women Entrepreneurs in SMEs: Realising the Benefit of Globalization and the Knowledge-Based Economy (2001); Quantum Leaps, *The Roadmap to 2020: Fueling the Growth of Women's Enterprise Development* (2010), accessed at http://quantumleapsinc.org/index.html; The National Women's Business Council, *Best Practices in Supporting Women's Entrepreneurship in the United States: A Compendium of Public and Private Sector Organizations and Initiatives* (2004), accessed at http://www.nwbc.gov/research/best-practices-supporting-womens-entrepreneurship-compendium-public-and-private-sector; S. Bulte, C. Callbeck, C. Duplain, R. Fitzpatrick, K., Redman, and A. Lever, *The Prime Minister's Task Force on Women Entrepreneurs,* National Liberal Caucus Research Bureau, Information Management, 2003, previously available at http://www.liberal.parl.gc.ca/entrepreneur; B. Orser and C. Connell, *Sustaining the Momentum: An Economic Forum for Women Entrepreneurs* (2004), accessed at http://www.ic.gc.ca/eic/site/sbrp-rppe.nsf/eng/rd01308.html; and Taskforce for Women's Business Growth, *Taskforce Roundtable Report: Action Strategies to Support Canadian Women-Owned Enterprises,* University of Ottawa, Telfer School of Management, 2011, accessed at http://sites.telfer.uottawa.ca/womensenterprise.

53. I. Treurnicht, "We Must Draw More Women into Ambitious Entrepreneurship," *MaRS*, March 8, 2012. For a list of female-owned firms supported by MaRS, see http://www.marsdd.com/2012/03/08/draw-women-ambitious-entrepreneurship.

54. We were introduced to Debra by another visionary, the late Gwynneth Wallace of Wolfville. Meeting Debra Moore and other Atlantic entrepreneurial feminists motivated us to undertake exploratory research that led to the writing of this book. It seemed appropriate that Debra's story should lead the case studies about feminine capital and innovation.

55. The fair trade sector is governed by Fair Trade International, an international agency that certifies producers, oversees national initiatives, and monitors businesses. The Just Us! website describes the principles of fair trade as direct trade: no intermediaries; fair pricing; democratic and transparent organizations; protection of the environment; community development; long-term relationships; and access to credit for producers.

56. See http://www.justuscoffee.com.

57. Florin and Schmidt, "Creating Shared Value in the Hybrid Venture Arena."

58. Following the horrific 2013 factory collapse in Bangladesh that killed 1,127 garment workers, more municipalities are enacting fair trade. For example, in 2013 Toronto become the largest fair trade city in North America; see http://fairtradetoronto.ca/category/news/news-may-2013.

59. S. Krashinsky, "When Philanthropy's Part of the Business Model, Marketing Takes Care of itself," accessed May 23, 2013, at http://www.theglobeandmail.com/report-on-business/industry-news/marketing/when-the-product-is-the-message/article12114083.

60. TOMS Shoes of Los Angeles is among the first enterprises based on the "one-for-one" message.

61. Sir Richard's Condom Company donates one condom to a developing country for every condom purchased. "Wherever we make a contribution, we design an entirely new brand and ensure its cultural relevance with the help and guidance of local artists, healthcare providers, and others. The KORE Condom marks the first ever condom in Haiti designed by Haitians and written in Haitian Creole." Over the past three years, the firm has donated approximately three million condoms. See http://sirrichards.com.

62. See http://www.warbyparker.com/donors-choose.

63. These paradoxes were inspired by Florin and Schmidt, "Creating Shared Value in the Hybrid Venture Arena."

64. Former board member, Association of Women's Business Centers (http://www.awbc.biz; former member, board of directors, National Association of Women Business Owners (http://nawbo.org); board secretary of the Global Banking Alliance for Women (http://www.gbaforwomen.org/); member, Editorial Advisory Board, *International Journal of Gender and Entrepreneurship*, and former board director, International Council for Small Business (http://www.icsb.org/); member, National Advisory Board, *Enterprising Women* magazine.

65. The BRAC mission is "To empower people and communities in situations of poverty, illiteracy, disease and social injustice." See http://www.brac.net. The Grameen Bank, founded in the 1970s by Nobel Laureate (2006) Professor Muhammad Yunus, introduced market-based lending to the poor in India.

66. M. Bannick and P. Goldman, *Priming the Pump: The Case for a Sector Based Approach to Impact Investing*, OMIDYAR Network, September 2012.

67. "As of October, 2011, it has 8.349 million borrowers, 97 percent of whom are women. With 2,565 branches, GB provides services in 81,379 villages, covering more than 97 percent of the total villages in Bangladesh." See http://www.grameen-info.org. For information about BRAC, see http://www.brac.net/content/who-we-are-evolution#.UfJUkaDQ6fQ. The Grameen Bank is undergoing restructuring by the Central Bank and Government of Bangladesh. See "Sheikh Hasina Government Vows to 'Cleanse' Grameen Bank," July 25, 2013.

68. J. Parker, "Empowering Women Through Microfinance in India," *The Diplomat—Pacific Money: Economics and Business*, March 13, 2013.

69. M. Spence, B. J. Orser, and A. L. Riding, "A Comparative Study of International and Domestic New Ventures," *Management International Review* 51, no. 1 (2011): 3–21.

70. Ibid.

71. C. Seelosa and J. Mairb, "Social Entrepreneurship: Creating New Business Models to Serve the Poor," *Business Horizons* 48, (2005): 241–246.

72. B. J. Orser, M. Cedzynski, and R. Thomas, "Modelling Owner Experience: Linking Theory and Practice," *Journal of Small Business and Entrepreneurship* 20, no. 4 (2007).

73. B. J. Orser and A. L. Riding, *Management Competencies and SME Performance Criteria: A Pilot Study* (Ottawa: Industry Canada—Small Business Policy Branch, December 2003). The report investigated management competencies and the perceived relative importance to SME owners of a variety of success criteria.

74. Taskforce for Women's Business Growth, *Taskforce Roundtable Report*.

75. Orser, Cedzynski, and Thomas, "Modelling Owner Experience."

76. Orser, Riding, and Townsend, "Exporting as a Means of Growth."

77. S. Pleiter, "Making Waves," *Queen's School of Business Magazine*, Summer 2013. Accessed at http://qsb.ca/magazine/summer-2013/profiles/making-waves.

78. A good reputation-enhancing organizational legitimacy is associated with sustained competitive advantage, achieved through access to clients and customers, financing, quality employees, and cost advantages such as favorable pricing on supplies. Fischer and Reuber write that reputation and legitimacy are judgments, or sets of beliefs, held by stakeholders such as funders, clients, suppliers, and partner agencies. See Fischer and Reuber, "The Good, the Bad, and the Unfamiliar."

79. Seelosa and Mairb, "Social Entrepreneurship."

80. T. L. Thompson and J. C. Ndayambaje, "Innovating Fluid Learning Spaces: Choices, Designs, Technology, and Data," paper presented at the 2011 eLearning Africa Conference, Dar es Salaam, Tanzania, May 25–27, 2011.

81. Bannick and Goldman, *Priming the Pump.* "Established in 2004 by eBay founder Pierre Omidyar and his wife Pam, the organization invests in and helps scale innovative organizations to catalyze economic and social change. To date, Omidyar Network has committed more than $550 million to for-profit companies and non-profit organizations that foster economic advancement and encourage individual participation across multiple investment areas, including financial inclusion, entrepreneurship, property rights, consumer internet and mobile, and government transparency." Accessed at www.omidyar.com.

82. "In 2011, the Global Impact Investing Network and J.P. Morgan published a report predicting nearly $4 billion of impact investments in 2012, and as much as $1 trillion in the coming decade. . . . A 2012 Credit Suisse report affirmed J.P. Morgan's claim that impact investing is a $1 trillion-plus market opportunity. Although these predictions are at a minimum ambitious, and at a maximum wildly inflated, there is no doubt that impact investing has captured the world's imagination much as microfinance did before it." S. Dichter, R. Katz, H. Koh, and A. Karamchandani, "Closing the Pioneer Gap," *Stanford Social Innovation Review* (Winter 2013): 38.

83. T. L. Thompson, *Connecting the DOTs: Creating Alternative Learning Spaces* (2009). Digital Opportunity Trust response to the Cisco white paper *Equipping Every Learner for the 21st Century*, accessed at http://www.dotrust.org/blogs/news/connectingthedotscreating alternativelearningspaces.

84. R. Lawson, C. Alcock, J. Cooper, and L. Burgess, "Factors Affecting Adoption of Electronic Commerce Technologies by SMEs: An Australian Study," *Journal of Small Business and Enterprise Development* 10, no. 3 (2003): 265–276.

85. C. Chibelushi, "Learning the Hard Way? Issues in the Adoption of New Technology in Small Technology Oriented Firms," *Education and Training* 50, no. 8 (2008): 725–736; D. L. Lester and T. T. Tran, *Information Technology Capabilities: Suggestions for SME Growth* (City: Institute of Behavioral and Applied Management, 2008), accessed at http://www .ibam.com/pubs/jbam/articles/vol10/no1/JBAM_10_1_4.pdf. Also see http://www.ibam.com /index.html.

86. R. K. Kazanjian, "Relation of Dominant Problems to Stages of Growth in Technology-Based New Ventures," *Academy of Management Journal* 31, no. 2 (1988): 257–279.

87. K. Pemmaraju, "Cloud Adoption: The Difference Between Small and Large Companies," accessed September 22, 2010, at http://sandhill.com/article/cloud-adoption-the -difference-between-small-large-companies/#.

88. Orser, Riding, and Stanley, "Perceived Career Challenges and Response Strategies of Women."

89. J. Brinckmann reports on differences in the survival rate of technology versus other ventures in *Competence of Top Management Teams and the Success of New Technology-Based Firms: A Theoretical and Empirical Analysis Concerning Competencies of Entrepreneurial Teams and the Development of their Ventures* (City: Publisher, 2008). For example, among German-government-supported young technology ventures, the survival rate was about 60 percent in the first five years (E. B. Roberts, *Entrepreneurs in High Technology: Lessons from MIT and Beyond* [New York: Oxford University Press, 1991]). Spin-off companies from the

Massachusetts Institute of Technology have a survival rate between 70 and 85 percent within the first five years (Kennedy, C.R., 1985, 39). These compare to survival rates for corresponding venture types of between 20 and 40 percent.

90. Dichter, Katz, Koh, and Karamchandani, "Closing the Pioneer Gap."

91. N. Kabeer, *Reversed Realities: Gender Hierarchies in Development Thought* (London: Verso, 1994); L. Mayoux, *Jobs, Gender and Small Enterprises: Getting the Policy Environment Right* (Geneva: International Labour Office, 2001), accessed at http://www.ilo.org/wcmsp5/groups/public/—-ed_emp/—-emp_ent/documents/publication/wcms_111394.pdf.

92. J. Rowlands, *Questioning Empowerment: Working with Women in Honduras* (Oxford: Oxfam, 1997); Kabeer, *Reversed Realities*.

93. Kabeer, *Reversed Realities*.

94. Ibid.; A. M. Golla, A. Malhotra, P. Nanda, and R. Mehra, *Understanding and Measuring Women's Economic Empowerment: Definition, Frameworks, Indicators* (Washington, DC: International Centre for Research on Women, 2011).

95. An example of an emerging social funding vehicle is "social impact bonds." See L. Callanan, J. Law, and L. Mendonca, *From Potential to Action: Bringing Social Impact Bonds to the U.S.* (New York: McKinsey & Company, 2012).

Chapter 5

1. T. L. Thompson and J. Hudson, "Web2.0: Mapping Perceptions and Practices Survey Synthesis of Preliminary Research Report," working paper published by Digital Opportunities Trust, 2011.

2. The concept of *social capital* was first introduced by Pierre Bourdieu: P. Bourdieu, "The Forms of Capital," in *Handbook of Theory and Research for the Sociology of Education*, ed. J. G. Richardson (New York: Greenwood, 1985), 241–258. See also E. L. Hansen, "Entrepreneurial Networks and New Organization Growth," *Entrepreneurship: Theory & Practice* 19, no. 4 (1995): 7–19.

3. W. Stam, S. Arzlanian, and T. Elfring, "Social Capital of Entrepreneurs and Small Firm Performance: A Meta-Analysis of Contextual and Methodological Moderators," *Journal of Business Venturing* 29, no. 1 (2014): 152–173.

4. Accessed at http://womeninbiznetwork.com; http://www.thebossnetwork.org; http://youthbiz.org; http://youngfemaleentrepreneurs.com; http://startupprincess.com.

5. Accessed at http://www.forbes.com/2010/06/23/100-best-womens-blogs-forbes-woman-time-websites.html; http://www.forbes.com/sites/meghancasserly/2011/06/23/top-10-entrepreneurial -websites-for-women.

6. C. Elliott and J. Leck, "Formal Mentoring Programs: Gender Influences and Considerations for Program Design," in *Managing Diversity in Today's Workplace*, ed. M. Paludi (Santa Barbara, CA: Praeger, 2012), 79–101.

7. R. C. Mayer, J. H. David, and F. D. Schoorman, "An Integrative Model of Trust Formation," *Academy of Management Review* 20, no. 3 (1995): 709–734.

8. Steven Covey first introduced the notion of an emotional bank account in his book *The 7 Habits of Highly Effective People* (New York: Simon & Schuster, 1989).

9. One of the most recognized models of trust is presented by Mayer, David and Schoorman, "An Integrative Model." They identify ability, benevolence, and integrity as the key components of initial trust formulation. In our research with female entrepreneurs,

however, we discovered that respect was more commonly mentioned, particularly as relationships developed "in action" and over time. See also J. Leck and B. J. Orser, "Fostering Trust in Mentoring Relationships: An Exploratory Study," *Equality, Diversity and Inclusion: An International Journal* 32, no. 4 (2013): 410–425.

10. E. St-Jean, "Mentoring as Professional Development for Novice Entrepreneurs: Maximizing the Learning," *International Journal of Training and Development* 16, no. 3 (2012): 200–216; C. R. Wanberg, E. T. Welsh, and J. Kammeyer-Mueller, "Protégé and Mentor Self-Disclosure: Levels and Outcomes Within Formal Mentoring Dyads in a Corporate Context," *Journal of Vocational Behavior* 70, no. 2 (2007): 398–412; E. E. Maccoby, "Gender and Relationships: A Developmental Account," *The American Psychologist* 45, no. 4 (April 1990): 513–520; P. Tharenou, "Does Mentor Support Increase Women's Career Advancement More Than Men's? The Differential Effects of Career and Psychosocial Support," *Australian Journal of Management* 30, no. 1 (2005): 77–109; T. D. Allen, R. Day, and E. Lentz, "The Role of Interpersonal Comfort in Mentoring Relationships," *Journal of Career Development* 31, no. 3 (2005): 155–169.

11. P. J. Robson, S. Jack, and M. Freel, "Gender and the Use of Business Advice: Evidence from Firms in the Scottish Service Sector," *Environment and Planning C: Government and Policy* 26, no. 2 (2008): 292–314.

12. Tharenou, "Does Mentor Support Increase Women's Career Advancement More than Men's?"

13. Leck and Orser, "Fostering Trust in Mentoring Relationships."

14. St-Jean, "Mentoring as Professional Development for Novice Entrepreneurs."

15. Hansen, "Entrepreneurial Networks and New Organization Growth."

16. K. Klyver and S. Grant, "Gender Differences in Entrepreneurial Networking and Participation," *International Journal of Gender and Entrepreneurship* 2, no. 3 (2010): 213–227; S. Terjsen and S. E. Sullivan, "The Role of Developmental Relationships in the Transition to Entrepreneurship: A Qualitative Study and Agenda for Future Research," *Career Development International* 16, no. 5 (2011): 482–506; Mayer, David, and Schoorman, "An Integrative Model"; T. B. Kregar, A. F. DeNoble, and B. Antončič, "The Entrepreneur's Personal Network Structure and Firm Growth," *International Journal of Innovation and Regional Development* 4, no. 3/4 (2012): 232–249; Hansen, "Entrepreneurial Networks and New Organization Growth."

17. A. Greve and J. W. Salaff, "Social Networks and Entrepreneurship," *Entrepreneurship Theory and Practice* 28, no. 1 (2003): 2; N. Lin," Building a Network Theory of Social Capital," *Connections* 22, no. 1 (1999): 28–51; N. Lin, "Building a Network Theory of Social Capital," in *Social Capital: Theory and Research*, ed. K. Cook and S. Burt (New Brunswick, NJ: Transaction, 2001), 3–29; P. J. Peverelli, L. J. Song, Z. Sun, and J. Yu, "Extending Network Analysis with Social Inclusions: A Chinese Entrepreneur Building Social Capital," *Frontiers of Business Research in China* 5, no. 1 (2011): 121–143.

18. J. D. Leck, B. J. Orser, and A. Riding, "An Examination of Gender Influences in Career Mentoring." *Equality, Diversity and Inclusion: An International Journal* 32, no. 4 (2013): 410–425.

19. Ibid.; A. Bandura, "Human Agency in Social Cognitive Theory," *American Psychologist* 44, no. 9 (1989): 1175–1184. Bandura contends that there are three important components to learning: observational learning, self-efficacy, and self-regulation.

20. B. J. Orser, M. Cedzynski, and R. Thomas, "Modelling Owner Experience: Linking Theory and Practice," *Journal of Small Business & Entrepreneurship* 20, no. 4 (2007): 387–408; B. Smith and E. Morse, *Entrepreneurial Competencies: Literature Review and Best Practices* (Ottawa: Industry Canada, Small Business Policy Branch, 2005).

21. A. Bandura, "Exercise of Personal Agency Through the Self-Efficacy Mechanism," in *Self-Efficacy: Thought Control of Action,* ed. R. Schwartzer (Washington, DC: Hemisphere, 1992): 3–38.

22. C. Chen, P. Greene, and A. Crick, "Does Entrepreneurial Self-Efficacy Distinguish Entrepreneurs from Managers?" *Journal of Business Venturing* 13, no. 4 (1998): 295–316.

23. F. Wilson, J. Kickul, and D. Marlino, "Gender, Entrepreneurial Self-Efficacy, and Entrepreneurial Career Intentions: Implications for Entrepreneurship Education," *Entrepreneurship Theory and Practice* 31, no. 3 (2007): 387–406.

24. R. J. Burke and C. A. McKeen, "Mentoring in Organizations: Implications for Women," *Journal of Business Ethics* 9, no. 4–5 (1990); Leck, Orser, and Riding, "An Examination of Gender Influences in Career Mentoring"; V. E. Schein, R. Mueller, T. Lituchy, and J. Liu, "Think Manager—Think Male: A Global Phenomenon?" *Journal of Organizational Behavior* 17, no. 1 (1996): 33–41.

25. St-Jean, "Mentoring as Professional Development for Novice Entrepreneurs."

26. Ibid.

27. J. Becker-Blease and J. E. Sohl, "The Effect of Gender Diversity on Angel Group Investment," *Entrepreneurship Theory and Practice* 35, no. 4 (2011): 709–733. Also see J. Becker-Blease and J. E. Sohl, "Do Women-Owned Businesses Have Equal Access to Angel Capital?" *Journal of Business Venturing* 22, no. 4 (2007): 503–521.

28. C. Brush, N. Carter, P. Greene, and M. Hart, *Gatekeepers of Venture Growth: A Diana Project Report on the Role and Participation of Women in the Venture Capital Industry* (Kansas City, MO: Kauffman Centre for Entrepreneurial Leadership, 2004).

29. Becker-Blease and Sohl, "The Effect of Gender Diversity on Angel Group Investment."

30. Klyver and Grant, "Gender Differences in Entrepreneurial Networking and Participation."

31. D. J. Levinson, C. N. Darrow, E. B. Klein, and M. Levinson, *Seasons of a Man's Life* (New York: Random House, 1978); D. J. Levinson, *Seasons of a Woman's Life* (New York: Alfred A. Knopf, 1996); K. E. Kram, "Phases of the Mentor Relationship," *The Academy of Management Journal* 26, no. 4 (December 1983): 608–625; K. E. Kram, *Mentoring at Work: Developmental Relationships in Organizational Life* (Glenview, Ill.: Scott, Foresman, 1985).

32. Kregar, DeNoble, and Anton?i?, "The Entrepreneur's Personal Network Structure and Firm Growth."

33. A. Anderson, S. Jack, and S. Dodd, "The Role of Family Members in Entrepreneurial Networks: Beyond the Boundaries of the Family Firm," *Family Business Review* 18, no. 2 (June 2005): 135–154. Also see Klyver and Grant, "Gender Differences in Entrepreneurial Networking and Participation"; S. Robinson and H. Hubberud, "Sources of Advice in Entrepreneurs: Gender Differences in Business Owners," *International Journal of Entrepreneurship* 13, (2009): 83–101; A. Smith-Hunter and J. Leone, "Evidence on the Characteristics of Women Entrepreneurs in Brazil: An Empirical Analysis," *International Journal of Management & Marketing Research* 3, no. 1 (2010): 85–102; L. Renzulli and H. Aldrich, "Family

Matters: Gender, Networks, and Entrepreneurial Outcomes," *Social Forces* 79, no. 2 (2000): 523–546; L. Foss, "Research on Entrepreneur Networks: The Case for a Constructionist Feminist Theory Perspective," *International Journal of Gender and Entrepreneurship* 2, no. 1 (2010): 83–102; and D. Cetindamar, V. K. Gupta, E. E. Karadeniz, and N. Egrican, "What the Numbers Tell: The Impact of Human, Family and Financial Capital on Women and Men's Entry into Entrepreneurship in Turkey," *Entrepreneurship & Regional Development* 24, no. 1–2 (January 2012): 29–51.

34. Hansen, "Entrepreneurial Networks and New Organization Growth."

35. C. Dawson, N. Fuller-Love, E. Sinott, and B. O'Gorman, "Entrepreneurs' Perceptions of Business Networks: Does Gender Matter?" *International Journal of Entrepreneurship and Innovation* 12, no. 4 (2011): 271–281.

36. S. Robinson and H. A. Stubberud, "Sources of Advice in Entrepreneurship: Gender Differences in Business Owners' Social Networks," *International Journal of Entrepreneurship* 13 (2009): 83–101.

37. S. Wasserman and K. Faust (eds.), *Social Network Analysis: Methods and Applications* (Cambridge, UK: Cambridge University Press, 1994).

38. T. Fenwick and S. Hutton, "Women Learning Themselves: Exploring Relations Between Desire and Knowledge Production of Women Entrepreneurs," paper presented at the International Conference of the Canadian Association for the Study of Women in Education, Edmonton, University of Alberta, May 2000.

39. Cetindamar, Gupta, Karadeniz, and Egrican ("What the Numbers Tell") found that family capital was positively associated with entry into entrepreneurship (as measured by family size), as was basic education and higher income. Women with larger families were somewhat more likely than men to engage in entrepreneurship. For example, a study of women entrepreneurs in Brazil found that 97 percent rely on family and friends for assistance of all types, including financial. The women reported having difficulty gaining access to financial capital, and lack of support from formal networks.

40. N. Carter, W. Gartner, K. Shaver, and E. Gatewood, "The Career Reasons of Nascent Entrepreneurs," *Journal of Business Venturing* 18, no. 1 (2003): 13–39; A. Greve and J. W. Salaff, "Social Networks and Entrepreneurship," *Entrepreneurship Theory and Practice* 28, no. 1 (2003): 1–22; Klyver and Grant, "Gender Differences in Entrepreneurial Networking and Participation," p. 222.

41. Robinson and Stubberud, "Sources of advice in entrepreneurship."

42. Ibid.

43. Ibid.

44. M. Bogren, Y. von Friedrichs, R. Øystein, and W. Øystein, "Networking Women Entrepreneurs: Fruitful for Business Growth?" *International Journal of Gender and Entrepreneurship* 5, no. 1 (2013) 60–77.

45. St-Jean proposes nine distinct functions that an entrepreneurial mentor can fulfill: reflector, motivator, confidant, integrator, support, guide, model, and one who provides confrontation and reassurance. See St-Jean, "Mentoring as Professional Development for Novice Entrepreneurs."

46. T. Allan and L. Eby, "Relationship Effectiveness for Mentors: Factors Associated with Learning and Quality," *Journal of Management* 29, no. 4 (August 2003): 469–486; T. Allen, R. Day, and E. Lentz, "The Role of Interpersonal Comfort in Mentoring Relationships," *Journal*

of Career Development 31, no. 3 (2005): 155–169; K. E. Kram, *Mentoring at Work: Developmental Relationships in Organizational Life*; C. Elliott, J. D. Leck, B. J. Orser, and C. Mossop, "An Exploration of Gender and Trust in Mentoring Relationships," *Journal of Diversity Management* 1, no. 1 (2007): 1–11.

47. R. Noe, "Women and Mentoring: A Review and Research Agenda," *Academy of Management Review* 13, no. 1 (January 1988): 65–78; Leck, Orser, and Riding, "An Examination of Gender Influences in Career Mentoring."

48. St-Jean, "Mentoring as Professional Development for Novice Entrepreneurs."

49. Allen, R. Day, and E. Lentz, "The Role of Interpersonal Comfort in Mentoring Relationships"; E. Maccoby, "Gender and Relationships: A Developmental Account."

50. Elliott, Leck, Orser, and Mossop, "An Exploration of Gender and Trust in Mentoring Relationships."

51. Ibid.

52. Leck and Orser, "Fostering Trust in Mentoring Relationships."

53. T. Allen, L. T. Eby, M. Poteet, E. Lentz, and L. Lima, "Career Benefits Associated with Mentoring for Protégés: A Meta-Analysis," *Journal of Applied Psychology* 89, no. 1 (2004): 127–136.

54. L. Kwoh, "Reverse Mentoring Cracks Workplace," *The Wall Street Journal*, November 28, 2011, accessed August 28, 2013, at http://online.wsj.com/article/SB10001424052970 2037648045770600514610940004.html?mod=wsj_valettop_email. According to Kwoh, "Reverse mentoring was championed by Jack Welch when he was chief executive of General Electric Co. He ordered 500 top-level executives to reach out to people below them to learn how to use the Internet. Mr. Welch himself was matched with an employee in her 20s who taught him how to surf the Web. The younger mentors earned visibility."

55. M. Harvey, N. McIntyre, J. Thompson Heames, and M. Moeller, "Mentoring Global Female Managers in the Global Marketplace: Traditional, Reverse, and Reciprocal Mentoring," *The International Journal of Human Resource Management* 20, no. 6 (2009), 1352.

56. C. Casal and C. Caspar, "Building a Forward-Looking Board," *McKinsey Quarterly*, February 2014, 1–8, at p. 5.

57. K. Somerville, C. Elliott, and C. Gustafson, "Increasing Women's Participation on Corporate Boards in the United States," paper presented at the Mustang International Academic Conference, Las Vegas, February 21, 2013).

58. Many of the best practices associated with establishing boards of directors are appropriate for setting up a board of advisors. Note, however, that members do not typically sit on both boards.

59. EY Report, 2013.

60. B. Moses, "The Networking Gender Gap, and How to Bridge It," *Globe and Mail*, October 3, 2011, accessed at http://www.theglobeandmail.com/report-on-business/careers/career-advice/the-networking-gender-gap-and-how-to-bridge-it/article4183138.

61. Cited in B. Moses, "The Networking Gender Gap."

62. M. Casserly, "Understanding How Women Network," Forbes, October 7, 2009, accessed at http://www.forbes.com/2009/10/07/networking-relationships-connections-forbes-women-entrepreneurs-men.html.

63. As of the writing of this book, Sandberg's goal of 1,000 Lean In circles, small support groups, being formed within a year has been exceeded, sixteen times over. The Lean

In Foundation says 16,023 of them have formed, in seventy-two countries (*Ottawa Citizen*, April 11, 2014).

64. A. Donnellon and N. Langowitz, "Leveraging Women's Networks for Strategic Value," *Strategy & Leadership* 37, no. 3 (2009): 29–36.

65. Quantum Leaps, *The Roadmap to 2020: Fuelling the Growth of Women's Enterprise Development* (Washington, DC: Quantum Leaps, 2010); Taskforce for Women's Business Growth, *Taskforce Roundtable Report: Action Strategies to Support Canadian Women-Owned Enterprises*, University of Ottawa, Telfer, 2011, accessed at http://sites.telfer.uottawa.ca/wo mensenterprise; Women's Enterprise Taskforce (2006–2009), accessed at: http://www.wom ensenterprisetaskforce.co.uk.

66. A. Hillsberg and D. Adelman, "Most Popular Social Media Sites Review: Why Women Are the Real Power Behind the Huge Success of Pinterest and Tumblr," FinancesOnline.com, accessed on April 24, 2014, at http://reviews.financesonline.com/most -popular-social-media-sites-review.

Chapter 6

1. S. Coleman and A. Robb, "A Comparison of New Firm Financing by Gender: Evidence from the Kauffman Firm Survey Data," *Small Business Economics* 33, no. 4 (2009): 397–411; O. Jung, *Financing Profile: Women Entrepreneurs* (Ottawa: Small Business Branch, Industry Canada, 2010).

2. S. Coleman and A. Robb, *A Rising Tide: Financing Strategies for Women-Owned Firms* (Stanford, CA: Stanford University Press, 2012).

3. D. Kelley, S. Singer, and M. Herrington, *Global Entrepreneurship Monitor, Global Report*, 2011, p. 13, accessed on March 24, 2014, at http://www.gemconsortium.org/docs/download/2409.

4. K. Hughes, "Exploring Motivation and Success Among Canadian Women Entrepreneurs," *Journal of Small Business & Entrepreneurship* 19, no. 2 (2006): 107–120.

5. Ibid.

6. A. L. Riding and B. J. Orser, *Beyond the Banks: Creative Financing for Canadian Entrepreneurs* (Toronto: John Wiley & Sons Canada, 1997).

7. S. Thornhill and R. Amit, "Learning About Failure: Bankruptcy, Firm Age, and the Resource-Based View," *Organization Science* 14, no. 5 (2003): 497–509.

8. The Global Entrepreneurship Monitor reflects a representative sample of the adult populations in seventy-seven countries, including 1.2 million interviews. Data are adjusted to reflect annual personal income to standardized U.S. dollars, corrected for purchasing power parity. See P. Reynolds, "Entrepreneurship in Development Economies: The Bottom Billions and Business Creation," *Foundations and Trends in Entrepreneurship* 893 (2012): 159.

9. Reynolds, "Entrepreneurship in Development Economies,"[1.]

10. B. J. Orser, A. L. Riding, and K. Manley, "Women Entrepreneurs and Financial Capital," *Entrepreneurship Theory and Practice* 30, no. 5 (2006): 643–665; B. J. Orser, A. L. Riding, and C. S. Swift, "Banking Experiences of Canadian Micro-Businesses," *Journal of Enterprising Culture* 1, nos. 3 and 4 (1994): 321–345; L. Feeney, G. H. Haines Jr., and A. L. Riding, "Private Investors' Investment Criteria: Insights from Qualitative Data," *Venture Capital: An International Journal of Entrepreneurial Finance* 1, no. 2 (1999): 121–145; M. Johne, "Self-Employed Face Latest Hurdles in Quest for a Loan," *The Globe and Mail*, March 24, 2014, B5.

11. M. Drolet, "Why Has the Gender Wage Gap Narrowed?" *Perspectives on Labour and Income* 23, no. 1 (Spring 2011): 1–13.

12. For statistics about U.S. venture capital investments by industrial area, see the Price-Waterhouse-Coopers Money Tree. Accessed at http://www.pwcmoneytree.com.

13. In contrast to bully investors profiled on reality television, many SME training centers offer comprehensive, feedback-driven elevator pitch training. For example, Springboard Enterprises' *Dolphin Tank* "isn't about Sharks or Dragons or a competition for the best idea, it's about channeling the expertise of the people in the room to provide connections and advice to help entrepreneurs take the next step." Springboard Enterprises, accessed on March 25, 2014, at https://sb.co/dolphin-tank.

14. Orser, Riding, and Manley, "Women Entrepreneurs and Financial Capital."

15. J.E.V. Johnson and P. L. Powell, "Decision Making, Risk and Gender: Are Managers Different?" *British Journal of Management* 5, no. 2 (1994): 123–138; G. N. Powell, "One More Time: Do Female and Male Managers Differ?" *The Executive* 4, no. 3 (1990): 68–75; J. P. Byrnes, D. C. Miller, and W. D. Schafer, "Gender Differences in Risk Taking: A Meta-Analysis," *Psychological Bulletin* 125, no. 3 (1999): 367–383.

16. G. Powell, "One More Time: Do Female and Male Managers Differ?"

17. B. J. Orser, A. Riding, and K. Manley, "Women Entrepreneurs and Financial Capital."

18. The mission of Women Advancing Microcredit International is to advance and support women working in microfinance and microenterprise development through education and training, by promoting leadership opportunities and by increasing visibility of women's participation and talent while maintaining a work-life balance. See http://www.waminternational.org.

19. For a summary profile of loan guarantee schemes among OECD member economics, see Organization for Economic Co-ordination and Development, *Financing SMEs and Entrepreneurs 2012: An OECD Scoreboard*, 2012.

20. For example, in the United States, the Small Business Administration also offers tools and checklists to assess credit worthiness. For the Small Business Administration loan application checklist, see http://www.sba.gov/content/sba-loan-application-checklist.

21. S. Myers and N. Majluf, "Corporate Financing and Investment Decisions When Firms Have Information That Investors Do Not Have," *Journal of Financial Economics* 13, no. 2 (June 1984): 187–221.

22. Riding and Orser, *Beyond the Banks*, 7.

23. Orser, Riding, and Manley, "Women Entrepreneurs and Financial Capital."

24. Ibid.

25. A. Riding, R. Singh, and B. J. Orser, "Gender and Financing Choices," *International Council for Small Business Conference Proceedings*, Dublin, June 11–14, 2014.

26. S. Coleman, "Access to Capital and Terms of Credit: A Comparison of Men- and Women-Owned Small Businesses," *Journal of Small Business Management* 38, no. 3 (2000): 37–52.

27. S. Coleman and A. Robb, "A Comparison of New Firm Financing by Gender: Evidence from the Kauffman Firm Survey Data." *Small Business Economics* 33 (2009): 397–411.

28. J. Wolken, "Firm, Owner, and Financing Characteristics: Differences Between Female- and Male-Owned Small Businesses," Working Paper no. 2002-18, accessed March 25, 2014, at http://www.federalreserve.gov/pubs/oss/oss3/ssbf98/FEDS_robbwolken.pdf.

29. L. Han, S. Fraser, and D. Storey, "Are Good or Bad Borrowers Discouraged from Applying for Loans? Evidence from US Small Business Credit Markets," *Journal of Banking & Finance* 33, no. 2 (February 2009): 415–424.

30. Ibid. Also see Riding, Singh, and Orser, "Gender and Financing Choices."

31. S. Coleman and A. Robb, *A Rising Tide: Financing Strategies for Women-Owned Firms* (Stanford, CA: Stanford University Press, 2012), p. 166.

32. S. Coleman and A. Robb, "A Comparison of New Firm Financing by Gender: Evidence from the Kauffman Firm Survey Data," *Small Business Economics* 33, no. 4 (2009): 397–411.

33. Orser, Riding, and Manley, "Women Entrepreneurs and Financial Capital." The study also reports that larger firms, firms with high financing coverage ratios, firms whose owners boast relatively high levels of experience, and firms with good banking relationships were less likely to be turned down for a loan. Firms that face relatively high expenditures on R&D, technology, and exporters are more likely to have loan applications declined. The study concludes, "That is, the issue is not so much that the firm is NAICs-designated as a KBI; rather, access to debt capital appears to be more a function of the nature of the R&D and technology the firm is undertaking."

34. A. L. Riding, "Business Angels and Love Money Investors: Segments of the Informal Market for Risk Capital," *Venture Capital* 10, no. 4 (2008): 355–369.

35. L. Feeney, G. H. Haines Jr., and A. L. Riding, "Private Investors' Investment Criteria: Insights from Qualitative Data," *Venture Capital: An International Journal of Entrepreneurial Finance* 1, no. 2 (1999): 121–145.

36. Ibid.

37. National Venture Capital Association, *Venture Capital Disbursements (MoneyTree Data), Recent Stats and Studies*, 2012, Price Waterhouse Coopers/National Venture Capital Associated MoneyTree Report, Thomson Reuters, accessed at http://www.nvca.org/index .php?option=com_content&view=article&id=344&Itemid=103.

38. T. Fan and P. Phan, "International New Ventures: Revisiting the Influences Behind the 'Born-Global' Firm," *Journal of International Business Studies* 38, (2007): 1113–1131.

39. J. Hagedoorn, "Understanding the Rationale of Strategic Technology Partnering: Inter-Organizational Modes of Cooperation and Sectoral Differences," *Strategic Management Journal* 14, (1993): 371–385; R. Gulati and H. Singh, "The Architecture of Cooperation: Managing Coordination Costs and Appropriation Concerns in Strategic Alliances," *Administrative Science Quarterly* 43, (1998): 781–814; T. Khanna, R. Gulati, and N. Nohria, "The Dynamics of Learning Alliances: Competition, Cooperation and Relative Scope," *Strategic Management Journal* 19, (1998): 193–210.

40. Ibid.

41. C. Brush, N. Carter, P. Greene, M. Hart, and E. Gatewood, "Women and Equity Capital: An Exploration of Factors Affecting Capital Access," *Frontiers in Entrepreneurship*, proceedings from the 12th Annual Entrepreneurship Research Conference, Arthur M. Blank Center for Entrepreneurship, Babson College, Babson Park, Massachusetts, 2000; Orser, Riding, and Manley, "Women Entrepreneurs and Financial Capital."

42. C. Brush, N. Carter, E. Gatewood, P. Greene, and M. Hart, *The Diana Project: Women Business Owners and Equity Capital: The Myths Dispelled* (Kansas City, MO: Kauffman Centre for Entrepreneurial Leadership, 2001).

43. Ibid.; these studies are part of the Diana Project, a global initiative to better understand women's entrepreneurship. For more information about The Diana Project, visit http://www.dianaproject.org.

44. R. T. Harrison and C. M. Mason, "Does Gender Matter? Women Business Angels and the Supply of Entrepreneurial Finance," *Entrepreneurship Theory and Practice* 31, no. 3 (2007): 445–472.

45. C. Brush, N. Carter, P. Greene, and M. Hart, *Gatekeepers of Venture Growth: A Diana Project Report on the Role and Participation of Women in the Venture Capital Industry* (Kansas City, MO: Kauffman Centre for Entrepreneurial Leadership, 2004).

46. For statistics about U.S. venture capital investments by industrial area, see the Price-Waterhouse-Coopers Money Tree, accessed at http://www.pwcmoneytree.com.

47. Brush and others, *The Diana Project.*

48. L. Bigelow, L. Lundmark, J. McLean Parks, and R. Wuebker, "Skirting the Issues: Experimental Evidence of Gender Bias in IPO Prospectus Evaluations," *Journal of Management* 40, no. 6 (2014): 1732–1759. doi: 10.1177/0149206312441624

49. See T. Greenwald, "Crowdfunding," *MIT Techology Review*, May-June 2012, accessed athttp://www2.technologyreview.com/article/427675/crowdfunding.

50. T. Prive, "What Is Crowdfunding and How Does It Benefit the Economy?" *Forbes*, November 27, 2012, accessed at http://www.forbes.com/sites/tanyaprive/2012/11/27/what-is-crowdfunding-and-how-does-it-benefit-the-economy.

51. See various websites.

52. R. T. Harrison, "Crowdfunding and the Revitalisation of the Early Stage Risk Capital Market: Catalyst or Chimera?" *Venture Capital: An International Journal of Entrepreneurial Finance* 15, no. 4: 283–287.

53. A. Tomczak and A. Brem, "A Conceptualized Investment Model of Crowdfunding," *Venture Capital: An International Journal of Entrepreneurial Finance* 15, no. 4: 335–259.

54. E. Mollick, "The Dynamics of Crowdfunding: An Exploratory Study," *Journal of Business Venturing* 29, no. 1 (2014): 1–16.

55. P. Belleflamme, T. Lambert, and A. Schwienbacher, "Individual Crowdfunding Practices," *Venture Capital: An International Journal of Entrepreneurial Finance* 15, no. 4: 313–333.

56. Harrison, "Crowdfunding."

57. C. Farr, "Indiegogo Founder Danae Ringelmann: 'We Will Never Lose Sight of Our Vision to Democratize Finance,'" VentureBeat, women2.0, February 24, 2014, accessed at http://women2.com/2014/02/24/indiegogo-founder-danae-ringelmann-will-never-lose-sight -vision-democratize-finance.

58. S. Castellanos, "How Online Fundraising Levels the Playing Field for Women," *Boston Business Journal*, March 7, 2014, accessed at http://upstart.bizjournals.com/money/loot/2014/03/07/shereen-shermak-launch-angels.html.

59. G. Stengel, "5 Tips for Women Investing in Entrepreneurs Via Crowdfunding," *Forbeswomen*, March 13, 2013, accessed at http://www.forbes.com/sites/geristengel/2013 /03/13/5-tips-for-women-investing-in-entrepreneurs-via-crowdfunding.

60. For information about The National CrowdFunding Association, visit http://www .nlcfa.org/main.html.

61. G. Stengel, "5 Tips for Women."

62. G. Powell and D. Ansic, "Gender Differences in Risk Behaviour in Financial Deci-

sion-Making: An Experimental Analysis," *Journal of Economic Psychology* 18, no. 6 (1997): 605–628.

63. Ibid.

64. See http://www.karmijnkapitaal.nl.

65. Astia's mission is to fund high-potential, high-growth women-led startup firms. See http://www.astia.org.

66. "Golden Seeds is an investment firm that pursues above market returns through the empowerment of women entrepreneurs and the people who invest in them." See http://www.goldenseeds.com.

67. The Pipeline Fellowship mission is to train "women philanthropists to become angel investors through education, mentoring, and practice. Fellows commit to invest in a woman-led for-profit social venture in exchange for equity and a board seat." For information about The Pipeline Fellowship, see http://www.pipelinefellowship.com/home.

68. Organization for Economic Co-Operation of Development, *OECD/INFE Policy Guidance on Addressing Women's and Girl's Needs for Financial Awareness and Education*, 2013, accessed at http://www.oecd.org/daf/fin/financial-education/G20-Women-Girls-Fin -Ed-Policy-Guidance-2013.pdf.

69. D. Markow and K. Bagnaschi, "What American Teens and Adults Know About Economics: Executive Summary," *National Council on Economic Education*, April 26, 2005.

70. FLatWorld Initiative. Accessed at http://www.finrafoundation.org/web/groups/foun dation/@foundation/documents/foundation/p240590.pdf.

71. A. L. Hung, J. Yoong, and E. Brown, "Empowering Women Through Financial Awareness and Education," OECD Working Papers on Finance, Insurance and Private Pensions, No. 14, OECD Publishing, 2012, accessed at http://dx.doi.org/10.1787/5k9d5v6kh56g-en.

72. ANZ Banking Group, *ANZ Survey of Adult Financial Literacy in Australia*, October 2008, accessed at www.anz.com/Documents/AU/Aboutanz/AN_5654_Adult_Fin_Lit_Report _08_Web_Report_full.pdf.

73. These two challenges were originally advanced by the OECD, in Hung, Yoong, and Brown, "Empowering Women Through Financial Awareness and Education."

74. S. Coleman and A. Robb, "A Comparison of New Firm Financing by Gender: Evidence from the Kauffman Firm Survey Data," *Small Business Economics* 33, no. 4 (2009): 397–411; O. Jung, *Financing Profile: Women Entrepreneurs* (Ottawa: Small Business Branch, Industry Canada, 2010).

75. Organization for Economic Co-operation of Development, *OECD/INFE Policy Guidance.*

76. For example, the Women's Enterprise Centre of Manitoba (Winnipeg), My Gold Mine accounting and financial training program. Information is based on a review of My Gold Mine and interviews with Sandra Altner, president of the center.

Chapter 7

1. N. MacNeil, "Entrepreneurship Is the New Women's Movement," *Forbeswoman*, June 8, 2012.

2. See Government of New Brunswick, Women's Issues Branch, Executive Council Office, *Gender Based Analysis Guide* (Fredericton, NB: Women's Issues Branch, Executive

Council Office, 2003), 9, accessed at http://www.gnb.ca/0012/womens-issues/genderanaly sis2003.pdf. See also http://www.womenpresidentsorg.com.

3. The engagement of women in entrepreneurship varies considerably by country, on the basis of provision of marriage and property rights, education, culture, customs, and tradition. Access to land and financial and human capital, as well as costly, complex legal requirements have more of a negative effect on female than male entrepreneurs. As a result, many women conduct trade in the informal economy, without access to social and economic safety nets for themselves and their employees. See A. Ellis, D. Kirkwood, and D. Malhotra, *Economic Opportunities for Women in the East Asia and Pacific Region* (Washington, DC: World Bank, 2010).

4. J. Rowlands, *Questioning Empowerment: Working with Women in Honduras* (Oxford: Oxfam, 1997); L. Mayoux, *Jobs, Gender and Small Enterprises: Getting the Policy Environment Right*(Geneva: International Labour Office, 2001); N. Kabeer, *Reversed Realities* (London: Verso, 1994).

5. See the following sources of related information: Ernst & Young, *Groundbreakers: Using the Strength of Women to Rebuild the World Economy* (New York: Ernst & Young Publications, 2009); European Commission, Enterprise Directorate General, *Good Practices in the Promotion of Female Entrepreneurship: Examples for Europe and Other OECD Countries* (Vienna: Austrian Institute for Small Business Research, December 2002); *Promoting Entrepreneurship Amongst Women: Best Reports*, No. 20-2004, (Luxembourg: Office for Official Publications of the European Communities, 2004), accessed at http://ec.europa.eu/enterprise/newsroom/cf/_getdocument.cfm?doc_id=4094; Organisation for Economic Co-operation and Development, *Women Entrepreneurs in SMEs: Realising the Benefits of Globalisation and the Knowledge-Based Economy*, (Paris: Organisation for Economic Co-operation and Development, 2001); Organisation for Economic Co-operation and Development, *OECD Accelerating Women's Entrepreneurship Forum* (Istanbul: Organisation for Economic Co-operation and Development, June 5–7, 2004); Organisation for Economic Co-operation and Development, *Women Entrepreneurs in Small and Medium Enterprises*, (Paris: OECD, 1998); Quantum Leaps, *The Roadmap to 2020: Fueling the Growth of Women's Enterprise Development* (Washington, DC: Quantum Leaps, 2010); National Women's Business Council, *Best Practices in Supporting Women's Entrepreneurship in the United States: A Compendium of Public and Private Sector Organizations and Initiatives* (Washington, DC: National Women's Business Council, June 2004); F. Weicker, *Impact Assessment of the Women Enterprise Initiative (WEI)*, prepared on behalf of Industry Canada, Western Economic Diversification Canada, 2008, accessed at http://www.wd.gc.ca/images/cont/11188-eng.pdf; B. J. Orser and A. L. Riding, "Gender-Based Small Business Programming: The Case of the Women's Enterprise Initiative," *Journal of Small Business and Entrepreneurship* 19, no. 2 (2006): 143–166.

6. For example, see Women's Enterprise Taskforce (2006–2009), accessed at http://www.womensenterprisetaskforce.co.uk; S. Bulte, C. Callbeck, C. Duplain, R. Fitzpatrick, K. Redman, and A. Lever, *The Prime Minister's Task Force on Women Entrepreneurs* (Ottawa: National Liberal Caucus Research Bureau, Information Management, October 2003),accessed at http://www.liberal.parl.gc.ca/entrepreneur; B. J. Orser and C. Connell, *Sustaining the Momentum: An Economic Forum for Women Entrepreneurs* (Ottawa: Industry Canada, Multimedia Services Section, Communications and Marketing Branch, March 2005),accessed at

http://www.ic.gc.ca/eic/site/sbrp-rppe.nsf/eng/rd01308.html; Taskforce for Women's Business Growth, *Taskforce Roundtable Report: Action Strategies to Support Canadian Women-Owned Enterprises*, University of Ottawa, Telfer School of Management, 2011, accessed at http://sites.telfer.uottawa.ca/womensenterprise.

7. G. Kirton and A-M. Greene, "What Does Diversity Management Mean for the Gender Equality Project in the United Kingdom? Views and Experiences of Organizational 'Actors,'" *Canadian Journal of Administrative Sciences* 27, no. 3 (2010): 249–262.

8. For example, see D. Walker and B. Joyner, "Female Entrepreneurship and the Market Process: Gender-Based Public Policy Considerations," *Journal of Developmental Entrepreneurship* 2, no. 4 (1999): 21–31; E. McGill, "Poverty and Social Analysis of Trade Agreements: A More Coherent Approach?" *Boston College International & Comparative Law Review* 27, no. 2 (2004): 429–452; Mayoux, *Jobs, Gender and Small Enterprises*; S. Gammage, H. Jorgensen, E. McGill, and M. White, *Trade Impact Review: Framework for Gender Assessments of Trade and Investment Agreements* (Washington, DC: The Coalition for Women's Economic Development and Global Equality, 2002) (The Women's EDGE Coalition recently published a country case study based on this framework.); M. White and others, *Women's Economic Development and Global Equality, NAFTA and the FTAA: A Gender Analysis of Employment and Poverty Impacts in Agriculture*, 2003 (Both reports can be obtained from the Women's EDGE Coalition, accessed at http://www.womensedge.org); European Commission Enterprise Directorate-General, *Good Practices in the Promotion of Female Entrepreneurship: Examples from Europe and Other OECD Countries* (Vienna: European Commission and the Austrian Institute for Small Business Research, 2002); Women's Enterprise Taskforce, *Greater Return on Women's Enterprise—GROWE: The UK Women's Enterprise Task Force's Final Report and Recommendations*, 2009.

9. See Quantum Leaps Inc. at http://www.quantumleapsinc.org. Virginia Littlejohn is the CEO of Quantum Leaps, past member of IBM's Advisory and Research Board, advocate to U.S. Small Business Administration's Office of Women's Business Ownership, past-president of the U.S. National Association of Women Business Owners, and advocate for the Women's Business Centers, the census of women-owned businesses and the National Women's Business Council.

10. For additional information about these indices, see N. Kabeer, *Women's Economic Empowerment and Inclusive Growth: Labour Markets and Enterprise Growth*, SIG Working Paper 2012/1 (Ottawa: Department for International Development and the International Development Research Centre, 2012): 9; OECD Gender Equality, accessed at http://www.oecd.org/gender; The World Bank & The International Bank for Reconstruction and Development, *Women, Business and the Law: Removing Barriers to Economic Inclusion* (Washington, DC: The International Bank for Reconstruction and Development/The World Bank, 2012), accessed at http://wbl.worldbank.org/~/media/FPDKM/WBL/Documents/Reports/2012/Women-Business-and-the-Law-2012.pdf; GEM, accessed at http://www.gemconsortium.org; Social Institutions & Gender Index, accessed at http://genderindex.org.

11. Global Entrepreneurship and Development Institute, *Gender Global Entrepreneurship and Development Index* (GEDI, 2013). A seventeen-country pilot analysis of the conditions that foster high-potential female entrepreneurship. Accessed at http://i.dell.com/sites/doccontent/corporate/secure/en/Documents/Gender_GEDI_Executive_Report.pdf.

12. "The 15 economies with no legal differences between women and men in the areas

measured are Armenia, Canada, the Dominican Republic, Estonia, Hungary, Kosovo, Mexico, Namibia, the Netherlands, New Zealand, Peru, Puerto Rico (U.S.), the Slovak Republic, South Africa and Spain" as cited in The World Bank, *Women, Business and the Law: Removing Restrictions to Enhance Gender Equality*, 2013, 8–9, accessed at http://wbl.worldbank.org/~/media/FPDKM/WBL/Documents/Reports/2014/Women-Business-and-the-Law-2014-Key-Findings.pdf.

13. S. Djankov, "Opportunities for Women," Doing Business 2008 presentation, slide 10, Cited in EY (Ernst & Young), *Unleashing the Power of Women Entrepreneurs: Women in the Workplace*, n.d., accessed at www.ey.com/womenentrepreneurs.

14. J. Demetriades, *Gender Equality Indicators: What, Why and How, Prepared for the OECD DAC Network on Gender Equality* (Paris: OECD, 2009).

15. Our thanks to Dr. Patricia Greene for alerting us to several of the indices and describing how they are being used.

16. See the Canadian Council for Small Business and Entrepreneurship, accessed at http://www.icsb.org/ccsbe.

17. See Women's Enterprise Centre of Manitoba, accessed at http://www.wecm.ca.

18. T. Scarlett, *Women's Enterprise Initiative: Generating Significant Economic Impacts in Western Canada* (Edmonton: Alberta Women Entrepreneurs Association, 2010), accessed at https://www.wecm.ca/documents/Scarlett_Tracey_Diana_conference_2010_paper.pdf.

19. D. Smallbone, S. Johnson, B. Virk, and G. Hotchkiss, *Young Entrepreneurs, Women Entrepreneurs, Ethnic Minority Entrepreneurs and Co-Entrepreneurs in the European Union and Central and Eastern Europe* (London, U.K.: Middlesex University Business School, Centre for Enterprise and Economic Development Research, 2000).

20. European Commission, Enterprise Directorate General, *Good Practices in the Promotion of Female Entrepreneurship*, Vienna, Austrian Institute for Small Business Research, December 2002, accessed at http://www.tecninvest.com/_research/Female_Entrepreneurship-en.pdf.

21. For information about the ChallengeHER Campaign, see http://www.sba.gov/community/blogs/challengeher-creating-procurement-access-and-opportunity-women-owned-small-businesse.

22. See Goldman Sachs, "10,000 Small Businesses," accessed at http://www.goldmansachs.com/citizenship/10000-small-businesses/US/index.html.

23. See Goldman Sachs, "10,000 Women," accessed at http://www.goldmansachs.com/citizenship/10000women.

24. See Government of New Brunswick, Women's Issues Branch, Executive Council Office, *Gender Based Analysis Guide*, 9. See also http://www.womenpresidentsorg.com.

25. Walker and Joyner, "Female Entrepreneurship and the Market Process."

26. M. Karl, *Women and Empowerment: Participation and Decision-Making* (London: Zed Books and the United Nations Non-Governmental Liaison Service, 1995), 14, as cited in OECD, Development Assistance Committee (DAC), *Source Book on Concepts and Approaches Linked to Gender* (Paris: OECD, 1998), 10, accessed at http://www.oecd.org/social/gender-development/31572047.pdf.

27. E. Cadwalader, "Policy Analysis: Identification of Barriers to Participation for Women in University Technology Transfer Activities," *Association for Women in Science (AWIS) Magazine* (Winter 2013); Council of Canadian Academies, *Strengthening Canada's*

Research Capacity: The Gender Dimension, The Expert Panel on Women in University Research (Ottawa: Council of Canadian Academies, 2002), accessed at http://www.scienceadvice.ca/ uploads/eng/assessments%20and%20publications%20and%20news%20releases/Women_ University_Research/WUR_fullreportEN.pdf; C. Moss-Racusin, J. F. Dovidio, V. L. Brescoll, M. J. Graham, and J. Handelsman, "Science Faculty's Subtle Gender Biases Favor Male Students," *Proceedings of the National Academy of Sciences* 109, no. 41 (2012): 1–6.

28. A rare case of public awareness about gender bias in awarding of academic funds and honorifics is evidenced in the report *Strengthening Canada's Research Capacity.* The expert panel reported that bias stems from the results of the very first Canada Excellence Research Chairs Competition in 2008. None of the nineteen appointed chairs was female. Media coverage and subsequent public outrage resulted in the minister of industry calling for an investigation about why women had not been selected to receive any of the $10 million research grants. Council of Canadian Academies, *Strengthening Canada's Research Capacity.*

29. B. J. Orser and S. Hogarth-Scott, "Case Analysis of Canadian Self-Employment Assistance Programming," *Entrepreneurship & Regional Development* 10, no. 1 (1998): 51–69.

30. See Government of New Brunswick, Women's Issues Branch, Executive Council Office, *Gender Based Analysis Guide*, 9.

31. Paraphrasing of McGill, "Poverty and Social Analysis of Trade Agreements."

32. McKinsey & Company, *Women Matter: Gender Diversity, a Corporate Performance Driver* (New York: McKinsey & Company, 2007). Also see McKinsey & Company, *Women Matter 2: Female Leadership, a Competitive Edge for the Future* (New York: McKinsey & Company, 2008).

33. In Canada, SME contract compliance is not without precedent. "Enacted in March 1996, the Canadian federal government established mandatory set-aside requirements for Aboriginal goods and services valued in excess of $5,000 destined for Aboriginal populations. In addition to mandatory set-asides for Aboriginal goods destined for Aboriginal communities, the federal government has articulated voluntary set-asides for goods and services that are not destined to Aboriginal communities." See B. J. Orser, *Procurement Strategies to Support Women-Owned Enterprise* (Ottawa: WEConnect International in Canada, 2009), 23. Available upon request from Ottawa: WEConnect International in Canada.

34. Article 8 of the Uruguay Round Agreement on Subsidies and Countervailing Measures (SCM Agreement). As cited by McGill, "Poverty and Social Analysis of Trade Agreements."

35. Mayoux, *Jobs, Gender and Small Enterprises*, 5. An example of SGBA is the development of My Gold Mine by the Women's Enterprise Center of Manitoba.

36. J. A. Kovsted, *Gender Equality: Women's Empowerment and the Paris Declaration of Aid Effectiveness: Issues Brief 6. Integrating Gender Equality Dimensions into Public Financial Management Reforms* (Paris: OECD, 2010), accessed at www.oecd.org/dac/gender/ effectiveness.

37. D. Smallbone, R. Athayde, and L. Meng, *Minority Business Diaspora Interchange: Procurement Opportunities for Small Firms and Black and Minority Ethnic (BAME) Enterprises in Three English Regions* (Kingston Hill, Surrey, UK: Small Business Research Centre, Kingston University, 2007).

38. For example, to learn about Walmart's Global Women's Economic Empowerment

Initiative, including the symbol for "women-owned firms" and a commitment to purchase $20 billion of goods from U.S. women-owned firms by 2016, visit http://walmartstores.com/women.

39. Better Regulation Task Force and the Small Business Council (UK),"Government: Supporter and Customer," 2003, accessed at http://archive.cabinetoffice.gov.uk/brc/government_responses/smallbusinessresponse.html; Canadian Federation of Independent Business, "Mandate 230: Marketing Your Business Survey: Canadian Federation of Independent Business," 2008, accessed at http://www.cfib.ca/research/reports; Chartered Institute of Purchasing & Supply, *Supplier Diversity* (Stamford, UK: The Chartered Institute of Purchasing & Supply, 2012), accessed at http://www.cips.org/documents/PPT0202_SupplierDiversity_Briefing.pdf.

40. A. Glover, *Accelerating the SME Economic Engine: Through Transparent, Simple and Strategic Procurement* (London: HM Treasury, November 2008), accessed at https://www.gov.uk/government/organisations/hm-treasury.

41. E. Vazquez and A. Sherman, *Buying for Impact: How to Buy from Women and Change Our World* (Charleston, SC: Advantage, 2013).

42. K. Higgins, *Gender and Free Trade Agreements: Best Practices and Policy Guidance* (Ottawa: The North-South Institute, 2013), accessed at http://www.nsi-ins.ca/wp-content/uploads/2013/03/2013-Gender-and-FTAs-Best-Practices-and-Policy-Guidance.pdf. Also see D. Rubin, C. Manfre, and K. N. Barrett, *Promoting Gender Equitable Opportunities in Agricultural Value Chains: A Handbook* (Washington, DC: United States Agency for International Development, 2009).

43. This section draws on the helpful work of McGill, "Poverty and Social Analysis of Trade Agreements." For a review of gender-based trade assessment, see http://www.bc .edu/dam/files/schools/law/lawreviews/journals/bciclr/27_2/07_FMS.htm; Rubin, Manfre, and Barrett, *Promoting Gender Equitable Opportunities in Agricultural Value Chains*; and B. McLaren, *Free Trade Agreements in Peru and Columbia: Monitoring Impacts from a Gender Perspective*, (Ottawa: The North-South Institute, March 2013), accessed at http://www.nsi-ins .ca/publications/free-trade-agreement-latin-america-gender.

44. McGill, "Poverty and Social Analysis of Trade Agreements"; See Gammage, Jorgensen, McGill, and White, *Trade Impact Review*; and White and others, *Women's Economic Development*.

45. McGill, "Poverty and Social Analysis of Trade Agreements."

46. Higgins, *Gender and Free Trade Agreements*.

47. McLaren, *Free Trade Agreements in Peru and Columbia*.

48. Departamento Administrativo Nacional de Estadística (DANE), Dirección de Impuestos y Aduanas Nacionales de Colombia, *Cifras Sobre el Comercio Exterior*, 2012.

49. Departamento Nacional de Planeación, *Adgenda Internapara la Productividad y la Competitivdad*, Documento Conpes No. 3297, (Bogota: Consejo Nacional de Politica Economica y Social, Republica de Columbia, DNP, 2004).

50. K. Camacho Reyes, *Las Confesiones de las Confecciones: Condiciones Laborales y de Vida de las Confeccionistas de Medillin*, Ensayos laborales, (Medellin: Escuela Nacional Sindal, 2008).

51. Daniel Chudnovsky and A. López, "Working Group on Development and Environment in the Americas, Discussion Paper Number 12, Foreign Investment and Sustainable

Development in Argentina, The Working Group on Development and Environment in the Americas, April 2008.

52. Reyes, *Las Confesiones de las Confecciones.*

53. Kirton and Greene, "What Does Diversity Management Mean for the Gender Equality Project in the United Kingdom?"

54. Introduced in Canada by the Conservative government, "Gender-based Analysis Plus (GBA+) is an analytical tool the federal government uses to advance gender equality in Canada. The 'plus' in the name highlights that Gender-based Analysis goes beyond gender, and includes the examination of a range of other intersecting identity factors (such as age, education, language, geography, culture and income). GBA+ is used to assess the potential impacts of policies, programs or initiatives on diverse groups of women and men, girls and boys, taking into account gender and other identity factors. GBA+ helps recognize and respond to the different situations and needs of the Canadian population." Accessed on October 27, 2013, at http://www.swc-cfc.gc.ca/gba-acs/intro-eng.html.

55. J. Siltanen and A. Doucet, *Gender Relations in Canada: Intersectionality and Beyond* (Don Mills, ON: Oxford University Press, 2008), 87, as cited in B. Clow, A. Pederson, M. Haworth, and J. Bernier, *Rising to the Challenge: Sex and Gender-Based Analysis for Health Planning, Policy and Research in Canada* (Halifax: Atlantic Centre of Excellence for Women's Health, 2009), accessed at www.acewh.dal.ca.

56. Kirton and Greene, "What Does Diversity Management Mean for the Gender Equality Project in the United Kingdom?"

57. Y. Due Billing and E. Sundin, "From Managing Equality to Managing Diversity: A Critical Scandinavian Perspective on Gender and Workplace Diversity," in *Handbook of Workplace Diversity*, ed. P. Prasad, J. Pringle, and A. Konrad (London: Sage, 2006), 95–120; L. Dickens, "Beyond the Business Case: A Three-Pronged Approach to Equality Action," *Human Resource Management Journal* 9, no. 1 (1999): 9–19; Kirton and Greene, "What Does Diversity Management Mean for the Gender Equality Project in the United Kingdom?"

58. N. Ahmad and A. Hoffman, *A Framework for Addressing and Measuring Entrepreneurship* (Paris: OECD Entrepreneurship Indicators Steering Group, November 20, 2007), accessed at http://www.oecd.org/industry/business-stats/39629644.pdf.

59. D. J. Storey, *Understanding the Small Business Sector* (London: Routledge, 1994).

60. For example, following the 2008–2009 economic recession, the U.S. government introduced a series of economic stimulus programs to support small businesses, including the following key acts: Economic Stimulus Act (2008)—$152 billion to extend tax rebates to low- and middle-income individuals, and for accelerated capital depreciation for small businesses; Emergency Economic Stabilization Act (2008)—$700 billion to establish the Troubled Asset Relief Program to assist financial institutions; American Recovery and Reinvestment Act (2009)—$787 billion for tax cuts, social programs, infrastructure investment, energy efficiencies and renewable energy investment, and small-business-related programs; Small Business Jobs and Credit Act (2010)—creation of a $30 billion small-business lending fund and provision of $12 billion in tax cuts to help small businesses and $504 million to SBA; America Invest Act (2011)—revision of patent laws from "first to invent" to "first to file," which simplifies and reduces the cost of patenting and provides for accelerated patent process; Jumpstart Our Business Startup Act (2012, JOBS Act)—liberalization of small equity issuance by allowing SMEs to raise capital via the Internet with minimal regulation

(such as crowdfunding). See G. Giuseppe Gramigna, "Adaptive Behavior: Bees Do It, Birds Do It, Small Businesses Do It, Even the SBA Does It: Do Researchers Do It?" presentation to the ICSB, 3rd Global Entrepreneurship Research and Policy Conference, George Washington University, October 11–13, 2012.

61. A. Lundstrom and L. Stevenson, *Patterns and Trends in Entrepreneurship/SME Policy and Practice in Ten Economies 3, Entrepreneurship Policy in the Future Series,* (Orebo: Swedish Foundation for Small Business Research, Orebo University, 2002).

62. R. Sharp (ed.), *Budgeting for Equity: Gender Budget Initiatives Within a Framework of Performance Oriented Budgeting* (New York: United Nations Development Fund for Women, 2003). Also see R. Sharp and R. Broomhill, "Budgeting for Equity: The Australian Experience," *Feminist Economics* 81, no. 1 (2002): 25–47.

63. This point builds on insights advanced by Naila Kabeer: "Women's practical gender needs reflect the roles and responsibilities associated with their position within the socio-economic hierarchy, and hence varied considerably across context, class, race and so on. Strategic gender interests, on the other hand, were based on a deductive analysis of the structures of women's subordination and help out the promise of a transformative feminist politics based on shared experiences of oppression." N. Kabeer (ed.), *Women's Economic Empowerment and Inclusive Growth: Labour Markets and Enterprise Development* (Ottawa: Department for International Development and International Development Research Centre, 2013), 6, accessed at http://www.idrc.ca/EN/Documents/NK-WEE-Concept-Paper.pdf.

64. J. Schalkwyk, *Culture, Gender Equity and Development Cooperation* (Ottawa: Canadian International Development Agency, Prepared on behalf of the OECD, 2000), 6, accessed at http://www.oecd.org/social/gender-development/1896320.pdf; Development Assistance Committee, *DAC Sourcebook on Concepts and Approaches Linked to Gender Equality* (Paris: OECD, 1998), accessed at http://www.oecd.org/social/gender-development/31572047.pdf.

65. Mayoux, *Jobs, Gender and Small Enterprises,* 11; A.M.J. Stranger, "Gender-Comparative Use of Small Business Training and Assistance: A Literature Review," *Education & Training* 46, no. 8/9 (2004): 464–473.

66. J. Byrne and A. Fayolle, "A Feminist Inquiry into Entrepreneurship Training," in *The Theory and Practice of Entrepreneurship: Frontiers in European Entrepreneurship Research,* ed. D. Smallbone, J. Leitao, M. Raposo, and F. Welter (Cheltenham, UK: Edward Elgar, 2010).

67. This section draws heavily from B. J. Orser, C. Elliott, and S. Findlay-Thompson, "Women-Focused Small Business Programming: Client Motives and Perspectives," *International Journal of Gender and Entrepreneurship* 4, no. 3 (2012): 236–265.

68. Byrne and Fayolle, "A Feminist Inquiry into Entrepreneurship Training."

69. P. Braidford and I. Stone, "Women's Business Centres: Lessons Learned from USA, Sweden and Canada," *Proceedings, Institute for Small Business & Entrepreneurship Conference,* Belfast, November 5–7, 2008; Byrne and Fayolle, "A Feminist Inquiry into Entrepreneurship Training."

70. Orser, Elliott, and Findlay-Thompson, "Women-Focused Small Business Programming."

71. See S. Vinnicombe and V. Singh, "Women-Only Management Training: An Essential Part of Women's Leadership Development," *Journal of Change Management* 3, no. 4 (2002): 294–306; Orser, Elliott, and Findlay-Thompson, "Women-Focused Small Business Programming"; N. Pernilla, "Business Counselling Services Directed Towards Female Entrepreneurs:

Some Legitimacy Dilemmas," *Entrepreneurship & Regional Development* 9, no. 3 (1997): 239–258; M. Tillmar, "Gendered Small-Business Assistance: Lessons from a Swedish Project," *Journal of European Industrial Training* 31, no. 2 (2007): 84–99; M. Godwyn, N. Langowitz, and N. Sharpe, *The Impact and Influence of Women's Business Centers in the United States* (Wellesley, MA: The Centre for Women's Leadership at Babson College, 2005); Braidford and Stone, "Women's Business Centres."

Chapter 8

1. J. Rowlands, *Questioning Empowerment: Working with Women in Honduras* (Oxford: Oxfam, 1997), as cited by L. Mayoux, *Jobs, Gender and Small Enterprises: Getting the Policy Environment Right* (Geneva: International Labour Office, 2001); N. Kabeer, *Reversed Realities* (London: Verso, 1994), as cited by Mayoux, *Jobs, Gender and Small Enterprises.*

2. EY (Ernst & Young), *Growing Beyond—High Achievers: Women Make All the Difference in the World*, accessed at http://www.ey.com/GL/en/Issues/Driving-growth/Growing -Beyond—-High-Achievers—-Women-make-all-the-difference-in-the-world.

3. International Monetary Fund (IMF, K. Elborgh-Woytek, M. Newiak, K. Kochhar, S. Fabrizio, K. Kpodar, P. Wingender, B. Clements, and G. Schwartz), "Women, Work, and the Economy: Macroeconomic Gains from Gender Equity," 2013, accessed at http://www .imf.org/external/pubs/ft/sdn/2013/sdn1310.pdf; Simeon Djankov, "Opportunities for Women," Doing Business 2008 presentation, slide 10, cited in EY (Ernst & Young), *Unleashing the Power of Women Entrepreneurs: Women in the Workplace*, accessed at www.ey.com/ womenentrepreneurs.

4. E. Gamberoni and J. G. Reis, *Gender-Informing Aid for Trade: Entry Points and Initial Lessons Learned from the World Bank* (Washington, DC: Poverty Reduction and Economic Management Network, July 2011); "Information from 20 semi-industrialized countries suggests that for every one-percentage-point increase in the share of household income generated by women, aggregate domestic savings increased by roughly 15 basis points." Goldman Sachs, *Education. Empowerment. Economic Opportunity* (New York: Goldman Sachs, 2009), 15; A. M. Golla, A. Malhotra, P. Nanda, and R. Mehra, *Understanding and Measuring Women's Economic Empowerment: Definition, Frameworks, Indicators* (Washington, DC: International Center for Research on Women, 2011).

5. A. de Haan and N. Miller, "Forward," in *Women's Economic Empowerment and Inclusive Growth: Labour Markets and Enterprise Development*, ed. N. Kabeer (Ottawa: International Development Research Centre, 2013), 3, accessed at http://www.idrc.ca/EN/ Documents/NK-WEE-Concept-Paper.pdf.

6. J. Downing, "Gender and the Growth of Microenterprises," *Small Enterprise Development* 2, no. 1 (March 1991): 4–12.

7. UNICEF "The State of the World's Children—2007 Report", Chapter 2, cited by EY (Ernst & Young), *Unleashing the Power of Women Entrepreneurs.*

8. The annual WEConnect International Conference is affiliated with the U.S. Women's Business Enterprise National Council.

9. B. Orser, and J. D. Leck, "Physician as Feminist Entrepreneur: The Gendered Nature of Venture Creation and the Shirley E. Greenberg Women's Health Centre," in *Women's Entrepreneurship and Growth Influences: An International Perspective*, ed. C. G. Brush, E. J. Gatewood, A. M. de Bruin, and C. Henry (Cheltenham, UK: Edward Elgar, 2010).

10. For information about Entrepreneurship 101, visit the incubator program, a University of Toronto and MaRS Innovation partnership, described at http://marsinnovation.com.

11. B. Orser, "Growth Strategies of Women Entrepreneurs in Technology-Based Firms," *Small- and Medium-Sized Enterprise Review* 3, no. 1 (June 2010): 9.

12. Quantum Leaps, *The Roadmap to 2020: Fueling the Growth of Women's Enterprise Development* (Washington, DC: Quantum Leaps, 2010), accessed at http://www.quantumleapsinc.org/publications/Roadmap-2020-June.pdf.

Glossary

1. See Government of New Brunswick, Women's Issues Branch, Executive Council Office, *Gender Based Analysis Guide* (Fredericton, NB: Women's Issues Branch, Executive Council Office, 2003), 9, accessed at http://www.gnb.ca/0012/womens-issues/genderanalysis2003.pdf.

2. D. Walker and B. Joyner, "Female Entrepreneurship and the Market Process: Gender-Based Public Policy Considerations," *Journal of Developmental Entrepreneurship* 2, no. 4 (1999): 21–31.

3. M. Karl, *Women and Empowerment: Participation and Decision-Making* (London: Zed Books and the United Nations Non-Governmental Liaison Service, 1995), 14.

4. Adapted from N. Ahmad and A. Hoffman, *A Framework for Addressing and Measuring Entrepreneurship* (Paris: OECD Entrepreneurship Indicators Steering Group, November 20, 2007), 4, accessed at http://www.oecd.org/industry/business-stats/39629644.pdf.

5. B. J. Orser, M. Cedzynski, and R. Thomas, "Modelling Owner Experience: Linking Theory and Practice," *Journal of Small Business & Entrepreneurship* 20, no. 4 (2007): 387–408; B. Smith and E. Morse, *Entrepreneurial Competencies: Literature Review and Best Practices* (Ottawa: Industry Canada, Small Business Policy Branch, 2005).

6. J. L. Borgerson, "On the Harmony of Feminist Ethics and Business Ethics," *Business and Society Review* 112, no. 4: 477–509, at p. 483.

7. H. Ahl, *The Scientific Reproduction of Gender Inequality* (Copenhagen: CBS Press, 2004), 16.

8. Borgerson, "On the Harmony."

9. Saskatchewan Women's Secretariat, *Gender-Inclusive Analysis: A Guide for Policy Analysts, Researchers, Program Managers, and Decision-Makers,* (Regina: Saskatchewan Women's Secretariat, 1998), 8.

10. See Government of New Brunswick, Women's Issues Branch, Executive Council Office, *Gender Based Analysis Guide*, 9.

11. M. C. Suchman, "Managing Legitimacy: Strategic and Institutional Approaches," *Academy of Management Review* 20, no. 3 (1995): 574.

12. A. J. van Weele, *Purchasing and Supply Chain Management: Analysis, Strategy, Planning and Practice*, 5th ed. (Andover, UK: Cengage Learning, 2010).

13. See Government of New Brunswick, Women's Issues Branch, Executive Council Office, *Gender Based Analysis Guide*, 9. See also Women's Presidents' Organization at http://www.womenpresidentsorg.com.

14. M. L. Barnett, "Waves of Collectivizing: A Dynamic Model of Competition and Cooperation Over the Life of an Industry," *Corporate Reputation Review* 8, no. 4 (2006):

272–292; D. L. Deephouse, *Acceptability Versus Favorability: Distinguishing Between Organizational Legitimacy and Organizational Reputation*, unpublished manuscript, Louisiana State University, 1999; R. C. Mayer, J. H. David, and F. D. Schoorman, "An Integrative Model of Trust Formation," *Academy of Management Review* 20, no. 3 (1995): 709–734.

15. A. Bandura, "Human Agency in Social Cognitive Theory," *American Psychologist* 44, no. 9 (1989): 1175–1184.

16. Mayer, David, and Schoorman, "An Integrative Model," 712.

Glossary

Angel: an individual who invests personal capital directly in a business owned by others. Also referred to as an informal investor.

Archangel: an individual who marshals informal capital by establishing syndicates of other angel (informal) investors.

Being female: refers to how feminine traits are expressed in decisions and actions by women.

Bootstrap financing (or bootstrapping): small amounts of seed capital used in early stages of firm maturation.

Cash flow: the amount and flow of funds in a firm over a designated period of time. Cash flow differs from the amounts indicated on an income statement, given that it does not include noncash items and expenses such as depreciation.

Cash flow conversation: the difference between the operating cycle (inputs of cash) and the payment cycle (that is, the interval between the purchasing of raw material and labor and the cash payment for them).

Credit history: a review of a firm's credit relationships. For new business owners who have not held mortgages or credit cards in their own name, the lack of credit history is particularly problematic for securing financing.

Debt: a financial obligation to a lender. The amount of debt and interest payable are agreed upon as occurring over a designated period of time.

Discouraged borrower: business owners who choose not to apply for external financing, even when financing is needed, and when they might otherwise be eligible for financing. Fear of denial is cited as a reason for this behavior.

Diversity: refers to a wide range of attributes such as Indigenous or Aboriginal status, physical and mental abilities, age, race, ethnicity, family status, sexual orientation, and geographic location and how they can interact with gender in ways that will produce different outcomes for men and women.[1]

Economic gender discrimination: occurs when a person of one sex does not meet program application or usage criteria, and the reason is a lack of qualifications associated with the person's gender.[2]

Empowerment: a "process of awareness and capacity building leading to greater participation, to greater decision-making power and control, and to transformative action."[3]

Entrepreneurial activity: enterprising human actions in pursuit of social and economic value, by identifying and exploiting new products, processes, or markets.[4]

Entrepreneurial feminism: feminist values enacted within the venture creation process.

Entrepreneurial identity gap: a schism between that which is personified as female or feminine and that which is described as entrepreneurial, as defined by male-oriented norms.

Entrepreneurial self-efficacy: confidence and a positive self-assessment of competencies and knowledge domains essential to creating and managing new ventures.[5]

Entrepreneurs: those persons (business owners) who seek to generate social and economic value by identifying and exploiting new products, processes, or markets.

Entrepreneurship: the phenomenon associated with entrepreneurial activity.

Equity: a financial investment that results in a portion of firm ownership.

Feminine capital: an aggregation of those elements of entrepreneurial capacity that incorporate "the feminine." It is both individual and collective.

Feminine versus masculine: feminine traits are *typically* associated with females; masculine traits are typically associated with males. Feminine and masculine traits and behavior are reinforced through socialization, including in media and academic research. As a result, male and female entrepreneurs and students learn to adopt certain behaviors. Such behaviors are not naturally or "essentially connected to either sexed bodies."[6]

Feminism: the recognition of men's and women's unequal conditions and the desire to change this.[7] Feminism assumes that women are often viewed as subordinate to men and that women's experiences' are distorted or omitted to the extent that research has focused primarily on public spheres of life to the exclusion of less visible, less dramatic, private female spheres. Feminism is therefore an intellectual commitment and communal effort to end sexism, in all forms, including sexism in the marketplace.

Feminist entrepreneurs: change agents who employ entrepreneurship to improve girls and women's quality of life and well-being.

Gender: a social construction[8] that, for the purpose of this work, informs behavior that can be viewed along a continuum of "masculine" and "feminine." Gender is seen to differ in time (such as throughout the venture creation process), place (such as within public and private spheres), and context (such as different economic conditions).

Gender equality: when women and men enjoy the *same* status and experience equal conditions for fully realizing their human rights to contribute and benefit from participating in a range of political, economic, social, and cultural endeavors.[9]

Gender equity: beyond equal treatment to the fairness of results, it requires the differential treatment of groups in order to end inequality and foster autonomy. Therefore, to level the playing field for men and women, measures may be necessary to compensate for the historical and social disadvantages that women have experienced.[10]

Intrapreneurs: entrepreneurs who seek to create change within large institutional settings.

Know-how: the skills or the capability to do something, or knowledge in action. It is also called "tacit knowledge," that which is difficult to articulate, codify, or measure.

Know-what: explicit knowledge about facts. This type of knowledge can be easily codified, processed, and stored (often in books, on websites, in databases, or in management information systems).

Know-who: information about "who knows what" and "who knows how to do what." Know-who incorporates social capital, relationships that enable access to experts.

Know-why: scientific knowledge such as the principles and laws of nature.

Legitimacy: the perception that the actions of one entity (founder, firm) are desirable, proper, or appropriate within the socially constructed system of norms, values, and beliefs.[11]

Mainstream strategies: building gender issues into existing program paradigms. This includes redesigning budgets, policies, and programming with a gender perspective.

Patient capital: a loan in which the terms of repayment are delayed in order that the borrower can earn revenue to pay back the capital and interest outstanding.

Procurement: the acquisition of goods, services, or works from an external source. It is favorable that the goods, services, or works are appropriate and that they are procured at the best possible cost to meet the needs of the purchaser in terms of quality and quantity, time, and location.[12]

Public policy: a means by which government, at federal, state/provincial, territorial, and municipal levels, carries out its decisions, through various courses of action including the development and implementation of acts, regulations, guidelines, programs, and standards.[13]

Reputation: a set of beliefs held by an external group of stakeholders, such as investors, clients, and suppliers that is an assessment or measure of favorability.[14]

Self-efficacy: one's confidence in a given knowledge domain. It is based on self-perceptions of one's skills and abilities.[15]

Sex: two categories (male and female) into which humans are divided on the basis of their reproductive functions.

Supplier diversity: a business program that encourages purchasing from small businesses owned by women, veterans and service-disabled veterans, LGBT (lesbian, gay, bisexual, and transgender), and other historically underutilized vendors.

Sweat equity: the unpaid time and energy exerted by the business owner during the incubation, gestation, and early startup phase of operation. While it is not a monetary form of equity, owners should document their time and others' in-kind contributions to demonstrate to potential investors the type and level of management activity.

Term loan: a long-term loan offered by a financial institution to a business in which the borrower agrees to repay interest and capital over a designated period of time.

Trade credit: credit, most often unsecured, extended by suppliers to buyers.

Trust: "the willingness of a party to be vulnerable to the actions of another party based on the expectation that the other will perform a particular action important to the trustor, irrespective of the ability to monitor or control the other party."[16]

Venture capital: capital invested in growing enterprises by individuals or venture capital firms when risk is a significant element of the environment.

Women's enterprise: a community of female-founded and owned firms (corporations, partnerships), self-employed workers, and social ventures (such as nonprofits, cooperatives, nongovernment organizations, charities, other).

Women's entrepreneurship: the domain of knowledge about women's enterprise, including curricula, research, and advocacy.

Working capital: the difference between the firm's current assets and current liabilities.

Index